ADULT DEPARTMENT

WE SERVE

*A History
of the Lions Clubs*

PRESENTED TO THE

FOND DU LAC PUBLIC LIBRARY

BY

Fond du Lac Evening Lions Club

WE SERVE

A History
of the Lions Clubs

Paul Martin

REGNERY GATEWAY
Washington, D.C.

Library of Congress Cataloging-in-Publication Data

Martin, Paul, 1922–
We serve : a history of the Lions clubs / Paul Martin.
p.   cm.
Includes index.
ISBN 0–89526–534–6 (cloth : alk. paper)
1. Lions International—History.   I. Title.
HS2705.L53M37   1991
369.5—dc20   90–23618
CIP

Published in the United States by
Regnery Gateway
1130 17th Street, NW
Washington, DC 20036

Distributed to the trade by
National Book Network
4720-A Boston Way
Lanham, MD 20706

1991 printing
Printed on acid free paper
Manufactured in the United States of America

Contents

Foreword

by H. C. Petry, Jr.
Past International President
(1950–51)

SINCE 1917, many millions of men, women, and young people have chosen to help those in need under the banner of Lions Clubs International. This book tells the story of those who founded our association and worked to make it what it has become: the world's largest humanitarian service club organization.

It is, to me, an astonishing story. Particularly so, since its scope could permit specific mention of only a small fraction of what our members have done in our nearly 75 years of existence. Consider this: the individual exploits of perhaps 100 clubs are told in the book by way of example; yet, as I write, we have just under 40,000 Lions clubs, 5,600 Lioness clubs, and 4,500 Leo clubs working in 171 countries and areas around the world. Every one of their stories could have been told.

Mr. Paul Martin, who spent more than two years in researching and writing this book, clearly could not do so. But I believe the stories he has told typify and exemplify the magnificent work that has been, and continues to be, done. A Lion himself, Paul is uniquely qualified to tell the Lions' story. A longtime contributor to THE LION Magazine, he has reported firsthand on our activities in many parts of the world. This experience has given proper perspective to his research in our archives, and to the many interviews he conducted with knowledgeable Lions around the world.

Finally, let me assure you that this is the story of what Lions, Lionesses, and Leos have done to help people, rather than a dry, "corporate" history. Paul has included only as much information about the organization and growth of the association as he felt was necessary to put the rest into perspective.

"We Serve" is both the title of this book, and our motto. Why this is so is truly the "rest"—and best—of the story.

WE SERVE

A History
of the Lions Clubs

CHAPTER ONE

How It Began

FIVE-YEAR-OLD Francisco lived in a world of total silence. Born deaf, he had never heard his mother's lullabies, his father's words of encouragement, the laughter of friends, or the sounds of the small town in Honduras where he lived. Then, one day, the Lions of Louisiana reached over the miles and brought him to their internationally-famed Lions-Saints Eye and Ear Clinic in New Orleans.

An exhaustive examination revealed that Francisco's problem was a rare condition that required two uniquely engineered hearing aids. Designed for the little boy's needs, these were precisely fitted and Francisco flew home prepared to enjoy a dimension of living that had been blocked to him before the Lions intervened.

Each hearing aid cost $2,000.* The $4,000 for the hearing aids, along with other expenses, were borne by the Lions.

In India, in the state of Kerala, Lions have helped more than 20,000 persons restore their sight through transplanted corneas. Money raised through the Lions Fair and All India Exhibition has paid for the corneas. Along with that, the Lions have built a permanent eye bank, bringing sight and hope to those who had neither before the Lions stepped in.

About an hour from Paris in the town of Nivillers near Beauvais, French Lions are rebuilding young lives. A project of the Paris (Doyen)

---

* Unless otherwise noted, all monetary figures reported in this book are in United States currency.

Lions Club, the Youth Culture Technical Center is designed for boys who are orphans or from broken homes. Among its more than 1,000 success stories is a 25-year-old professor at Beauvais Technical High School. Sixteen when he arrived at the center, the youth was a difficult discipline case. Rebellious, angry, and unwilling to take direction, he gradually responded to the program at the Lions-sponsored facility.

"The instructors worked with me to improve my academic skills," he explained, "and during my two years there I was trained as an electrician. I got a job in industry when I left and went to night school to learn more about my trade and teaching. I studied hard and went back to see my old instructors at the Technical Center whenever I needed encouragement. Three years ago a teaching job opened up at the Technical High School in Beauvais and I was hired. It's a new life for me."

This young man was facing jail when he arrived at the facility in Nivillers nine years ago. He was sent to the Lions' project by the French court system because of his history of delinquency. Without the intervention of the Lions, chances are he would be in jail today, instead of a happy and productive citizen.

Since its first tentative beginnings, Lions Clubs International had by 1991 become a robust force for good with nearly 40,000 clubs in more that 170 countries. Approximately 1.4 million men and women proudly call themselves "Lion."

When the record is studied and the score added up, the history of Lions shows clearly and eloquently that human beings can grow together.

"The ultimate test of what a truth means," said William James, "is the conduct it inspires." Lionism's principles offer a fresh and positive vision of goodwill and brotherhood, worldwide.

Cutting across all national, racial, and cultural boundaries, Lions Clubs International's activities have included:

- Sight conservation and work with the blind.
- Hearing conservation and work with the deaf.
- Citizenship, educational, health, and social services.
- Drug education and prevention programs.
- Diabetes detection and research.
- Work for international cooperation and understanding, including international youth camp and youth exchange programs.

A meeting of practical-minded visionaries at the LaSalle Hotel in Chicago, Illinois, on June 7, 1917, set the stage for the organization, later that year in Dallas, Texas, of today's international association.

The minutes of the meeting state that it had been organized by Melvin Jones, a Chicago insurance man and secretary of The Business Circle. Jones had invited The International Association of Lions Clubs of Evansville, Indiana, the Vortex Club of St. Louis, Missouri, and the Business and Professional Men's Association of St. Paul, Minnesota. He had also invited the Optimist and Exchange Clubs, but the Exchange Clubs did not attend.

Dr. William Woods, an Evansville, Indiana, physician, is listed on the minutes of that meeting as "President, International Association of Lions," and as representing 27 Lions clubs listed under his name. The corporate records of the State of Indiana, USA, show that on October 24, 1916, Dr. Woods, Carmi Hicks, and C. R. Conen filed Articles of Incorporation for a non-profit corporation titled The International Association of Lions Clubs. All Lions clubs chartered after August 30, 1916, were organized under that name and by June 1, 1917, there were 35 clubs that had received charters from The International Association of Lions. On May 16 of that year Melvin Jones asked Dr. Woods to attend the Chicago meeting "with a view to lining up our organization with yours."

The minutes of the meeting show that Edwin J. Raber and W. J. Livingston then introduced the following resolution:

"That the Board of Directors of the Business Circle of Chicago enter into negotiations with Dr. W. P. Woods of The International Association of Lions Clubs, and with other clubs with reference to the affiliation of these clubs and that said Board of Directors have full power to make and complete all arrangements for said affiliation and any act they do on the premises shall be the act of this club and binding thereon," and that "The motion was seconded by A. F. Sheahan and unanimously adopted by the Business Circle."

The minutes also show that later in the LaSalle Hotel meeting Dr. Woods invited the various clubs represented to join The International Association of Lions. Woods is quoted as stating:

"Whereas all clubs represented here today have different names, and whereas the Lions clubs have an international organization, with approximately thirty clubs in different parts of the United States, and whereas the Lions clubs are not now represented in any other cities represented by the other clubs; therefore, as president of The International Association of Lions Clubs, I hereby extend an invitation to these clubs to accept charters in The International Association of Lions Clubs and become a part and parcel of our organization. If you accept this invitation, there will be no membership charged, and all we ask is to adopt our name and pay dues to The International Association, which are at the rate of $1.00 per member, payable semi-annually in advance."

The St. Louis club accepted the offer and received its Lions Club charter on July 25, 1917.

Determined to make an informed decision, Melvin Jones wrote a letter on June 19, 1917, to J. T. Coleman, secretary of the Ardmore, Oklahoma, Lions Club. Jones said: "Dr. W. P. Woods, your international president, has extended to our organization an invitation to accept a charter and the name of The Lions Club. We have about decided to do so, and our decision will no doubt be influential in getting other clubs in other cities to do the same thing.

"Before making a final decision we would like to have you tell us about your organization in Ardmore. How many members have you? How often you meet and any other information you care to write to help us in our decision.

"Your early reply will be appreciated."

J. T. Coleman replied that in his judgment, "the Lions Club is a very valuable organization for any city. I know it is a success in other cities in this county.

"I have given the matter considerable thought and say without hesitation that I can recommend it to the business and professional men of any city."

The Chicago club received its Lions club charter on August 2, 1917.

On July 21, 1917, Dr. Woods notified all clubs, "the first convention of the Lions Clubs will be held in the City of Dallas, State of Texas, on the 8-9-10 of October, of this year."

Millions of lives have been transformed because of what happened during those three days. Countless human beings can see, hear, walk, work, and are alive because of the extraordinary association that was organized in that gathering. It began on a Monday morning, October 8,

1917, and today men, women, and children on every continent benefit from that legacy.

Headlines in *The Dallas Morning News* for that day declared: "Lions' International Meeting Opens Today." The delegates were welcomed by Mayor Joe E. Lawther in the Palm Garden of the Adolphus Hotel at ten o'clock in the morning.

With a prophetic look at the Lions' future, Mayor Lawther said, "Your organization is made up of men who accomplish things; men who recognize no obstacles."

In addition to Dr. Woods, 36 delegates and eight alternates took part in the meeting. Twenty-two Lions clubs were represented at the Dallas convention and six other clubs were still in existence or being formed at the time. Twenty-three Lions clubs have functioned continuously since then and in the convention of 1951, they were officially designated "Founder Club of Lions."

The first day of the convention the delegates elected officers. L. H. Lewis, president of the Dallas Lions Club, was elected by acclamation. However, he refused the post and asked the delegates to name Dr. Woods to the position. They did, and elected the rest of the officers by acclamation: L. H. Lewis, Dallas, Texas, first vice president; E. N. Kaercher, St. Louis, Missouri, second vice president; Melvin Jones, Chicago, Illinois, secretary-treasurer. R. A. Kleinschmidt, Oklahoma City, Oklahoma, and James L. McRee, Memphis, Tennessee, were named directors for three years. H. F. Endsley, Texarkana, Arkansas, and Roger Wheles, Shreveport, Louisiana, were chosen directors for two year terms.

There were two directorships for a one-year term and these were filled by ballot. A. V. Davenport of Tulsa, Oklahoma, and C. J. Kirk of Houston, Texas, were elected to these directorships. Nine states were represented at the convention: Arkansas, Colorado, Illinois, Indiana, Louisiana, Missouri, Oklahoma, Tennessee, and Texas. Texas and Oklahoma brought the largest delegations and received two seats each on the Board of Directors. The 22 Lions clubs represented at the Dallas Convention included Texarkana, Arkansas; Denver and Colorado Springs, Colorado; Chicago, Illinois; Shreveport, Louisiana; St. Louis, Missouri; Ardmore, Chickasha, Muskogee, Oklahoma City, and Tulsa, Oklahoma; and Memphis, Tennessee. Texas had the largest turnout with clubs from Abilene, Austin, Beaumont, Dallas, Fort Worth, Houston, Paris, Port Arthur, Waco, and Wichita Falls.

At the time of the convention Lions clubs were operating in Little Rock, Arkansas, and Pueblo, Colorado, as well as El Reno and Okmulgee, Oklahoma. Clubs in Oakland, California, and Temple, Texas, were being organized and began functioning soon after.

The delegates voted to open membership to women as well as men. The convention retained the Lions' emblem, the head of a Lion holding a club in its mouth marked "International." The group chose purple and gold as the Lions' colors and Melvin Jones was authorized to open a headquarters in Chicago.

W. J. Power of St. Louis spoke in favor of changing the name of the organization from Lions to Vortex. E. N. Calvin of Waco, Grant Richardson of Shreveport, and others contended that the name of Lions should be kept. The motion to retain the name Lions was passed by a vote of 24 to six.

The January 1931 issue of *The Lion* featured this interpretation of the association's name:

"Our name was not selected at random, neither was it a coined name. From time immemorial, the lion has been the symbol of all that was good, and because of the symbolism that name was chosen. Four outstanding qualities—Courage, Strength, Activity and Fidelity—had largely to do with the adoption of the name. The last mentioned of these qualities, Fidelity, has a deep and peculiar significance for all Lions. The lion symbol has been a symbol of Fidelity through the ages and among all nations, ancient and modern. It stands for loyalty to a friend, loyalty to a principle, loyalty to a duty, loyalty to a trust."

The report of the committee on constitution and by-laws was received with little debate, and most of the provisions were adopted without difficulty. However, there was a heated argument about an amendment to the constitution offered by W. A. Lybrand and J. C. Leonard of Oklahoma City. A principle that has become a guiding precept in Lionism's program of international service, the amendment stated: "No club shall by its by-laws, constitution or otherwise hold out the financial betterment of its members as its objects." After a stormy session, the amendment passed.

The United States had entered World War I six months before the

Dallas convention and the delegates voted to support the war effort and the Liberty Loan. The secretary was instructed to transmit a copy of that motion to President Woodrow Wilson.

Austin, Texas, and St. Louis, Missouri, asked to be the site for the 1918 convention and the delegates chose St. Louis.

The first convention of Lions Clubs International closed on October 10, 1917. Dr. Woods had been elected international president of the association. The Lions Objects and Code of Ethics were drafted. Altered only a little during the years, they embody the moral strength and spirit of the association. Harnessing a diversity of voices, the delegates created documents of coherence, logical consistency, and social vision.

Perhaps unaware of the extraordinary movement they had created, the delegates relaxed with a sightseeing tour of Dallas and a show at the Majestic Theater.

The Board of Directors met after the convention ended and Dr. Woods reported that the association had $72.05 in the bank. However, he had spent $446.80 for which he had not been reimbursed.

Now, for the first time, Lionism had the structure to prepare for its international destiny. At that small gathering in Dallas it gained the form designed to make it a worldwide force for goodwill and brotherhood.

That was still in the future, but 27-year-old Fabrizio is among many who give thanks for that beginning. His life really began when he was 19 and arrived at the Lions-supported National Association for Families of Handicapped Children and Adults. Located in Biella, 60 miles west of Milan in northern Italy, it draws clients from a 50-mile radius who are spastic, brain-injured, or severely retarded.

When Fabrizio came to the center, he had no skills and no opportunities. Suffering from brain damage, his future was bleak. After three years at the Lions-sponsored facility, Fabrizio went to work in a nearby shop as a mechanic and has been working successfully at this new trade for five years.

"It's great to be able to go to work every day," he said. "They taught me how to handle tools and I can do my job now. I learned how to plan my life so I can get to work on time and do other things I used to have trouble with."

Fabrizio may not be able to find Dallas on the map, but that's where the seeds of his new life were planted in 1917.

In the country of Zambia in Africa hundreds of blind children have received a special education in the Lions School for the Blind that opened in May 1974. A project of the Ndola Lions Club, the school is open to children from all over Zambia. They attend free-of-charge and, for seven years, are enrolled on a boarding school basis.

Each child receives a basic primary education, plus instruction in social studies, religion, nature study, physical education, and hand-icrafts. Physical conditioning plays a major role in the youngsters' lives. They enjoy the usual sports, including tree climbing and an obstacle course that has an anthill as one of the obstacles. Music and dancing are also part of the curriculum. Each child returns home with specialized knowledge, new skills, and a better ability to cope with blindness.

These boys and girls may never visit Texas, but what happened there at the Adolphus Hotel reached into the future to bring them better lives. Lions Clubs International emerged from Dallas with a sharpened vision of its worldwide role.

For the present, however, service was confined to the United States. During the rest of 1917 and into the following year, Lions clubs generally concentrated on projects to support the nation's war effort. This ranged from bond drives, collections of books and magazines, entertaining servicemen, help for war orphans and widows, and fund-raising for the Red Cross.

1918 CONVENTION

Seventy-nine delegates or alternates from 24 cities participated in the 1918 Convention in St. Louis, Missouri. Held October 19–21 in the Marquette Hotel, the meeting welcomed almost double the number of the previous year's turnout with ten states represented. Twenty St. Louis Lions were there and 20 from Oklahoma's seven clubs. Seventeen Texas Lions attended, as did seven Lions from Chicago and six from Arkansas.

Significantly, 17 of the 24 clubs on hand had sent delegates to the first convention and five delegates represented the new clubs. Ten states were there. Oklahoma had the largest delegation with Missouri second.

An unusual event occurred early in the convention; R. A. Kleinschmidt of Oklahoma City moved to declare all offices vacant and to permit the nominating committee to fill all offices. The motion passed. This unseated several directors with one or two years left to serve. Also, it placed elective power in the hands of a few rather than the majority.

A nominating committee was elected and then resigned immediately. The chairman reported "two or three members of that committee, I believe, should be elected as officers and directors, and the committee does not want to nominate any of its members." Following an understanding that members could nominate from their own numbers, the committee was re-elected.

The officers the committee nominated were elected: L. H. Lewis, Dallas, Texas, president; Jesse Robinson, Oakland, California, first vice president; Dr. C. C. Reid, Denver, Colorado, second vice president; F. C. Brinkman, Jr., Shreveport, Louisiana, third vice president; Melvin Jones, Chicago, Illinois, secretary-treasurer.

The Constitution and By-Laws Committee proposed an amendment to the constitution eliminating women from membership in Lions clubs.

The Committee on Club Ethics made some minor changes in the Code of Ethics adopted in Dallas the year before. However, almost all of these 1918 changes were restored at the convention in 1919.

The delegates applauded news of the association's solvency. The secretary-treasurer reported receipts of $2,360.83 and expenditures of $1,944.68 between October 9, 1917, and August 15, 1918. The bank balance in The Northern Trust Company in Chicago showed $488.20

The Oakland Lions Club asked for the 1919 Convention but then withdrew in favor of Chicago, which became the site for Lions convention number three. Momentum was growing with each convention.

New clubs were forming. At the St. Louis Convention some of Melvin Jones' earlier efforts were rewarded when the Cirgonian Club of Los Angeles, California, wired the convention: "Cirgonian Club of Los Angeles expresses its desire to affiliate with the Lions Clubs. Please instruct us what to do. Send us the constitution, by-laws, literature, etc. Sorry we cannot send delegate to convention. We rely upon you to represent us." The Lion governor for the Pacific Coast was authorized to induct the new club. Jones had corresponded with the Cirgonian Club during 1916–17.

He had been working in a small office in the Insurance Exchange

Building, 175 W. Jackson Boulevard in Chicago. The rent was $12.50 a month and a stenographer received $40. The convention voted to increase Jones' salary from $400 a year to $750 and authorized him to find a larger office in the same building.

The Finance Committee recommended publishing a magazine with all of the association's income above office expenses and the secretary's salary used for the magazine. Melvin Jones was authorized to handle this as he thought best.

The Board voted to purchase 1,000 lapel buttons with the association emblem. It voted in favor of a motion raising dues from $1.00 to $2.00 effective January 1, 1919, and kept the charter fee at $10.00 until September 1, 1919.

G. M. Cunningham was given the post of national organizer. He was to receive a stipulated sum per member and pay his travel and organization expenses from that sum.

The first district officers were appointed. G. M. Cunningham was made district governor of Texas; Jesse Robinson of Oakland, California, was named district governor of California, Nevada, Oregon, and Washington. Leon T. Kahn of Shreveport, Louisiana, became district governor of Louisiana.

In closing the convention, President Lewis announced his plans to visit every Lions club in existence, at his own expense. He declared the convention adjourned at 1:00 p.m. on August 21, 1918.

The first issue of *The Lion* appeared in November 1918. Twenty-eight pages plus cover, with dimensions of 6 ½" x 9", it summarized the St. Louis Convention, listed new clubs and reported on the activities of seven existing clubs. The first issue included an expanded list of district governors, rather than the three named by the Board of Directors on August 21. The governors included: T. J. Parker, Little Rock, for Arkansas; Louis K. Cameron of Denver for Wyoming and Colorado; G. W. Milligan of Chicago for Illinois; E. J. Wenner, Waterloo, for Iowa; William J. Repke, St. Paul, for Minnesota; A. V. Davenport of Tulsa for Oklahoma; and John E. Lippett, Memphis, for Tennessee. Robinson and Davenport had been appointed at the board meeting and Louisiana had a new district governor, F. C. Brinkman of Shreveport who replaced Leon I. Kahn.

Although invariably cheerful about the present and optimistic about the future, even Melvin Jones might have had difficulty envisioning the magazine's vigorous growth. Destined to be published in 19 different languages, it would become the multilingual voice of Lionism's limitless world.

The expansion program was still evolving. G. M. Cunningham was joined by S. A. Hicks and the two men worked mainly in the western United States. By the end of the first fiscal year they had organized new clubs in Colorado, Wyoming, Missouri, Oklahoma, and Texas. Then, development stumbled.

Some 548,000 Americans died in the 1919 influenza epidemic, including Lion Cunningham's son. Few clubs were holding meetings and many were delinquent in their dues. President Lewis had an appendectomy, his wife became seriously ill, and he was unable to visit the existing clubs or promote new ones. Momentum slowed, then ground to a full stop.

However, when the future looked gloomiest, a large club that had owed dues for a year, paid in full. Several others that had been on the verge of expiring returned to life. Cunningham resumed work and organized 11 Lions clubs in four states in less than five months.

In many instances, club activities the first two years provided a preview of the association's international role in decades ahead. World War I had ended, but famine, sickness, and misery remained. Early in 1919 the Lions Club of Houston, Texas, sponsored a concert featuring Belgian musicians from the Brussels Conservatory. The performance raised more than $1,000 for the Belgian Relief Committee to help suffering children in that country. The concert was only the latest in the Houston Lions Club's projects to reduce pain in war-ravaged Europe.

In 1918, the Corsicana, Texas, Lions Club voted to furnish a drinking fountain for each school building in the city. That small project signalled the first step in the cooperation between Lions and educators. By the mid-1980s that beginning in Corsicana had grown to hundreds of schools constructed by Lions worldwide. In Mexico, especially, Lions clubs are recognized for their leadership in building and equipping schools.

Charged with energy, Lions Clubs International was vigorous and growing as members headed to Chicago and the 1919 convention. Blending brains and determination in a climate of friendly cooperation,

Lionism's founders fashioned a bold blueprint for lives devoted to helping others. They worked with meticulous care to design the practical approach that is reflected in the association's success in every part of the free world.

With an air of expectancy, Lions converged on Chicago for the Third International Convention. They were poised for a distinguished role that would soon move onto the international stage.

It was the end of the beginning.

CHAPTER TWO

Lionism's Explosive Growth

Section One—Through the end of 1945

Lionism's growth by decades:

1920:   6,451 members, 113 clubs, two nations
1930:   79,414 members, 2,202 clubs, four nations
1940:   120,251 members, 3,432 clubs, eight nations

In February 1973, Lions Clubs International welcomed its one-millionth member with appropriate ceremony when Barney Gill joined the Oceana Lions Club in Virginia Beach, Virginia. It had taken fifty-five-and-a-half years to reach this milestone. A decorated war hero, star athlete, and retired U.S. Army Lieutenant Colonel, Gill was inducted by the club secretary, Ray Campbell. At that time, Barney Gill was executive director of the United Drug Abuse Council, the planning and coordinating agency for all drug related programs in southeastern Virginia.

"I had all those years of training and background working with young people, in athletics and in the army," said Gill. "I figured it was a shame to let all that experience go to waste. When the chance to help kids who have drug problems came along I jumped at it. You can't go through life without getting involved. That's why I took the job I have now and why I became a Lion."

"When Ray asked me to join the Lions I thought about it a long time," Gill continued. "I had talked to many different service clubs and business clubs throughout the state. That gave me a chance to look them over and evaluate them. They were all doing good work, but the work that the Lions were doing impressed me most. Their job is helping people and that's where I belong, too."

However, that was all in the future when Lions gathered for their Third International Convention in Chicago in July 1919. At a luncheon held in the Red Room of the LaSalle Hotel, on the first day of the convention, a young attorney decided what the word Lions should mean: *L*iberty, *I*ntelligence, *O*ur *N*ation's *S*afety. The educational committee recommended that his suggestion be adopted.

The first state convention was held in Muskogee, Oklahoma, on May 28, 1919. The delegates voted to support the Boy Scout organizations and to urge extension of such clubs in areas where they did not exist. Three weeks later Texas held a one-day state convention in Waco.

At the end of 1917 the association numbered 25 clubs and had a membership of 800. One year later membership had nearly doubled to 1,526 in 28 clubs. By 1919, 2,364 Lions met in 42 clubs. As 1920 closed, 113 clubs served 6,451 members.

Lions became international on March 12, 1920, with the Border Cities Lions Club established in Ontario, Canada. It included the communities of Ford, Walkerville, Windsor, Sandwich, and Ojibway. The club was later named Windsor. Clubs were formed in Toronto and Hamilton, Ontario, shortly after that.

Two hundred and eighty-four delegates representing 32 clubs from nine states attended the 1920 International Convention in Denver. They elected Jesse Robinson of Oakland, California, president. Melvin Jones was elected secretary-treasurer, and he was soon thereafter named editor of *The Lion* magazine.

It was a busy convention in Denver. Delegates established a home office in Chicago and limited the size of a town in which a Lions club could be organized. They increased the number of directors from three to nine. The powers of the board were enlarged and an executive committee of five members was given authority to act on behalf of the board between its scheduled sessions. Financial problems had disappeared and the association was solvent and growing.

As it became more professional in appearance and content, the magazine claimed an increasingly important role in the organization. The early issues of 28 pages contained a blend of articles of national interest, news of individual clubs, and essays describing the host cities of new clubs. Readers profited from specific tips on ways to hold better meetings, attract new members, and retain old ones. As it evolved, the magazine gradually expanded coverage of service projects provided by various clubs.

Several stories concerned clubs that had adopted lion cubs as mascots. Some brought them to the table during regularly scheduled club luncheons and fed them bowls of milk. Understandably, as the lions grew larger and stronger the club members quickly lost interest in having them at lunch.

Offering something for everyone, one issue included a sample menu for a ladies' night program. The menu carried the suggestion, "Remember, they love flowers and music."

In March 1920, the magazine described the establishment of a wives' club, the first recorded in the association's central publication. It was called "The Lioness Club of Quincy, Illinois." The club was organized "for the express purpose of being a helpmate organization to the Lions and Quincy." Mrs. Lois Dudley of Benton Wells was its first president.

The next month's issue of the magazine devoted its cover to displaying the new Lions emblem as it appears today. The design was submitted by the Oklahoma City Lions Club and had been adopted at a Board of Directors meeting in January 1920.

Lionism was flying high in 1921. Famed World War I aviator and ace Eddie Rickenbacker was the special guest of the Stockton, California, Lions Club. He spoke to the group and then entertained them with an exciting array of aerial maneuvers.

The Lions song, "Don't You Hear Those Lions Roar?" was first introduced at the Omaha, Nebraska, convention in 1924.

Written by Robert Kellogg of the Hartford, Connecticut, Lions Club, it was performed by the Pittsburgh Quartet. It has been sung countless times since in restaurants, meeting halls, convention arenas, and anywhere else that Lions gather.

A Lion is likely to turn up almost anywhere. One, Admiral Richard E. Byrd, Jr., flew over the North Pole May 9, 1926, with famed aviator Floyd Bennett. A member of the Washington, D.C., Lions Club, Admiral Byrd sent a letter that was read during the annual convention in San Francisco, California, July 21–24, 1926. It said in part: "We carried the Lions Club flag with us to the top of the world and felt it the greatest possible honor to do so."

On November 28 and 29, 1929, Admiral Byrd and his chief pilot, Bernt Balchen, flew to the South Pole. Now Lions had been to both the top and bottom of the earth.

The news was all good at the convention. Spirits soared when Melvin Jones announced that the previous year had seen the greatest growth in the association's history with 186 new clubs organized. Significantly, 50 of these clubs had been formed without an organizer's help, demonstrating the growing extension efforts of enthusiastic Lions.

Jones also told the audience about a new Lion song book that included music with the lyrics. He gave them the news that the magazine's name was now *The Lion* and membership stood at 49,230.

China became the third Lion nation when a club began meeting in Tientsin on October 1, 1926. Truly international, the Tientsin club's 55 members included Chinese, British, German, Italian, French, Japanese, Austrian, Hungarian, and United States members.

Mexico was next with formation of a club in Nuevo Laredo on March 15, 1927. In part, that was the result of efforts by Waco, Texas, and Tulsa, Oklahoma, Lions who had entertained high ranking Mexican officials travelling in the United States in 1922.

The number of Lions clubs passed 1,000 in 1926.

United States clubs formed outside the continental United States. Clubs appeared in Honolulu, Hawaii, on September 30, 1926, San Juan, Puerto Rico, on December 22, 1936, and Anchorage, Alaska, on June 6, 1944.

Cuban Lions held their first meeting in Havana, on June 23, 1927. Lionism in Cuba was strong and vigorous for more than three decades but became inactive after the 1959 revolution.

A second Chinese club was established in Tsing-tao in 1927, with prospects for others in Peking, Shanghai, and Hangchow. Chinese Lions were active in those years, founding an eye clinic in Tsing-tao and sponsoring a Boy Scout troop and establishing a soup kitchen in Tientsin.

World War I hero Sergeant Alvin York of Tennessee spoke to the international convention in Miami, Florida, in 1927. Decorated by 12 governments, York remained unassuming in the midst of his fame. He had been named by French Marshal Foch as the greatest soldier of the war. His decorations included the Medal of Honor from the United States.

A new publication appeared, *The Lions International Monthly Letter,* the forerunner of today's *Leadership Update.* Fresh in its approach, the letter offered suggestions for programs and activities along with up-to-the-minute news of particular interest to club presidents and secretaries.

Calling for "an aggressive campaign in foreign extension so that Lionism may have the stimulation of world contact," International President Ray Riley set the tone for the 14th International Convention in Denver, Colorado, July 15–18, 1930. Members cheered when they learned that 8,935 new Lions had been inducted during the previous fiscal year and 398 new clubs had begun meeting.

In 1930, club totals stood at 2,202 and membership was now 79,414. Lionism marched steadily forward. The figures represented a robust increase during the previous decade from 113 clubs and 6,451 members in 1920.

The unquenchable spirit of the membership has made Lions Clubs International the most successful service organization in the world. The Great Depression severely tested that spirit.

In 1931, Lions in Toronto, Ontario, Canada, hosted the first convention held outside the United States. Membership hit a high of 80,456 with 2,491 clubs but began to dip the following year. Triggered by the bleak economic picture, the slide continued.

In the 15th year of Lions Clubs International, 1932, International President Julien C. Hyer of Fort Worth, Texas, asked members to reach deep within themselves to keep the association growing.

In an address titled "Real Lionism Means Actual Sacrifice," Hyer urged Lions not be quitters but to be a steadying influence. "There are members in every club," Hyer said, "who are facing a real problem in business. They need your help. Along with the blind and the under-privileged let us give close attention to our own membership. Some of our best leaders of other days are wavering financially. The Lion looks after the inmates of his own den." He urged members to "sacrifice everything but our membership."

Despite these kinds of efforts, dwindling bank accounts made club dues impossible for many. There were 79,203 Lions in 1932, 75,022 the next year, 77,218 twelve months later, and 78,871 members with 2,707 clubs in 1935.

The association received a major international publicity boost with the Chicago World's Fair in 1933 and 1934. When "The Century of Progress" opened on May 27, 1933, Lions Clubs International was represented. Visitors from every continent learned about Lions from members manning a booth in the Social Science Division at the Fair. Some 5,000 Lions representing 1,309 clubs were there, too.

Amelia Earhart, an honorary member of the New York City Lions Club, completed a record-breaking, nonstop flight from Los Angeles to Mexico during the 1935 International Convention in Mexico City. Members stood and cheered when the record was announced during the gathering. Appearing on a Mexico City radio broadcast, Earhart congratulated the organization for "doing its full share toward the furtherance of Lionism and international relationships."

There was more good news at the convention. Melvin Jones told the assembly that 171 new clubs had been formed with a membership gain of 7,500. Finances were solid and the net worth was nearly $4,000.

Membership reached a new high of 85,539 and three more nations welcomed Lions clubs: Panama, Costa Rica, and Colombia. Clubs totalled 2,725. With the exception of China, all the early international growth was confined to the Western Hemisphere.

In Cut Bank, Montana, population 1,500, the Lions stalking new members brought in 45 in a single week in 1936 and claimed "the biggest percentage of increase ever made by a single club."

At the International Convention in Providence, Rhode Island, in 1936, International President Richard Osenbaugh told the group: "Today we face a wider citizenship, a citizenship not only of the city, not only of the state, not only of a nation. As Lions we face the responsibility of the citizen of the world. It is our work to hold and maintain the proper environment and to build the proper type of future men to carry on."

The trend of internationalism set the tone at the Providence convention and a new article was added to the constitution. It provided for the formation of an International Council made up of one representative from each country in which Lionism was established. A representative was to be chosen by the clubs of that country. The council was designated to meet each year at the same time and place as the international convention and advise the board of directors on the conduct of the association with regard to international cooperation and understanding.

Melvin Jones was in the spotlight during the 1937 convention in Chicago. Past International President Roderick Beddow dedicated the entire event to him. Fifteen members of the Chicago (Central) Lions Club were on stage the second morning in Chicago's Civic Opera House. In a moving ceremony, Jones was given a medallion in his own image designed by a noted artist. Clubs were urged to observe the birthday of Melvin Jones by bringing in new Lion members during the week of January 13. The tradition is still observed with the month of January titled Founders and Rededication Month.

International President Frank Birch's 1938 New Year's message to Lions of the world was highly optimistic. "Lionism was never in a more flourishing condition than it is today," he exclaimed. "There are more clubs in the association than ever before—2,890 as this is written. There are approximately 94,000 Lions in the eight countries of Lionism.

"Almost without exception, clubs are more active. Attendance is improving, finances are better, membership is on the upgrade, activities are more varied and more worthwhile."

President Birch's optimism was founded on solid achievement. Later in 1938 membership passed 100,000 and statistics showed that Lions Clubs International was leading the way as the largest service organization in the world. However, the world picture was growing gloomier.

With the Hitler-Stalin Pact, August 23, 1939, it became clear that the world was rushing toward war. On September 1, Hitler invaded Poland from the west and a few days later Stalin's armies smashed into that ravaged nation from the east. Six years would pass before the struggle ended.

By the end of fiscal year 1939 the association counted 120,251 members with 3,432 clubs in eight countries. Until two years after the war's end, all of the growth would occur in the Western Hemisphere.

As the war in Europe spread in 1940, International President Alexander Wells said, "In the present period of strife, turmoil and great unrest throughout the world and the prevalence of so much confused thought and ill-advised action . . . one cannot but feel a deep concern for . . . the need for a stabilizing influence. In Lionism, I feel we have such a stabilizer and inasmuch as it has been truly said that Lionism represents a true cross-section of the best in citizenship, everywhere, much of our feeling of concern may to a very large extent at least be allayed."

Wells' statement came at the time in the spring of 1940 when France, Norway, Denmark, Belgium, the Netherlands, and Luxembourg had surrendered to Germany. One month later Italy declared war on Great Britain and France.

During these war years Lionism came to Guatemala when its first club began meeting in Guatemala City, on October 29, 1941. The year 1942 saw clubs founded in San Salvador, El Salvador, on February 4; Tegucigalpa, Honduras, on April 18; and Managua, Nicaragua, on December 4.

Venezuela established its first club, Barquisimeto (Central), in 1943, and a Lions club came to Lima, Peru, in 1944.

When World War II finally ended in August 1945, there were 218,184 members meeting in 4,856 clubs in 14 nations for a net gain of 40,605 over the previous year. Much of the world needed rebuilding. Lions Clubs International moved into the post-war period poised for vigorous expansion.

Section Two—1946 through 1970

Lionism's growth by decades:

1950: 402,841 members, 8,055 clubs, 28 nations
1960: 613,376 members, 15,077 clubs, 91 nations
1970: 906,579 members, 24,391 clubs, 126 nations

Three new countries joined the family of Lionism during fiscal year 1945–46: Netherlands Antilles, Bermuda, and Ecuador.

As the association celebrated its 30th anniversary at the Waldorf Astoria Hotel in New York in October 1947, it had become the largest and most active service organization in the world. At home in 19 nations, membership stood at 325,690.

At the board meeting before the anniversary celebration, Melvin Jones suggested forming a committee to establish a permanent headquarters. The McCormick Building location in Chicago was becoming cramped as the workload grew and employees were added.

One of the association's most inspiring clubs was formed in Kalaupapa, on the island of Molokai in Hawaii. The date was April 24, 1948. Kalaupapa is a leper colony founded in the 19th century by Father Damien. The charter members all suffered from Hansen's Disease— leprosy. Among the most active Lions anywhere, they provide a compelling tribute to the vision of the organization's founders. The members built a cross on a high point of land on Molokai, near their colony. A bronze plaque at the base reads: "Love Never Faileth."

Lionism came to Europe in 1948, propelled in large part by the work of Melvin Jones, International President Fred W. Smith, Assistant Secretary General Roy Keaton, and future French Lion A. A. DeLage.

President Smith was slated to represent the Association at a meeting of nongovernmental organizations in Geneva, Switzerland, May 17-21, 1948. A. A. DeLage, instructed by Melvin Jones, had gone to Europe in January 1948 with the aim of establishing the first club in Europe. He stopped in Paris to look at the possibilities and then went on to Geneva.

In March he and Keaton talked with 20 key leaders in Geneva about starting Europe's first Lions club. When the 20 men in Geneva asked for more time to discuss the proposal, Keaton and DeLage flew to Stockholm, Sweden, and met with leaders there.

International President Smith presented a charter to the Geneva Lions Club on May 19, and to the Stockholm Lions Club on May 23. The Stockholm Lions Club, however, completed organizational requirements before the Geneva Lions and is considered Europe's first Lions club.

In April 1949, the International Board of Directors gathered in Chicago and learned from Secretary General Jones that 160 acres in 31 lots had been purchased for a Lions Clubs International City. This "city" would be located 27 miles southwest of Chicago's Loop. Jones proposed that it would be a home for International Headquarters and staff employees. The corporation, known as Liondom, was authorized by the board to take title to the land and to complete negotiations for additional property. Obviously, the proposal required more study and analysis before any definite action could be taken on building and incorporating Lions International City.

At the 1949 Convention in New York City Melvin Jones told members that 291 acres in 35 lots had been purchased, well within the 400 acres authorized by the board. By the time the board again met in October in Niagara Falls, Ontario, 300 acres were owned by the association. Jones presented a sketch of his proposed city. It revealed an administration building and a residential section of 160 lots, a parking area, and a monument in front of the administration building in tribute to contributors to the city. Water and sewage installations were contemplated and the entire cost of the city was estimated at $2 million. An additional 40 acres was purchased prior to the April board meeting. Pledges from Lions to help finance the purchase of land totalled $110,000.

England welcomed Lionism the next year. "The highlight of my year as international president," said Walter C. Fisher, "was in presenting the charter to the first Lions club in England—the London Club in March 1950. Bruce Malcolm, our District A Secretary, went to London in the fall of 1949 and was instrumental in organizing the club. Our contact in London was Colonel Edward Wyndham, the charter president of the new club. This contact resulted from the war effort of Canadian Lions. During the war, the Canadian Lions pooled their money raising efforts and sent nearly $5,000 to England to help house the thousands of children who were orphaned by the war. Colonel Wyndham was connected with the Waifs and Strays Society, which administered our money."

"The biggest thrill of my year as International President," he continued, "came as a result of the same project. My wife, Alice, and I were granted a half hour private audience with Her Majesty the Queen, an honor which no other International President has ever had."

In the two years that elapsed between Europe's first Lions club and the English club, Lionism had been welcomed in Australia, Chile, France, Bolivia, Norway, the Philippines, Guam, and Denmark. At the end of 1950, 8,055 clubs in 28 countries served 402,841 members.

Delegates to the 1950 International Convention in Chicago were given a special preview of Lions International City. Many boarded Illinois Central trains and rode to the site of the proposed future home of Lionism. Construction had not begun and a considerable amount of property still needed to be purchased.

It was at the Chicago convention that Melvin Jones retired as chief managing officer of the association, a position he had held for 33 years. Now 71, Jones said he would devote his energies primarily to the development of Lions International City. Furthermore, he said he would give his "cooperation and help to build this great association to higher heights."

Jones assumed the title of secretary general for life. R. Roy Keaton was appointed director general of Lions Clubs International and, as such, became the chief managing officer of the association. Melvin Jones was also to become executive secretary of Liondom, the corporation founded to exercise control over Lions Clubs International City. Jones maintained an office in International Headquarters as prescribed by the board of directors.

The International Board meeting was held in Honolulu, Hawaii, in the spring of 1951. A significant result of the Honolulu board meeting was to suspend plans for Lions Clubs International City. Pledges had lagged. Although the board was in favor of acquiring a permanent home for the association, the members said, "It is no longer feasible, right or proper, to encourage the solicitation of or to accept funds for the purpose of building a Lions Clubs International City, but (the Association) will accept funds for Lions Clubs International and earmark and use all such funds to acquire such a home."

At the Atlantic City, New Jersey, International Convention the board members voted to find a permanent home for Lions Clubs International. After careful study, the Research Committee decided to buy a building and remodel it for International Headquarters. That was the end of the dream of Lions Clubs International City.

Led by Third Vice President Dodge the committee selected a site on the northeast corner of Michigan Avenue and Lake Street in downtown Chicago. It was a six floor building. Transportation was excellent for the staff. The total cost of the building was $750,000 and another $250,000 would be required for remodeling.

On August 29, 1952, International President Edgar M. Elbert and Secretary Byrd made the necessary arrangements and 209 North Michigan Avenue in Chicago became Lions Clubs International Headquarters. A large purple and gold Lions' emblem was placed high on the building's south wall. For nearly 20 years it greeted visitors from many parts of the world.

The flag ceremony at the Mexico City Convention in 1952 presented six new nations: Iceland, Germany, Japan, Belgium, Brazil, and the Netherlands. There were now 449,029 Lions, 9,595 clubs, and 38 Lion nations.

Lionism came to the Philippines in 1949. Although the Philippines and Japan had been bitter enemies during World War II the Filipino Lions decided to carry the message to Japan in 1952. Speaking to the convention in 1952, International President Elbert told of a moving event he had experienced as first vice president. He said, "How it encouraged me to have taken an active part in establishing Lionism in the land of Japan, to have heard Kin-ichi Ishikawa, president of the first Lions club in Tokyo say, and I quote him, 'Filipinos should detest and hate us, but then, from these same Filipinos came an invitation for us to join Lions Clubs International. International Director Manuel J. Gonzales, on the occasion of our Charter Night, presented to me a Filipino flag. I presented him with a Japanese flag. When I hugged his flag to my bosom, I could not push back the tears. From all over the world of Lionism, letters of congratulations have come to us since our Charter Night. We Japanese have qualities which are intrinsically good and beautiful. We can contribute these to the rest of the world through Lions Clubs International.' "

Elbert called the year 1952–53 the beginning of the glory years of the association. At the end of 1953 there were 46 nations in the world of Lions.

"During my year as international president I met with more than two score of the world's prominent leaders. These included President Miguel Aleman of Mexico, Prime Minister Sir Winston Churchill of Great Britain, King Gustav Adolphus VI of Sweden, Pope Pius XII, Prime Minister Schuman of France, and Prime Minister Ebert of West Germany. I also had the privilege of meeting with President Dwight D. Eisenhower. Each welcomed me with extraordinary warmth and kindness. They were delighted that their nations belonged to global Lionism."

"We Serve" became the association's official motto at the International Convention in New York City in 1954. More than 6,000 suggested mottos had been submitted. The winner was created by Lion D. A. Stevenson of Font Hill, Ontario, Canada.

It symbolizes the moving spirit of Lionism: to help others, to tear away the shrouds of ignorance and distrust that separate one human being from another. The dominant theme for more than seven decades, "We Serve" is daily translated from words to living reality on every continent.

Steadily more global in consciousness and performance, International Headquarters developed an international language department in the 1950s. Specially trained employees were handling correspondence in Spanish, French, German, Italian, and Finnish. Today, correspondence, newsletters, reports, and other types of communication are handled in the official languages of Lionism by the District and Club Services Division. In addition to English, a complete translation service is provided in Spanish, Portuguese, German, Italian, Finnish, French, Swedish, Japanese, and Korean. Staff members research at all levels of the association to make sure that materials are reliable and useful to members around the world.

Famed humanitarian Dr. Albert Schweitzer became an honorary Lion in 1957. While visiting French West Africa, then International President John L. Stickley made Dr. Schweitzer a member of the Ysounde Lions Club in the Cameroons. Dr. Schweitzer also received the Lions Humanitarian Award. In a letter to President Stickley, Dr. Schweitzer wrote, "I hope that the movement of Lions progresses. It has such a good influence on men of our era."

In the middle of 1958 John H. Vogt was named executive administrator of the International Headquarters. He became head of the fast-growing office staff and chief of administrative affairs. A native of Fort Madison, Iowa, Vogt came to Lions Clubs International from a top executive post with the Ford Motor Company.

The 14,000th Lions Club was organized at Bastad, Sweden, during fiscal 1958–59 and Lions Clubs International entered the 1960s with 606,740 members and 14,723 clubs in 104 countries and geographic areas. It arrived at the South Pole when a group of U.S. scientists and military personnel established the southernmost Lions club in the world. South Pole Antarctica became the 101st area on the Lions' map with the organization of the 59ers Club. The men were based at the Pole's Amundsen-Scott station for Geophysical Year research, and the 49ers Club of Las Vegas thought it a great idea that they symbolically plant the flag of Lionism on the polar cap. The idea began when Air Force Major A. G. Thompson spoke to the 49ers Lions Club and told them that there was one spot on earth they didn't have a Lions club, the South Pole. The Lions moved from there. Major Thompson was with the 12th Air Force, headquartered in Waco, Texas. When the Waco Lions learned of the plan, they decided to join in the extension effort. The 59ers Club was chartered with 16 members.

THE PASSING OF A LEGEND

Lions at the 44th International Convention in Atlantic City in 1961 were saddened by the death of Melvin Jones. He died in his home in Flossmoor, Illinois, on the afternoon of Thursday, June 1, 1961. He was 82 years old. Although partially incapacitated by a stroke two years before, he appeared regularly at his office in the International Headquarters building to greet visiting Lions and lend his counsel to the growing Lions association. He had never missed an international convention. At the Chicago convention the year before, Jones was helped from his wheelchair to acknowledge a sustained standing ovation from appreciative Lions from around the world.

Much of the association's success and international growth could be attributed to Jones. In a tribute, International President Finis Davis said: "Once in every generation or era a man appears and in his fleeting hour on the stage leaves an indelible imprint on the lives of his fellow men, and upon generations yet to come.

"Such a man was Melvin Jones. All over the world today he is the symbol of man's concern for his fellow man; the guiding spirit of a great movement for human welfare; the eternal inspiration for men of good will who find unselfish rewards in human service."

A charter member of the Bird City, Kansas, Lions Club when it was organized in May 1929, Vernon Shahan recalled his friendship with Melvin Jones during an interview in 1988.

"I first met Melvin back in the 1930s because I was attending a number of charter nights," he reminisced. "He reminded me a lot of my father because they were about the same size and the same age. I'm 81 now. His ability to organize and get things done made quite an impression on me. I found him to be a man of principle. He was a real guiding light and a genius to get this organization going as well as it has. He constantly stressed the concept of service to the community and working on an international scale."

As Lions mourned the loss of a long-time leader, there was also good news at the Atlantic City convention. Members cheered when President Davis told them that 17,000 new Lions were inducted during the year and 800 new clubs had been established. Lionism was now in 113 nations with 630,000 active members.

In 1965, there were 19,435 clubs and more than 760,000 members. Lionism continued its dramatic expansion. The 20,000th Lions club was organized in 1966, the Walnut Creek (Rossmoor) Club in California.

As Lions moved into the golden anniversary year, 1967, membership had passed the 800,000 mark. One nation in particular was enjoying spectacular growth, Japan. Since the Tokyo Lions Club, Japan's first, was organized in 1952, Japan's growth rate in new clubs and members has been one of the largest anywhere in the world. In 1967, only 15 years after it joined Lionism's international family, Japan had the second largest membership of any country in the association, a position it holds to this day.

In only three years, from 1964 to 1967, Japan experienced a 67 percent increase in clubs and a 37 percent gain in members.

France was the largest Lion country in Europe, with Sweden and Italy not far behind.

Lionism's Golden Anniversary was recognized by nations and communities in many parts of the world. A number of countries issued commemorative postage stamps recognizing the association's 50th year. The stamp issued by the United States depicted International President

Lindsay's theme, "Search for Peace." Other countries issuing anniversary stamps included Brazil, Senegal, Colombia, Morocco, Paraguay, Bolivia, Luxembourg, Australia, Chad, the Philippines, the Central African Republic, Upper Volta, Dahomey, French Somaliland, Nigeria, Peru, Korea, Monaco, Belgium, Japan, Iran, Chile, Cameroon, El Salvador, Vietnam, Ethiopia, and Ecuador.

There were 118 countries hosting Lions clubs, with 837,344 members and 21,479 clubs. Lives were changed as members served their communities, their countries, and the world. Past International President Jorge Bird said in his farewell address: "I returned from my world travels convinced that Lionism is at its peak of enthusiasm and accomplishments. Its spirits are high, its mood confident and optimistic. Its presence is secure and its future glows with promise." He was ending his term at the 1968 International Convention in Dallas, Texas.

In 1970, Lion Wilburn L. Wilson became executive administrator at International Headquarters. A member of the Chicago (Central) Lions Club, he had served on the International Headquarters staff since 1932 and been treasurer since 1944.

Steadily building on past success, Lions Clubs International moved into the next decade with confidence, commitment, and awareness of Melvin Jones' observation: "You can't get very far until you start doing something for somebody else."

Section Three—1971 to 1990

   1980: 1,288,398 members, 33,864 clubs, 146 nations
   1990: 1,368,991 members, 39,415 clubs, 166 nations

"This building is a temple built without hands," declared International President Dr. Robert D. McCullough on April 21, 1971, at the dedication of the new International Headquarters building in Oak Brook, Illinois. "It was built by the hearts of 950,000 Lions around the world."

The 108,000 square foot, tri-level structure doubled the space of the former building at 209 North Michigan in downtown Chicago. With continuing worldwide growth, even the new structure became too small by the middle of the next decade. Extensive remodelling to create more space expanded the building by about 30 percent. The new space was completed in 1986. Today, the 400 staff members there and in other parts of the world serve the needs of Lions, Lionesses, and Leos in 171 nations and geographical areas.

It is, as Dr. McCullough observed, "a memorial to those who have served Lionism from the beginning."

The year 1971 also marked the formation of the 25,000th club when 32 charter members met for the first time as the Fred, Texas, Lions Club. Silsbee, Texas, Lions sponsored the new club.

More than 30,000 Lions and their families were on hand for the 1971 International Convention in Las Vegas, Nevada.

Newly-installed International President Robert J. Uplinger of Syracuse, New York, announced as his theme for 1971–72, *Lionism Is Commitment*. "It would be wonderful if I, by some miracle, could manage to distill into a serum all of the motivation and psychology necessary for this commitment and then inject it into each one of our nearly one million members. Of course, this would be impossible. But if you will assume with me that I have such power, I would suggest that there are three main ingredients which I would mix into the serum to energize our theme for this year of 1971–72—*Lionism Is Commitment*."

The 55th International Convention in 1972 was held in Mexico City. The flag ceremony introduced two new island countries to the family of Lionism, Nevis in the British West Indies and Macao, a Portuguese colony in the Far East.

Lions gathered in Miami Beach, Florida, for the 1973 International Convention and incoming president Tris Coffin of Montreal, Quebec, Canada, introduced his 1973–74 theme to the Convention—*One Million Men Serving Mankind*.

More than one million Lions serving in clubs in 528 districts and 149 countries and geographical areas around the world were ready to answer President Coffin's call.

California's Governor Ronald Reagan welcomed Lions in San Francisco in July 1974, for the 57th International Convention. He said, "The scope of your many activities is an impressive demonstration of what active and concerned citizens can accomplish by working together. Your efforts are helping to make this a better world for everybody. . . . The people around this globe have discovered the real meaning of brother-hood through such things as helping the blind as you do, helping crippled children, educating the disadvantaged and any number of good works of compassion from one human being to another. And because this help stems from humanitarian concern for people, it represents something very special and very precious, especially in today's world where there's so much cynicism and distrust."

Johnny Balbo became international president in 1974. Lionism flourished in 136 countries with more than 27,000 clubs and more than a million members carrying the message.

By 1975, the International Headquarters building was mortgage-free. Past International President Balbo said, "During the March 1975 board meeting in Oak Brook, Illinois, Lions Clubs International reached a new milestone. We had the pleasure of burning the mortgage of the International Headquarters building. In less than four years, we had paid off all our indebtedness on our new building."

"I visited many heads of state, as did other International Presidents before me," said Past President Balbo. "Two of these visits, though, stand out in my mind. One was to His Holiness, Pope Paul VI, and the other to Dr. Rudolf Kirschlager, President of Austria. Both spoke of the strong force our association was for peace around the world. Pope Paul talked about the great humanitarian services performed by Lions club members around the world. He was well versed in our goals."

Past International President Balbo continued, "Dr. Kirschlager said, 'Russia, Red China and the United States would never make peace in the world. Peace comes from the family—your family, my family, the entire family of Lions Clubs International is a strong force for peace in the world.' "

The third session of the international convention in Dallas in 1975 brought memories to many long-time Lions. A special tribute was paid to the memory of Helen Keller who, at the international convention 50 years earlier, offered her challenge to the Lions to take up the cause of the visually handicapped. Actress Carolyn Jones read Miss Keller's challenge to the Lions of 50 years before.

This was followed by an address by Dr. Richard Kinney, at that time director of the Hadley School for the Blind in Winnetka, Illinois, the world's foremost correspondence school for the visually handicapped.

"Lions," said Dr. Kinney, deaf and blind himself, "you are playing a tremendous role in attacking the most terrible blindness of all—the blindness of ignorance and prejudice that sets one man against another, one race against another, one nation against another. . . . It was once said, 'Live and let live' but Lionism has raised this principle to that nobler 'Live and help live.' "

During their travels, international presidents encounter a variety of stirring experiences. "One of the most beautiful moments for me occurred at a Multiple District 111 meeting in Germany," recalled Past International President Harry J. Aslan. "A German Lion came up to me and said, 'President Aslan, I want to relate a story to you. Thirty-one years ago I came to the United States. I came to Dallas in 1944 as a prisoner of war after I was captured by the American army. Thirty-one years later, in 1975, I came back to Dallas and you installed me as a District Governor.'

"This had profound meaning and it touched me deeply," continued Lion Aslan. "And I said to District Governor Dr. Friedrich Bocker, 'Lionism is a force, a humanitarian force that recognizes that we can put aside animosities, hatreds and jealousies. Through Lionism, enemies have become friends. Through Lionism, we can join together serving people on a human level, recognizing the value of the human being.' "

The 1976 International Convention in Hawaii was the largest in Lionism's history. A record total of 1,420 new Lions clubs were established during the year. Membership had reached an all-time high of 1,158,650.

In September 1976, the 30,000th Lions club was established and received its charter from International President Joao Fernando Sobral of Sao Paulo, Brazil. The landmark club was the Callaway, Minnesota, Lions Club sponsored by the Detroit Lakes, Minnesota, Lions.

At the 1978 International Convention in Tokyo, also one of the best attended in association history, incoming International President Ralph A. Lynam, in his inaugural address, spoke of what a privilege it is to be a part of the family of Lionism. "We must cherish and protect this tremendous international flavor of our organization," he stressed, "for a better world is within our reach."

The year 1978 saw another change in the administrative leadership of the association with General Counsel and Secretary Roy Schaetzel replacing the retiring W. L. Wilson as executive administrator. Schaetzel had joined the International Headquarters staff in 1964 as assistant general counsel and was appointed to his most recent position in 1969. A member of the Chicago (Central) Lions Club, he vowed upon assuming his new duties to provide the board of directors and Lions worldwide with the administrative productivity, efficiency, and adaptability they need and desire.

Through nearly all of Lionism's history *The Lion* magazine has been a highly effective means of informing members of the work of their fellow members.

Today there are 29 editions of the magazine published in 19 languages—English, Spanish, Japanese, French, Swedish, Italian, German, Finnish, Flemish, Icelandic, Turkish, Norwegian, Greek, Korean, Portuguese, Dutch, Danish, Chinese, and Thai. English language editions are published in North America (the Headquarters edition), Australia, New Zealand, England (British-Irish), Hong Kong, and India. The Headquarters and Spanish language editions are published at International Headquarters. The others are produced in areas of their distribution.

The Headquarters edition established in 1918 is the oldest. The Spanish edition was established in 1944. Six European editions began publishing in 1957—French, Finnish, Flemish/French, German, Italian, and Swedish. Soon Lions in other nations were printing their own editions of the magazine.

"The magazine's purpose is two-fold," says Robert Kleinfelder, senior editor of the Headquarters edition of *The Lion* since 1974. "One is to give credit to individual clubs and districts for services they have performed. The other is to inspire Lions to carry out similar projects and to be proud of what Lions, Lionesses, and Leos are accomplishing.

"By informing and inspiring, *The Lion* also makes its contribution to growth. The more pride individual Lions take in what they're doing, the more apt they are to found new clubs and to invite friends and business associates to join."

"The future of *The Lion* will parallel that of Lionism," he continued. "As Lionism grows and more Lions become aware of what a great tool the magazine can be, they will want to establish their own editions. Undoubtedly, there will be many more language editions in the coming years."

Fernando Fernandez, editor of the Spanish language edition since 1970 says, "The magazine helps by publishing details of significant projects of clubs in Latin America. Readers in Lima, Peru, see a story about how Lions in Monterrey, Mexico, built this big hospital. The club in Peru decides to undertake a project of the same scope. Most likely, the Peruvian club will get in touch with the club in Monterrey to get details on their project.

"The magazine becomes a 'how to' manual—how to get doctors together in a caravan, or set up a relief mission to a disaster-torn village. The inspiration, the practical points, the learning are all there."

The magazine also helps bind Lions together as brothers wherever they are. "Lions in Uruguay, Guatemala, Puerto Rico, Mexico— wherever—read about LCIF projects, international headquarters activities, membership drives, general programs and the activities of clubs throughout the world."

Fernandez, like Kleinfelder, feels *The Lion* helps attract new members. "I have seen *The Lion* in offices of doctors, dentists and opticians in Mexico and Puerto Rico. Patients thumb through it and are impressed by what Lions are doing. They are motivated to become members."

In the later 1970s Lionism expanded rapidly in Japan, Korea, the Philippines, Malaysia, and India. Since 1975 there has been rapid growth in Africa.

New clubs were chartered in Swaziland, Lesotho, Sierra Leone, Bophuthatswana, the Comoro Islands, Benin, Gambia, Ghana, and Equatorial Guinea between 1979 and 1982.

International presidents continued their tireless travel schedules. In his report to the membership at the 65th International Convention in Atlanta, Georgia, on June 30, 1982, outgoing President Kaoru "Kay" Murakami of Kyoto, Japan, said: "During the past 12 months, I spent only 14 days at home. The rest of my time was devoted to my work for Lionism. Right now, I am filled with deep satisfaction that I toiled to the limit of human possibility, both physically and mentally."

President Murakami told the group he traveled 764,344 miles, or the equivalent of 32.5 trips around the world. It is also equal to more than three trips to the moon.

International President Everett J. "Ebb" Grindstaff finished his term with a report to the membership at the convention in Honolulu, Hawaii, on June 22, 1983. Looking back at 12 months of positive effort he pointed with pride to "More than 140,000 new members added since July 1, 1982, 31,630 in our October Anniversary Membership Growth Program alone, an increase over last year. These statistics show that we have 1,346,179 Lions worldwide."

He noted that during his term, goals had been selected that would create increased continuity in association programs. Grindstaff declared, "This has been a year of achievement and a year during which foundations have been laid for continued involvement in specific activities in the years ahead."

With the slogan, "Join Hands in Service," Dr. James M. "Jim" Fowler served as international president in 1983–84.

During President Fowler's term the association produced a feature film, *New Challenges, New Opportunities*. Narrated in ten languages, it explores the technology available in Lions-supported learning facilities to enhance employment opportunities for the blind and visually impaired.

The Drug Awareness Program also expanded in many parts of the world. Reports streaming into International Headquarters showed that 265 districts named drug awareness chairmen. A *District Drug Awareness Chairman's Guide* was produced in all ten association languages and was distributed to the chairmen and to district governors. A drug awareness kit was produced consisting of a slide show, a cassette, a written script, and a drug awareness handbook. This provided information on setting up drug awareness programs, initiating activities, locating resources, and recognizing the harmful effects of drugs on young people and their families.

Under International President Fowler's leadership, a concise statement of the association's official program was created and distributed called *The Lions Drug Awareness Program*. *Drug Awareness: A Guide for Leo Clubs* was also provided. *Myth and Fact,* an English language pamphlet was produced exploring the truth about marijuana's harmful effects.

In his report at the 67th International Convention in San Francisco, California, in 1984, President Fowler announced that 908 new Lions clubs were organized during his term bringing the worldwide total to

38,806 Lions clubs in 157 nations and geographical areas. Worldwide membership totaled 1,353,350.

International President Bert Mason had good news for the Lions attending the 68th International Convention in Dallas, Texas, on June 19, 1985.

He reported the continuing enthusiastic support for the Lions' Drug Awareness Program and extensive use of Lions-created resource materials. Lions, Lionesses, and Leos were working together in drug education programs in communities on every continent.

President Mason announced that a Diabetes Awareness Kit, consisting of a handbook and slide presentation, was being developed. Diabetes awareness seminars, workshops, film presentations, and camps for children with diabetes were being implemented around the world.

United States President Ronald Reagan brought the delegates to their feet with his ringing support for Lions volunteerism in solving human problems. It was the first time a president still in office spoke to an international convention. Former U.S. Secretary of State Henry Kissinger also spoke to the Lions and their families at the Dallas gathering.

There was good news, too, in membership development: 144,567 new Lions donned the lapel pin during the year and worldwide membership stood at 1,347,775. Seven hundred and ninety-one new Lions clubs were organized between July 1, 1984, and July 1, 1985. Worldwide there were more than 37,000 clubs in 158 countries and geographical areas.

Determined to "Bring Quality to Life" during his term, International President Sten A. Akestam visited more than 40 nations with his wife, Martha, during 1986–87.

One of the highlights of his term occurred on January 7, 1987, when syndicated columnist Ann Landers printed President Akestam's letter urging those at high risk to seek diabetes testing.

He said, "The letter appeared in 1,200 newspapers and resulted in tremendous public interest, with more than 1,000 phone calls being received at International Headquarters. To meet the demand for additional information on diabetes, Lions clubs offered thousands of diabetes brochures available from our headquarters.

"These are only a few examples of how our membership is and can be involved in working on behalf of this important objective, the ultimate aim of which is to eliminate diabetes."

Akestam added, "Less than ten years ago, the Lions Clubs International Foundation had its first $1 million year. This past February, the Foundation had its first $1 million month. From July 1986 through April 1987, donations to LCIF totalled $4,187,455. That was a 67 percent increase over the same period last year."

During his term, club strength reached 38,700. The membership climbed to 1,352,177.

International President Judge Brian Stevenson emphasized the importance of the association's remaining sensitive to changing attitudes. At the 71st Annual Convention in Denver, Colorado, in 1988 he told the assembly: "The amendment to our International Constitution, eliminating the word 'male' as a condition for membership in a Lions club, has encouraged women the world over to become Lions. At present, approximately 10,000 women are members of clubs in 69 countries, and I am certain women will continue to demonstrate their wish to serve community and human needs through membership in Lions clubs."

At the same convention, incoming International President Austin Jennings pointed to a new area of potential membership growth. He said, "A scrutiny of demographics will show large influxes of people in the suburban areas, not to mention sections within our cities which are being populated more and more by young business and professional people. We need to arouse the interest of this 'new breed' of individuals to the benefits of serving through Lionism."

Immediately after the international convention, Executive Administrator Roy Schaetzel retired and Mark C. Lukas, manager of the executive services division and assistant executive administrator, was named to the top administrative post of the association. He joined the International Headquarters staff in 1979 as manager of the Lions Clubs International Foundation, was named to his most recent post in 1988, and is a member of the Sugar Grove, Illinois, Lions Club.

"A continuing challenge to our obligations as members of the association," Lukas observed, "is to give more than we receive. We must always maintain a spirit of purposefulness at International Headquarters and strive for quality in our every task. "Never," he emphasized, "should we be content with anything but our very best performance in whatever we undertake."

He further observed that one of the primary functions of the headquarters staff is to help the association's elected officials develop programs which are significant in scope and relevant to the over 1.5 million Lions, Lionesses, and Leos serving in nations around the world.

The next year at the Miami/Miami Beach, Florida, convention, as Jennings ended his term, he pointed to the addition of two new countries during the year and emphasized their importance. "With the establishment of the Budapest, Hungary, Lions Club and the Poznan, Poland, Lions Club, we have become the first service club organization to be represented in what is generally considered the Eastern Bloc. I attended the organizational meetings of both clubs, met with the new Lions and with their sponsoring Lions from Finland, organizers of the Budapest club, and Lions from Sweden, sponsors of the Poznan club. I realized fully what an important step this is for the expansion of Lionism."

A Lions Club was also organized that year in Tallinn, Estonia.

To develop the concept Jennings described in Denver in 1987, the Ad Hoc Committee on Membership Classification, chaired by then International Director Kay K. Fukushima, studied the situation and presented its findings to the International Board of Directors at the March 1988 board meeting. The conclusion of the committee was that the association's growth had been struggling in downtown metropolitan areas. This gave birth to a unique experimental approach. The concept is called "The New Urban Lions Club." One of the primary results of the March 1988 board meeting was to define just what was meant by a "quality member" and enable potential sponsors to ask appropriate questions of prospective members.

Fifty-four young professionals are active in a new urban Lions club operating in Sacramento (Crest), California. The sponsoring club is the Sacramento (Senator) Lions Club with Past International Director Fukushima serving as the Guiding Lion. The membership is primarily middle to upper level managers, male and female, in their late 20s to late 40s. Most of the members live in the suburbs and none of the members ever belonged to a service organization before. The new club meets twice a month and its primary service project concentrates on improving literacy.

In Toronto, Ontario, Canada, there is another "new" Lions club. Its roster is composed exclusively of medical personnel. Dr. William J. Copeman, a Lion for 35 years and past district governor of District A-5, suggested forming a doctors Lions club. The main objective of the club is to deal with various medical needs in Toronto, assist underprivileged children, and raise funds for research at the University of Toronto.

The club has been a major success. Lions clubs have long been involved in the needs of the medical community. For example, in northern Ontario, 15 medical centers now exist wholly or largely because of the generosity of Lions. Such projects as a dialysis camp for children with kidney disorders, dog guides for the blind, and highly technical treatment equipment for hospitals have all been made possible through funding by Lions.

Dr. Copeman explained, "A Doctors Lions Club would increase significantly the number and range of health oriented services Lions perform. In addition to its own activities, the Doctors Lions Club would encourage members of the existing Lions clubs in Toronto to become even more involved in health related projects."

The Doctors Lions Club was officially established on December 19, 1988, with Dr. Copeman as its charter president. It is already highly successful.

Other pilot programs are being developed. Studies continue by the Extension, Field Operations, and Membership Committee to learn the best ways to involve individuals in metropolitan areas in the worldwide activities of Lions Clubs International.

"The key to growth is member involvement," emphasized then International Director Jim Cameron of Urbana, Indiana. "Indiana led the United States and Canada in 1987 in net membership growth. A lot of credit goes to the caravan to Guatemala because people got personally involved. It created a great deal of enthusiasm in our state and a great deal of interest and good publicity for Lionism. One successful project leads to another. There's a winning attitude that makes you glad to be part of the project. You can't imagine how good you feel when you come back from a project like the Guatemala caravan. I think that's a major reason for the growth of Lionism in general and in Indiana in particular. It's because of the involvement of people helping people. I think that will remain the secret of Lions expansion throughout the world."

That expansion seems assured. New members will invigorate individual clubs and Lionism everywhere. Their enthusiasm, ideas and energy make it possible for the Lions' *We Serve* imperative to spread and remain relevant in a rapidly changing world.

Recognizing that membership growth is vital to the future of Lionism, the International Board of Directors adopted a resolution designed to strengthen every Lions club's drive to build its membership roster. Adopted at the June 1989 meeting in Orlando, Florida, the resolution provides for the establishment by each club of a three-member membership committee.

Before the resolution there was no formal mechanism for bringing in new members at the local level. The resolution established an organizational structure for membership which runs from local clubs through the zone and multiple districts.

A new club position, membership director, which automatically falls to the chairman of the membership committee, was created by the resolution. Each member is elected to a three-year term, consistent with the three-year term served by multiple district membership chairmen. In the second year, the elected member becomes a committee vice chairman, and in the third, chairman. This rotation system better prepares the committee chairman and assures continuity of the committee's work.

The club membership director is responsible for:

- developing a growth program for the club and presenting the plan to the board of directors for approval;
- encouraging Lions during meetings to bring new members into the club;
- setting up membership orientation sessions;
- serving as a member of the zone level membership committee.

The establishment of club membership committees provides a structure for growth. Unquestionably, Lions will prove equal to the task of inspiring vigorous growth into the 21st Century.

CHAPTER THREE

The Objects and Code of Ethics

"THROUGH the years the Objects and Code of Ethics have helped me to keep my eye on what's right and what's important," said Bill Jansky, past president of the Riverside Township Lions Club near Chicago, Illinois.

"The Objects and Ethics highlight the need for truth and honesty in all personal and business activities and they keep us aware of the importance of service as a fundamental principle in Lionism. I think it's significant that when Lions Clubs International began, the early members made a major point of stressing that none of us should use our Lions membership as a way to further our business. The Objects and Ethics remind us to carefully examine our motives and probe life goals as we measure actions on the basis of benefit to others."

Using truth and concern for others as measuring sticks, the Objects and Code of Ethics look beyond the profit of the moment. They offer a glowing vision of growth and service. Treating the individual as something more than a temporal fragment, they put man in proper perspective, recognizing that the welfare of each human being is linked with the welfare of all human beings.

Describing his first reading of the Code and the Objects, Past International President H. C. Petry, Jr., said, "I could not help but become personally interested in Lionism and recognize it as an organization of tremendous value and integrity." Following these documents in one's personal life "develops character and integrity in ways which might not happen otherwise. I thank the Lions for bringing my own personal commitment of time and resources for the benefit of those less fortunate than myself."

Past International President W. R. Bryan observed: "Like my religion, I find it difficult to put into words how the Lions Code has affected me. I would dare hope—perhaps pray—that my behavior as a Lion has had a positive influence on those with whom I came in contact around the world."

OBJECTS

To create and foster a spirit of understanding among the peoples of the world.

To promote the principles of good government and good citizenship.

To take an active interest in the civic, cultural, social, and moral welfare of the community.

To unite the clubs in the bonds of friendship, good fellowship, and mutual understanding.

To provide a forum for the open discussion of all matters of public interest; provided, however, that partisan politics and sectarian religion shall not be debated by club members.

To encourage service-minded men to serve their community without personal financial reward, and to encourage efficiency and promote high ethical standards in commerce, industry, professions, public works, and private endeavors.

CODE OF ETHICS

To show my faith in the worthiness of my vocation by industrious application to the end that I may merit a reputation for quality of service.

To seek success and to demand all fair remuneration or profit as my just due, but to accept no profit or success at the price of my own self-respect lost because of an unfair advantage taken or because of questionable acts on my part.

To remember that in building up my business it is not necessary to tear down another's; to be loyal to my clients or customers and true to myself.

Whenever a doubt arises as to the right or ethics of my position or action towards my fellow men, to resolve such doubt against myself.

To hold friendship as an end and not a means. To hold that true friendship exists not on account of the service performed by one to another, but that true friendship demands nothing but accepts service in the spirit in which it is given.

Always to bear in mind my obligations as a citizen to my nation, my state, and my community, and to give to them my unswerving loyalty in word, act, and deed. To give them freely of my time, labor, and means.

To aid my fellow men by giving my sympathy to those in distress, my aid to the weak, and my substance to the needy.

To be careful with my criticism and liberal with my praise; to build up and not destroy.

As Past International President Joseph M. McLoughlin noted, "No society can maintain high standards without the kind of public-spirited citizens who comprise Lions clubs."

The Objects and Ethics provide a framework of personal integrity, concern, and global vision. Compared with the concepts and goals of most private organizations in 1917 they were unusual. It was instantly evident to new members that Lions placed a high priority on meeting community needs and demonstrating high ethical standards in their personal lives.

Years after the Objects and Ethics had been adopted, Melvin Jones observed: "If a Lions club follows out its Objects, it will have the full program. It will be interested in world affairs, in national problems, in the needs of its own local community and in the welfare of individual members."

Sheila Gwin agrees. In 1979, when she was four and lived in Tonto Basin, Arizona, she nearly lost her arm. Returning from a hunting trip with her stepfather and a neighbor boy, Sheila was hit by a shotgun blast when a 12-gauge shotgun accidentally discharged. Her right arm was severed above the elbow.

"Sheila was flown to Scottsdale Memorial Hospital and the arm was brought along, packed in ice," said Jim Rush, past president of the Papago Mountain Lions Club in Scottsdale. "She was on the operating table for nearly 15 hours as a team of microsurgeons worked to restore the limb. She's had eight operations in all. When the Papago Mountain Lions heard of Sheila's plight they began raising money to help. A fund was established for her at a local bank. The Lions offered to administer and coordinate it to pay for operations and subsequent therapy."

The Arizona Lions state convention in 1980 featured an appeal to help Sheila and the response was overwhelming. A member of the Papago Mountain Lions Club told the assembled Lions about the child and said, "Next year we'll have this girl here and she'll sign her name using the right arm that was severed." In fact, the next year Sheila appeared at the convention and did just that. In all, the Lions raised $59,000 for the youngster.

"It's now 1987 and Sheila Gwin has about 95 percent use of her right arm," said Jim Rush. "If a person didn't know there had been an accident he wouldn't be able to tell what had happened. It's important to emphasize that this was a combined project of Lions clubs of Arizona with help from many other sources. The Papago Mountain Lions Club coordinated the effort, and doctors and hospitals donated immense amounts of services for the girl."

"The Objects of Lionism come to life with something like that," Rush continued. "Two years ago we flew in an eight-year-old girl from Nicaragua for corrective surgery. She had been born with a cleft palate and an operation in Nicaragua had been botched so badly she couldn't talk. She couldn't eat because food would fall out of her mouth. Skilled surgery repaired the condition and now she's perfectly normal. This is what Lionism is all about: reaching out in our own community or across thousands of miles to help another human being. The Objects and Code of Ethics give us a guide for expanding our lives."

Legend has it that Melvin Jones had made an exhaustive study of every code found in history. He had examined the thoughts of Hammurabi of Babylon (2250 B.C.), the Napoleonic Code, the Mosaic

Commandments, the Justinian Codex; and he had been struck by one feature common to all of them. Said Jones, "They were all legal codes filled with negative commands. That was not what we were looking for. What we finally got was what you might call a 'leadership code,' and there isn't a 'Thou shalt not' in it."

Much of the work on the Code of Ethics was done by G. M. Cunningham, who was then secretary of the Houston Lions Club. He wrote the first draft and sent it to Melvin Jones who sent it on to R. E. Kleinschmidt and Walter Lybrand, attorneys who lived in Oklahoma City, for a legal review.

At the convention held in St. Louis in 1918, J. Hirsch was named chairman of a committee to determine whether it needed changes. K. H. Warren, D. F. Hurst, Arlie J. Cripe, and H. F. Endsley served on the committee with him. They discussed the code during two evening meetings and then voted for its adoption. The delegates agreed and the Code has been a foundation of Lionism ever since.

The Code of Ethics has remained unchanged, although through the years some alterations have been proposed. Melvin Jones said, "I recall that some delegate wanted a few amendments at the convention in Hot Springs in 1922. You should have heard the uproar."

Along with its permanence, for Past International President Lloyd Morgan, the Code is a practical guide to behavior enriched by the fact that "there is a warm feeling of satisfaction knowing that you are associated with others who believe as you do."

The Objects and Ethics make Lions international good neighbors. However, being a good neighbor calls for more than a few casual gestures. Many different things may be needed. It may come naturally, but more likely it requires precise planning and considerable effort. The good neighborliness of Lions around the world is reflected in numberless thoughtfully designed projects.

Take the experience of Martha. Totally blind and deaf, she entered the Florida Lions Conklin Center for the Multihandicapped Blind in Daytona Beach in the summer of 1981. Sixteen years old at the time, Martha was energetic and intensely interested in the world around her. Her academic skills were excellent, so the specially trained staff designed a program tailored specifically to her requirements. Martha was taught dressmaking using braille patterns, a regular sewing machine, needles, and thread.

"Along with learning to sew," Martha explained, "my instructors showed me how to cook in a regular kitchen and I can prepare anything I want now. I learned how to travel anywhere I want to go and gained a great deal of confidence in meeting people and functioning in unfamiliar situations. The Conklin Center taught me that my life doesn't have to be limited but I can continue to grow through new skills and experiences."

The multihandicapped students at the Florida Lions Conklin Center are all legally blind. Some are also deaf and suffer speech problems; others are retarded. Some have suffered brain damage and some have orthopedic handicaps and are confined to wheelchairs or use crutches. While not all will ultimately be able to hold a job, all will learn to take care of themselves in their homes.

Students at the center range in age from 16 to 69. One of them, a young man we'll call Gordon, spent two months at the facility in the summer of 1980. Deaf and nearly completely blind, he had lost most of his sight as a result of retinitis pigmentosa.

"During the two months I spent at the center," said Gordon, "I took part in what they call an 'enrichment program' that helped to sharpen my mobility skills and improved my speech, reading, and mathematics. They also taught me tactile sign language in case I eventually lose all of my sight. I learned other skills like house cleaning, preparing meals, and grocery shopping. I was given some tests to help determine what vocational direction would be best for me. At the end of two months I was far more independent and confident. I plan to continue my education after graduating from high school."

The Conklin Center began with a Lion's vision sparked by a 1972 survey showing that there were more than 1,250 multi-handicapped blind in Florida, with more than 700 of them classed as deaf-blind. These men, women, and children were receiving only custodial care and no formal education at all.

Led by the late Past International Director Millard B. Conklin, the Florida Lions organized the Florida Lions Aid to Blind and Sight. They obtained an eight-acre tract of land valued at $200,000 for the sum of one dollar. Money for construction came from many sources, including many Florida Lions clubs and the Florida Lions Foundation. It opened on January 28, 1979, the nation's first residential training center for the multihandicapped blind.

The center has live-in facilities for 16 students and a staff of 32, including 12 academic instructors, two instructors in independent living, and one recreational instructor. The program is individualized for each student. The nine members of the board of directors are all Lions.

Don Wedewer, a Lion who is director of the Florida Division of Blind Services, has been a major force in the Conklin Center's development. A veteran of World War II, Don lost his eyesight and both legs in the Battle of the Bulge in 1944. After discharge from the army he graduated from the University of Missouri in 1950 and received a Master's degree from the same school in 1952.

"Don Wedewer has always played a significant role in expanding training and educational opportunities for the blind," said Ed McCoy, director of the Conklin Center. "He's a man of outstanding ability with a great understanding of the needs of the blind. Whenever we've needed direction or help of any kind, Don has been right there to give us a hand."

One of the first students there—Bill—was totally blind, somewhat retarded, and possessed no work skills. Bill was, however, always well groomed and neatly dressed. In only four months at the Center he responded remarkably. Bill could travel to all parts of the facility and even take part in vocational classes across the street.

On February 27, 1981, after two years of intensive training, he graduated. Today he lives semi-independently and works full-time operating a power sewing machine in a Florida workshop—one of the skills he learned at the Center. Helpless and hopeless when he arrived, Bill has become a confident, optimistic young man. His life has been transformed.

Men and women of all ages are enjoying new freedom because the Florida Lions linked deeds with the words: "We Serve." Everybody benefits. Don Wedewer's office has found that every dollar spent on rehabilitating a blind person brings in $11 in taxes as a result.

The Objects and the Code of Ethics come to life in every part of the world when Lions work together. In his innaugural address in 1967, Past International President Jorge Bird said, "It seems that men too often forget that we are all creatures of God, that we are all brothers. At this very moment millions of human beings need our help and our spirit of service. We shall not remain indifferent to the great problems of our times. Let us remember that we are not Lions for ourselves. We are Lions for those who are not."

For more than seven decades Lions have demonstrated compassion, self sacrifice, and generosity in thousands of different ways. And, they've had fun doing it.

Take the giant cow built by the New Salem, North Dakota, Lions Club. They installed a fiberglass Holstein on top of the highest hill in the area. Thirty-eight feet high, 50 feet long, and 12,000 pounds, it can be seen for miles. Billed as the "World's largest cow," the huge Holstein is a joint project of the local dairy farmers and residents, sponsored by the New Salem Lions Club.

The area around New Salem is the leading dairy producing area in the state and the Lions thought that some kind of monument should be erected to honor the Holstein cow. They are quick to point out that their giant leading lady is more than "just another pretty face."

The rise and fall of civilizations is often marked by the rise and fall of values—and the documents which express those values—in the view of Robert J. Uplinger, international president from 1971 to 1972. "As history moved on, the world received the English Magna Carta, the Mayflower Compact, the Declaration of Independence, and other land-mark documents," Uplinger said. "When American culture changed from rural to urban at the time of World War I, Lions Clubs International adopted the 'Objects and Ethics' as we have them today. 'Objects and Ethics' has had a profound effect on all of our leadership and serves as a rule and guide for Lions everywhere."

The origins of the Lions movement in the business community are evident in the first three Ethics and in the final Object. However, in designing these standards the founders made it clear that this new service club was separating itself from the business community. They emphasized that a Lions club was not just another quasi-social arm of private business and the professions. Leaving absolutely no room for confusion, they declared that it was to be a private, non-political, non-sectarian association. This is demonstrated in the fifth Object.

The Objects had been debated, discussed, considered, explored, talked over, and examined at length and in depth by the time they came up for a vote at the 1919 convention in Chicago, Illinois. The meeting was small enough so that each representative had an opportunity to declare his views on the Objects. During a spirited discussion the delegates worked out their differences and then approved the Objects of Lionism at the association's 1919 Convention in Chicago.

Basically, the Objects and Ethics have served as guidelines for individual members; a set of principles for private and professional life and standards by which a person may become a better citizen. They stimulate thoughtful action and cooperation with other Lions and community leaders in improving conditions locally, nationally, and globally. The Objects and Ethics encourage Lions to become citizens of the world.

Past International President Edward M. Lindsey adds that working on the practical level as a Lion "made me more acutely aware of my fellow man and his plight, gave me a higher understanding of my citizenship obligations, a more sensitive compassion for those in need and a desire to live up to the almost spiritual aspects of the Lion's Code of Ethics and Objects."

Although the delegates to the early conventions were exclusively from Lions clubs in the United States, and clubs were not chartered outside the country until the 1920s, the founders envisioned a global mission. They foresaw the international goals of the new organization. They knew that future Lions would be concerned with providing help where it was needed. Although Lions Clubs International was born in the United States, its founders were certain it would take root and flourish on every continent.

Hence, the First Object: "To create and foster a spirit of understanding among the peoples of the world."

"There are no national borders to confine Lionism. It finds a home wherever men are willing and able to give of themselves for the benefit of their fellow man," said Joao Fernando Sobral, past international president.

Over and over, history has attested to the wisdom of the men who devised the Objects and Ethics. Where there's a need, Lions find a way to meet it. In 1973, the Lions of Morioka, Iwate, Japan, became increasingly concerned with the epidemic of deaths among young children in their nation. The annual mortality rate was more than 60,000 youngsters and growing each year.

A newspaper editor wrote: "Among all traffic fatalities, the most serious problem we face is that of pre-schoolers. During every spring and fall, Traffic Safety Weeks, protection of young children from traffic accidents, is always listed as one of the goals. But for the past two years, the number of victims has been on the rise. . . . We ought to determine what we are doing wrong and hasten to solve the problem."

The Morioka Lions voted to change this situation and made it a major service activity. By the end of 1973 they had developed a program called the "Leo Safety Method."

When the Morioka Lions began implementing the program they found that simply supplying informational literature to families was inadequate. It did not produce the desired results. They discovered that elementary school children could be taught to understand and obey traffic rules learned in school. However, pre-schoolers were unable to comprehend the rules. The Lions found that when young children dart into a busy street they are acting instinctively, not intellectually. So, the Morioka Lions designed a technique that appealed to a pre-schooler's instinct. The final method was engineered especially for pre-schoolers who would be instructed by their mothers at home.

The Leo Safety Method includes instructional materials and two instruments used in training the little boy or girl. The Leo Pendant is a necklace that helps the child tell the difference between a "safe zone" and a "danger zone." When the child is told to wear the pendant around his neck he knows he is about to enter an area of heavy traffic. When the necklace is removed the danger is no longer there. The child comes to understand this through repetition.

Another device employed in the program is a belt leash worn by a child when crossing the street. When coming to a crosswalk the mother pulls the belt and calls out "stop." The child learns to stop on his own after this is repeated again and again.

Major Japanese newspapers, along with radio and television stations, publicized the Leo Safety Program. Highly effective, the program spread to many other sections of Japan after its start in Morioka. Unquestionably, countless lives have been saved and injuries prevented by the Leo Safety Program.

"Wearing your Lions lapel pin identifies you to others as a person who cares about his community; who is willing to put this caring into humanitarian action," said the late Mathew Seishi Ogawa, then third international vice-president. And, as the Morioka Lions showed, they care about human beings of all ages.

Some years ago John W. Gardner, former U.S. Secretary of Health, Education and Welfare stated: "The society which scorns excellence in plumbing because plumbing is a humble activity and tolerates shoddiness in philosophy because it is an exalted activity will have neither good plumbing nor good philosophy. Neither its pipes nor its theories will hold water."

The Code of Ethics is a call to moral excellence and far from easy. It smoothes personal relations by basing them on truth and consideration for others. Stunning in its power and undeniable in its results, it offers a fresh and positive vision in the midst of a world often seething with tension, confusion, and uncertainty.

It reflects the words of Past International President Lloyd Morgan who observed: "The basic ideals of Lionism challenge every member to do his very best in whatever task he undertakes."

The ideals spotlighted in the Objects and Ethics provide a framework for harmonious action. They dissolve boundaries of nationality, culture, religion, and economics.

For example, a few miles from Quito, the visitor to Ecuador finds a monument marking the equator. Standing there with one foot in the Northern Hemisphere and the other in the Southern, he understands why Ecuadorians are fond of calling their country "The Middle of the World." Possessing a civilization dating back more than 10,000 years, Ecuador is an intriguing blend of ancient cultures and modern technology. Quito, a colorful city of more than 800,000 persons living 9,000 feet above sea level, offers an arresting view of colonial cathedrals, Indians selling blankets woven in brilliant colors and intricate designs, breathtaking scenery . . . and Lions helping others.

A children's rehabilitation center, founded in 1972 and sponsored by the Quito (Sixth of December) Lions Club, provides a comprehensive treatment program for handicapped Ecuadorian youngsters.

"We give special consideration to children whose parents are unable to pay for necessary treatment," said Dr. Luis Cueva, past president of the Lions club and a Quito surgeon. "This unit mainly treats children suffering from cerebral palsy, polio, congenital defects, or the effects of injuries. It operates in conjunction with the Eugenio Espejo Hospital."

The program aims at total rehabilitation of the youngsters and provides a wide-ranging approach to achieve this. All required surgical and medical care is available to correct physical problems. Medical care includes all types of therapy needed to bring maximum physical mobility to each child. Whenever necessary, the Sixth of December Club pays the costs of surgery and the hospital supplies medicines, food, and nursing care.

Hundreds of Ecuadorian boys and girls enjoy good health and vocational opportunities because the Lions went to work for them. These youngsters have *experienced* the message in the Objects and Ethics.

Mahatma Gandhi was the small, humble man who led India to freedom in 1947 after several decades of struggle. He once remarked: "Knowledge is useless unless we use it to *experience* a change within ourselves." The *experience* of millions of Lions throughout the world for more than seven decades has been reflected in countless service projects that have changed the lives of men, women, and children everywhere.

"We best meet the objects of Lionism if we serve in an unselfish manner," suggests Past International President Everett J. "Ebb" Grindstaff. "We are on this earth to be of service to our fellow man. We are asked to grow into a mountain, not shrink into a grain of sand." So successful have Lions been in implementing the objects and ethics that "there is no question that the thousands of projects that our local clubs, or districts, or multiple districts are involved in add up to more service than any other civic or service organization in the world."

Communication is usually thought of as written or verbal messages. Books, newspapers, magazines, radio, or TV, along with personal conversations are the usual methods of communication.

There is another type of communication that has nothing to do with words. It is the result of what a person is . . . or what a club is. It was described by Emerson when he said: "What you are speaks so loudly I can't hear what you say."

Past International President John L. Stickley made the same point when he wrote that he was more influenced by the way Lions and

Lionesses lived the Code and Objects than he was by the Code itself. "I came to realize that Lionism is one great ecumenical movement, binding together in a common cause people of all races, creeds, nationalities, and colors."

Practiced in the arena of day-to-day living, Lionism's principles build better human beings. The principles create individuals conscious of the needs of others and devoted to creating solutions for them.

Timeless and vigorous, the principles have been restated in every age. They are mirrored, for example, in the words of St. John Chrysostom who said, "Let us astound them by our way of life. For this is the main battle: If we do not exhibit a life better than theirs, nothing is gained. . . . Let us win them by our life . . . for this is more powerful than the tongue."

The beloved mystic from Antioch, Syria, was speaking nearly 16 centuries ago and outlining a way to deal with criticism. He could well have been describing the final paragraph in the Code of Ethics.

The Objects and Ethics have played an expanding role in Lionism's growth. Radiating joy and good fellowship, members of the association work tirelessly to improve the human condition. The first Object comes to life in such international programs as youth exchange and youth camps, the eye bank network, the Lions Clubs International Foundation, and countless projects involving Lions from different nations. The language of Lionism is universal.

The Lions Policy Position on Peace, drafted by the International Board of Directors and announced by Past International President Judge Brian Stevenson at the March 1988 Lions Day with the United Nations at UN Headquarters in New York, is among the most recent demonstrations of Lionism helping to promote the "spirit of understanding among people of the world."

Created by farsighted men of good will, the Objects and Ethics enable individuals of every nation and background to cooperate and help others. Demanding integrity and commitment, they point the way to lives of heightened meaning as they liberate a vitality for excellence. Energized by these principles, Lions serve and change the world.

CHAPTER FOUR

Helen Keller's Knights of the Blind

SIGNIFICANT human beings have played dramatic roles in Lionism's vigorous growth and development. Helen Keller spoke to the Ninth Annual Convention of Lions Clubs International and her eloquent appeal lit a flame that has blazed brilliantly ever since. While her appearance and speech were deeply moving, it is probably only in retrospect that one can measure the extent of her influence.

The meeting opened in the Convention Hall of the Breakers Hotel in Cedar Point, Ohio, at 10:40 A.M. on Tuesday, June 30, 1925. First Vice President Benjamin F. Jones called the assembly to order and soon after Helen Keller and her remarkable teacher, Anne Sullivan-Macy, were introduced to the group.

Helen Keller was one of the most extraordinary women in history. She was born on June 27, 1880, in Tuscumbia, Alabama, to well-to-do parents. Her father, Arthur Keller, was a former Confederate officer and her mother, Kate Adams, was related to Robert E. Lee.

An unusually bright, alert child, Helen contracted an illness when she was 18 months old that was diagnosed as congestion of the brain and stomach. It left her with neither sight nor hearing. Very soon she forgot the few words she knew and became completely speechless. Angered when her parents or the family servants failed to understand her signs she lashed out with kicks, screams, and tantrums.

In the 1880s the law in the United States still labeled deaf and blind persons as idiots—even though Braille (writing through raised dots read by touch) had been invented by Louis Braille, a blind Frenchman in 1826. In Scotland, teaching the deaf and blind had been started in 1793.

However, an enlightened physician who knew Helen sensed the spark within. He believed her intelligence could be developed once communication was established with her dark and soundless world.

Arthur and Kate Keller talked with Alexander Graham Bell who suggested that they hire a teacher from the Perkins Institution for the Blind in Boston. Nineteen-year-old Anne Sullivan, later Mrs. John Macy, arrived and Helen's life bloomed.

In her autobiography, *The Story of My Life,* Helen Keller wrote: "The most important day I remember in all my life is the one on which my teacher, Anne Mansfield Sullivan, came to me. I am filled with wonder when I consider the immeasurable contrast between the two lives which it connects. It was the third of March, 1887, three months before I was seven years old."

Helen's journey from that beginning in 1887 to the convention in Cedar Point, Ohio, in 1925 is told movingly in the words of her beloved teacher. On that Tuesday morning in Cedar Point, International President Harry A. Newman of Toronto, Ontario, introduced Helen Keller and Anne Sullivan-Macy. They were greeted by a standing ovation from the delegates. Helen sat down and Anne began to speak to the hushed audience.

Anne Sullivan-Macy said: "Lions and ladies: If you will be very good and very quiet, I will try to tell you Helen Keller's story, so that you may understand better, when she stands here and speaks to you, the tremendous obstacles that she has overcome.

"Few human beings, if you stop and think of it, have overcome such obstacles. Deaf, blind and mute from her nineteenth month, she has had to create a world of her own, with the help of the sense of touch and a great imagination. When Helen Keller was six and one-half years old, her father wrote to the School for the Blind in Boston to ask if it was possible to get a teacher for his little girl. Helen Keller, born in Tuscumbia, Alabama, had been blind and deaf as the result of illness from her nineteenth month. Now, at the age of six and one-half years, he wanted to get a teacher for her. It was arranged that I should go to Alabama, Helen's home, and teach her.

"I found Helen a very active, a very intelligent and a very destructive little creature. From the time when she lost her sight and hearing there was no means of communicating with her, so, of course, her family and her brothers and sisters could not talk with her. She knew nothing. She had forgotten the few baby words that she knew. She had absolutely no means of communicating with those around her except a few motions or signs which she made for herself.

"The first thing that I did was to try to teach her language. The only way possible of reaching that imprisoned little soul was through the manual alphabet, the hand spelling, because you can make the letters in the hand. The deaf people use the spelling into the air and the person they are speaking to reads what is said in the air. Helen Keller could not see, so the letters had to made in her hand. The first word she learned to spell was 'doll.' I gave her a new doll, knowing that a little child would be interested in a doll, whether she could see or whether she couldn't. Helen felt of the doll. She knew what it was—she had had dolls before. When she was satisfied, I took her hand and made the letters 'd-o-l-l' in her hand, pointed to the doll that she was holding and nodded my head.

"Helen looked puzzled. She felt my hand. Nobody had ever done anything like that before. Child-like, she immediately began to try to make the same motions with her fingers. I helped her to make the letters and after a few trials she actually spelled the word 'doll,' pointed to it and nodded her head, just as I had done.

"Her mother told me that she knew that Helen knew that the nod of the head meant 'Yes.' When Mrs. Keller would let her do anything, she would put the little hand on her face and nod her head. She also knew that a shake of the head meant 'No'; that is, that it meant something she must not do; but she never paid any attention to that sign.

"Helen learned about thirty words in that way. I would show her the object, I would show her a piece of cake, for instance, I would spell 'c-a-k-e' in her hand, point to the cake and indicate by my motions that when she made those signs, she could have the cake. It wasn't long before she could spell 'cake' and all the things that she liked to eat.

"But she did not understand for more than a month that every object had a name. If I gave her a new object, she would just feel of it and throw it aside. One day I was trying to make her understand that the cup and what was in the cup had a different name. She became confused, and when I put water in the cup, she would spell 'cup' for 'water,' and 'water' for 'cup,' and so on, until it occurred to me to take her out to the pump and let her hold the cup while I pumped. As the water gushed forth I spelled into her other hand, 'w-a-t-e-r.' She dropped the cup, a look of intelligence, of understanding, came into her face for the first time. In that moment it dawned on her mind that what I was doing with my hand meant that cool something that was flowing over her hand."

As the audience listened, enthralled, Anne Sullivan-Macy described the way Helen Keller learned to speak. Deaf from childhood, she had not heard a human sound since she was a 19-month-old baby. With dogged persistence and the help of her teacher, Helen mastered speech. Moving in its power, Anne's talk set the stage for the next act.

When she finished, Anne Sullivan-Macy sat down to resounding applause. President Newman thanked her and then introduced a five-member band from Joplin, Missouri. Each of the band members was blind and had become a musician after losing his vision. They played several tunes and Anne took the podium again.

She told the 5,000 listeners that when Helen Keller was 10 she begged to again learn how to speak. At first this seemed impossible, but then Anne Sullivan discovered that Helen could learn sounds by placing her fingers on her teacher's larynx and "hearing" the vibrations. That was even though she had forgotten voice and what a sound meant. She "heard" with her thumb on the throat at the larynx, her first finger resting on the lips, her second on the nose, and her hand resting on the cheek of the person who was speaking.

Now it was time for Helen Keller to address the convention. Helen spoke in her own words and Anne Sullivan-Macy repeated them.

Helen Keller began: "Dear Lions and Ladies. I suppose you have heard the legend that represents opportunity as a capricious lady who knocks at every door but once, and if the door isn't opened quickly, she passes on, never to return. And that is as it should be. Lovely, desirable ladies won't wait. You have to go out and grab 'em.

"I am your opportunity. I am knocking at your door. I want to be adopted. The legend doesn't say what you are to do when several beautiful opportunities present themselves at the same door. I guess you have to choose the one you love best. I hope you will adopt me. I am the youngest here, and what I offer you is full of splendid opportunities for service.

"Try to imagine how you would feel if you were suddenly stricken blind today. Picture yourself stumbling and groping at noonday as in the night, your work, your independence, gone. In that dark world wouldn't you be glad if a friend took you by the hand and said, 'Come with me and I will teach you how to do some of the things you used to do when you could see?'

"You have heard how through a little word dropped from the fingers of another, a ray of light from another soul touched the darkness of my mind and I found myself, found the world, found God. It is because my teacher learned about me and broke through the dark, silent imprisonment which held me that I am able to work for myself and for others. It is the caring we want more than money. The gift without the sympathy and interest of the giver is empty. If you care, if we can make the people of this great country care, the blind will indeed triumph over blindness.

"Will you not help me hasten the day when there shall be no preventable blindness; no little deaf, blind children untaught; no blind man or woman unaided? I appeal to you Lions, you who have your sight, your hearing, you who are strong and brave and kind. Will you not constitute yourselves Knights of the Blind in this crusade against darkness?

"I thank you."

Helen Keller sat down and received a prolonged standing ovation from the audience.

President Newman thanked Miss Keller and then Lion Ben Ruffin of West Virginia offered a resolution making Helen Keller an Honorary Member of Lions International. President Newman declared that the motion had been passed unanimously, "making Helen the first Lady Lion of the continent."

Lion Davis of Texas then said, "I move that we recognize Miss Keller's teacher as the second Honorary Member of Lions International." This was seconded by the entire convention.

Said Helen Keller, "I am happy and proud to be a Lion."

Misfortune is a lever that destroys some but lifts others to heights of strength and achievement. Helen Keller was a critical catalyst in Lionism's future.

Her impact on June 30, 1925, in Cedar Point, Ohio, is measured in the millions of lives that have been transformed by Lions' activities for the visually handicapped.

Helen Keller graduated from Radcliffe, the first deaf-blind person in history to graduate from college. She competed on equal terms with her peers who could see and hear and she graduated *cum laude*.

Helen wrote 13 books and countless articles that appeared in major magazines and newspapers. Her books were translated into 50 languages. She not only mastered English, but learned to speak in French and German as well. She made the world acutely conscious of its responsibility toward the handicapped.

"It has been a happy life," Helen Keller said before she died in 1968. "My limitations never make me sad. Perhaps there is just a touch of yearning at times. But it is vague, like a breeze among flowers. Then, the wind passes and the flowers are content."

It is a living tribute to Helen Keller and the power of her talk at Cedar Point that, today, it is estimated that 30 percent of all Lions service projects each year are in the field of sight (all sight-related projects are now incorporated in the SightFirst program).

At the 1925 Convention the delegates passed a resolution declaring Sight Conservation and Work for the Blind one of Lionism's major activities. In June 1976, the wording was altered to Sight Conservation and Work *with* the Blind. The change was made to reflect Lions' consideration for the independence of the visually handicapped.

Helen Keller provided a powerful impetus to Lions Clubs International's service for the blind. However, many clubs had been active in these kinds of projects before her talk at Cedar Point.

For example, the March 1924 issue of *The Lion* described the glee club concert promoted by the St. Paul, Minnesota, Lions to benefit the local Home for the Blind. The Lions rented a theater, sold more than $1,000 worth of tickets in a single week, ushered and coordinated all aspects of the program, and donated the proceeds to the Home for the Blind. The story noted that "Lion Gus Messing writes that the little affair was just sort of a training stunt for a lot of the new members the club has been taking in recently."

During 1924, President Newman spearheaded creation of two major service committees operating at the international level. Harry C. Hartman, a Seattle, Washington, Lion who was blind, was named chairman of the Committee for the Blind. Judge Hubert Utterback, of the Des Moines, Iowa, Lions Club, became chairman of the Committee for Handicapped Children. They were to work with First International Vice President Benjamin Jones.

After exhaustive study, Hartman, Utterback, and Jones found that of the large number of blind persons in the United States in 1920, a significant number could have been saved from blindness by proper medical care. Prevention of visual handicaps became an important emphasis for the association.

At the time of Helen Keller's talk to the Lions in 1925, the Major Activities Department at International Headquarters began to organize a listing of agencies designed to help the blind or those with other disabilities. The Lions were already involved in health camps, open air schools, milk funds, summer camps, scouting, and other activities.

Lions clubs developed a variety of programs to meet the needs in their own areas. In the July 1926 issue of *The Lion,* Harry Hartman, chairman of the International Committee on the Blind wrote: "The Secretary General's report to the convention last year showed that a total of 58 clubs had reported participation in work for the blind. These reports include subscriptions to the Juvenile Braille Magazine, as well as sight saving, employment and other less significant features. For the first 11 months of the present fiscal year 143 clubs from 34 states have reported efforts on behalf of blind people."

In the next few years Lions clubs helped the visually handicapped in myriad ways. The Sudbury, Ontario, Lions Club paid for restorative surgery for a sight impaired youngster. The Midland, Texas, Lions sponsored a program providing eye examinations for more than 1,400 boys and girls. The St. Augustine, Florida, Lions Club organized a blind Girl Scout Troop. The Lions gave the young ladies a flag and took them on several outings. In 1928, the Hollywood, California, Lions Club gave a press to a Braille publishing house. Many, many other projects for the blind were devised by Lions clubs in those years. The range was limited only by the ingenuity of the members.

During George A. Bonham's term as president of the Peoria, Illinois, Lions Club in 1930 he saw a problem. Soon after, he devised the solution. Bonham watched a blind man trying to cross a street, left helpless as traffic whirled about him. Futilely tapping his black cane on the pavement, the man was isolated in the center of drivers who did not understand his handicap.

Bonham pored over the problem. Suddenly he had the answer. Paint the cane white and put a wide band of red around it. When the blind person crosses a street let him extend it so that everyone can see and be aware of his blindness. George Bonham presented the idea to the Peoria Lions Club and the members voted unanimously in favor of it. Canes were painted and given to the blind in the city. The Peoria City Council passed an ordinance giving the right-of-way to a blind person using a white cane.

The international convention in Toronto, Ontario, in 1931 saw the introduction of a resolution describing the Peoria Lions Club's white cane program. The resolution said, in part: "The adoption of this plan is recommended to our clubs as part of our major activity, Blind Work. Full information as to this plan, including copies of the ordinances which have been adopted, may be obtained through our activities department."

By 1956 every state in the United States had passed White Cane Safety Laws giving any person using a white cane the right-of-way at crossings. These laws include protection for blind individuals who travel with guide dogs, as well.

During World War II the Veterans Administration set up a rehabilitation center for blind war veterans. Techniques for using white canes were refined at these facilities. The extended cane is moved in a semicircle in rhythm with the user's footsteps and a light touch on the ground at the end of each arc. This enables the blind person to feel such obstacles as gratings, steps, posts, walls, etc. State and private agencies have adopted these techniques for their own training centers.

Many Lions clubs use the white cane as a part of fund-raising programs for the visually handicapped. A lapel pin in the form of a small white cane is given to each contributor.

A number of electronic devices have been developed to aid the blind in traveling. For instance, the Beltone Ultra Sonic Aid was invented by Dr. Leslie Kay of New Zealand and has been called a "seeing ear for the blind." Operating like a tiny loudspeaker, the transmitter sends out sounds that bounce off objects in the blind person's path. They are picked up on the receiver as *beeps, chirps,* or *twitters*. After learning how to interpret the sounds, the blind person identifies the object and acts accordingly.

"The Nurion Laser Cane is another electronic aid for the blind," explained Lee Farmer, who worked as a technology transfer specialist at Hines Veterans Administration Hospital near Chicago until his retirement in 1986. "The Laser Cane emits three invisible light beams when the cane is activated. These consist of an upper beam, a straight-ahead beam and a downward beam. There are three audible signals which correspond with the light beams. The tones are high, middle and low pitched. These alert the user to objects which are either directly in front of the blind person, or above or below, such as a curb. While they work very well for some individuals, they are not for everyone."

For Stephen Miyagawa the cane is highly effective. A blinded veteran of the Korean War, he works as a darkroom technician at Edgewater Hospital in Chicago. He said, "I travel cross-town six days a week to and from work. That's 16 miles each way and I make three transfers on public transportation. In my daily travel I walk on elevated and commuter train platforms four or five times. As time passed, I began to appreciate the Laser Cane more and more.

"The upward channel which detects hanging objects and informs me of the height and closeness of objects is a special boon to me. Before the Laser Cane came into my life I had run into a three-inch pipe sticking out of a utility truck, the bed of a huge truck parked in my way, a sign post and a protruding box on a light post. All of these resulted in painful and expensive trips to the dentist."

Costing about $3,000, the Laser Canes are used mainly in the United States. In many instances, Lions clubs have provided them for blind persons.

On occasion, Lions have persuaded their legislators to assist in helping the blind. President Franklin D. Roosevelt signed the Randolph-Sheppard Bill on June 20, 1936, "whereby blind people are to operate vending stands inside government buildings." The co-authors of the bill, Representative Jennings Randolph of West Virginia and Senator Morris Sheppard of Texas were both Lions.

In 1964, President Lyndon Johnson issued a proclamation that marked the climax of the campaign by the blind to gain endorsement of their rights as pedestrians. With Johnson's proclamation the white cane became officially recognized.

"A white cane in our society has become one of the symbols of a blind person's ability to come and go on his own. Its use has promoted courtesy and opportunity for mobility for the blind on our streets and highways. To make the American people more fully aware of the meaning of the white cane, and of the need for motorists to exercise special care for the blind persons who carry it, Congress, by a joint resolution approved October 6, 1964, authorized the President to proclaim October 15, 1964, as White Cane Safety Day.

"Now, therefore, I, Lyndon B. Johnson, President of the United States of America, do hereby proclaim October 15, 1964, as White Cane Safety Day."

Through the adoption of the white cane laws, the blind have gained the legal right to travel, the right of physical mobility. They have gained the social right of movement. The activities of Lions clubs throughout the United States played a major role in expanded public awareness and favorable legislation.

The flame lit by Helen Keller has burned brightly down the decades.

It sparked invention—like the Banks Pocket Braille-Writer which allowed blind people to type messages to one another. Invented by a Lion, a physician blinded in World War I, the Braille-Writer's manufacture was accomplished by the club in San Diego.

They talked with Thomas J. Watson, president of IBM, to see if he would cooperate in its manufacture. Eager to help, Watson offered to produce the first thousand machines free for distribution by the Lions to blinded World War II veterans.

The machine uses a keyboard with six keys and a space bar. The cover lifts to show a roll of narrow paper tape on which Braille characters are printed by striking the keys. Dr. Banks invented the writer after 12 years of experimentation and development. Users of his machine sometimes say they "talk by the yard rather than the hour."

Keller's flame kindled the imagination of extraordinary people who accomplished extraordinary things.

There was the middle-aged high school teacher who became totally blind at age 55. He founded what amounted to a national correspondence university for the blind, teaching courses he designed on the basis of his experience as a successful teacher and blind person. And there were the members of Illinois clubs whose support helped the fledgling correspondence school grow.

There were the three inspired Lions in Detroit who set out with $400 and a prayer to found a school to train dog guides and provide training for blind people in how to use them.

Finally there were the hundreds of clubs and thousands of Lions who saw the potential in each of these achievements. They supported and magnified them by working to bring their benefits to thousands and thousands of blind people.

A case in point is the tremendous impetus given by Lions to the use of guide dogs as the eyes of the blind in the United States. The organized training of dogs to guide the blind began in Germany during World War I, but did not come to the United States until 1929 when the first such school began.

Those early training efforts showed the breeds best suited to the work are larger dogs like German shepherds, Labrador retrievers, golden retrievers, and boxers. Individual dogs are picked for training on the basis of good disposition, intelligence, physical fitness, and responsibility. Intensive training begins when the dog is about 18 months old and lasts for three to five months. Like a horse being trained for riding, a dog must first get used to the harness he will wear whenever he is guiding his blind owner. He learns instant obedience to such commands as "forward," "left," "right," and "sit." Most importantly, the dog learns to disregard any command which might place his owner in jeopardy, like an order to go "forward" into moving traffic.

After the dog successfully finishes his training—and many dogs can't make the grade—the owner and his prospective guide dog are trained to work together in a four-week program. Just as many of the dogs are unsuited to being guide dogs, many blind people find during training that they are not suited by temperament to work with dogs. Others find it impossible to entrust their own safety to a dog, however well trained.

Lion involvement with this complex and expensive process began in Detroit with the Uptown Lions Club which decided against all odds that they would provide dog guides for the blind. With tremendous enthusiasm, unbounded energy, and a healthy dose of ignorance about the size of the undertaking, Donald P. Schuur, Edward U. Martin, and Harold Davenport incorporated "The Lions Leader Dog Foundation" with the provision that dog training and students' room and board would be covered.

Also involved in the incorporation were Charles Nutting and S. A. Dodge, who was destined to become president of Lions Clubs International.

The incorporation was a simple act of faith by one club which was to give freedom and self respect to thousands of blind men, women, and children. In one of their many visits in search of a building to house the school, Schuur and Nutting fell through a rotting kitchen floor into a farmhouse basement. Undaunted, they finally founded the school in 1939 in a farmhouse near Rochester, Michigan, with four dogs housed in a dilapidated barn. Lions clubs all over the country bought dogs and underwrote the costs of individual students. In the years since, more than 6,000 blind people have been taught to see through their dogs' eyes, becoming self-sufficient, useful citizens in the process.

The influenza epidemic of 1915 marked the beginning of one of the most important and fascinating chapters in the Lions work for the blind. Once again, the story centers on extraordinary individuals. A pre-Christmas cold turned into influenza for William Allen Hadley, a 55-year-old teacher who headed the commercial department of Chicago's Lakeview High School. Two days later, he suffered a detached retina in one eye. Hadley had already lost the sight in his other eye when he was very young. Hadley's doctor and close neighbor, E. V. L. Brown, knew that Hadley was a voracious reader and shrewdly played on Hadley's pain at being deprived of his books. "Learn Braille and you can read again" was Brown's counsel. Hadley followed it.

Soon Hadley was tutoring high school students in his home in Winnetka, a Chicago suburb, and also typing manuscripts for an author friend. In 1919, a minister from Oklahoma who was visiting another Winnetka neighbor of Hadley made a startling suggestion on a summer evening as the two men were chatting on Hadley's front porch.

"You have proven you are a brilliant educator. There are thousands of students whom you could teach. And they are not further from you than your own mailbox. Why don't you teach other blind adults through correspondence courses?"

Hadley's letters to people working with the blind brought much encouragement and hundreds of letters from blind people eager to sign up.

One came from a farmer's wife in Kansas, who, like Hadley, had been an avid reader until she lost her sight. Hadley created his Braille correspondence course for this book-starved woman, using the Braille-Writer which was invented by Frank H. Hall of the Illinois School for the Blind in Jacksonville, Illinois.

Founded in 1849, the school's name was changed to Illinois School for the Visually Impaired in 1977. Lions have been involved for many, many years.

"Through the years Lions' support has played a key role in our school's ability to help the blind," said Dr. Richard Ulmsted, superintendent and a past president of the Jacksonville Lions Club. "There are clubs in the state that donate year after year to help keep us operating. Very often the Lions club in a community where one of our students lives will provide a Braille-Writer or a computer or some other item the student needs.

"The Low Vision Clinic here on campus is a statewide Lions' project that started in 1976. It's held twice a year and has become so successful that it has been extended from two days to three days for each session. We have a new all-weather track at the school that was dedicated in 1987. This was built with $75,000 raised by the District 1-G Lions. If I could single out one person who has been a driving force in helping our school it would be C. D. "Doc" Brewer of the Jacksonville Lions Club."

The farmer's wife from Kansas is just one of thousands who have benefited from the expertise of the school in Jacksonville, Illinois, since it opened in 1849. Between November 1920 and June 1921, her Braille "typed" exercises were mailed to Hadley who corrected them and sent them back, usually with a word of encouragement.

With his first student's successful completion of the course, Hadley knew that he could teach by mail. He put an ad in a Braille periodical which brought more than 100 inquiries. Hadley was in the correspondence school business in a big way. By 1932, his school was incorporated as the Hadley School for the Blind. The curriculum catalog of that year listed 14 courses including English grammar, psychology, salesmanship, typewriting, and Bible studies.

Hadley liked to refer to his school as the "University of Courage." When one applicant wrote on his application that his prior schooling was with the "University of Adversity," Hadley shot a note back: "We are making arrangements to transfer your credits from the University of Adversity to the University of Courage." In 1929, Elmer Selby, a member of the newly chartered Winnetka Lions Club and a reporter for the town's weekly paper walked by a stairway leading to the Hadley School offices. Selby, who had written a number of articles on the school for the paper, dropped in to see Hadley. The two chatted amiably for a time and the talk led Selby to suggest that the Winnetka Lions make the Hadley school its main project. The suggestion was eagerly accepted, and the enthusiasm quickly spread to other Lions clubs in Illinois. By 1936, more than 4,000 students had enrolled at Hadley since its founding. That year it served 654 students who took a total of more than 1,000 courses.

Beginning with the Winnetka Lions Club, the Lions of Illinois have played a major role in the growth and development of Hadley School. Through the years they have contributed more than a million dollars to its operation. Lions clubs in other parts of the world have taken an interest in Hadley's overseas branches, as well.

As one example, in 1969 the Mt. Prospect, Illinois, Lions Club gave $10,000 to help found the Hadley branch in Kenya. Jason Mutugi, a former Hadley student and a Lion is the director. The Lions Club in Sao Paulo is helping the Hadley office in Brazil. In Paris, the Lions are supporting the Hadley office.

Hadley School for the Blind remains the largest single educator of the blind in the world and by 1988 was teaching more than 8,000 students around the globe. It offers more than 100 home study courses for the visually handicapped and educates the blind in more than 78 countries. Between 1984 and 1988 enrollment more than tripled as a result of increased interest in technical courses.

The legacy of Helen Keller as it was transmitted and amplified by

Lions Clubs International helped form one extraordinary person after another.

There was the girl stricken in the late 20s with polio which blinded her and paralyzed her right side. Adopted by the Lions Club of Redondo Beach, California, Cecil Baker was educated at the University of Redlands. The Lions club also underwrote several eye operations. Cecil used her education "to do my little bit in helping free those without sight from the shackles of darkness and bring them light and truth. Without the generous-hearted Lions I would have never realized my dream."

About the same time, a young woman in Winnipeg, Manitoba, was thrown from her horse while riding to school. According to a report written by John Sturrock, secretary of the Winnipeg, Manitoba, club, two physicians who treated her over a two-year period believed her injuries had left her "hopelessly" blind. The Moosejaw, Saskatchewan, Lions Club didn't give up so easily. One of its own members, Dr. Frank McElrea, a chiropractor, treated the girl so successfully that 60 percent of her sight was restored.

R. V. Harris, a physician who was himself blinded at the age of 47, developed a program designed to help blind adults become self-supporting. He took it before the Lions Club of Savannah in 1930, which gave such a boost to Harris' effort that his organization, the Georgia Association of Workers for the Blind, quickly grew to "nearly 300 members as a result of the splendid cooperation and dynamic force of the Lions," according to an account written by Harris. "It was fortunate for the association that G. B. King was appointed chairman of the Lions Blind Work Committee and it gives me great pleasure to testify to the splendid work which he inaugurated and the enthusiastic support the Lions club has given him."

A blind girl, Lee Belmont, sponsored by the Paterson, New Jersey, Lions Club, spoke for countless thousands who came before and after her when she wrote on June 21, 1930, to District Governor Lawrence F. Kramer of the Paterson club to thank members "who have done much and will do a great deal more to promote the welfare of the blind."

Sometimes an abundance of work and caring is expressed in the sparse language of a report. Like this one in 1935 by the West Frankfort, Illinois, club: "Made a final payment for glasses for 83 cases. More than 2,600 children were examined . . . with the club footing the bills for those unable to pay. Credit for this work is due Lions Dr. A. S. Alberts and Dr. J. A. Johnson and school nurse Mary Kolesay."

There's a hint of the joy created by members of the Wichita, Kansas, club's three-day outing in the summer of 1935 for 25 blind men and women. "They swam or splashed in the pool, . . . they heard the gurgle of a rushing stream for the first time and they threw rocks in the water and enjoyed the splash," club secretary Lloyd F. Cooper said.

By the early 1940s, the Lions Club of Tampa was running a thriving eye clinic under the direction of Dr. Bill Hopkins, eye specialist and Lion member "who does all of his examinations free and doesn't receive one penny for his work," according to a report written by F. M. Sack, secretary. The clinic examined 45 to 100 kids, who were referred to the Lions by school physicians each month. PTAs and schools sent children who were "backward in their studies" when it was suspected that poor vision might be a cause. Financing came from the annual showing of a midnight movie at a local theater. The movie was sold to the club at cost by the theater management which donated the theater, ushers, and a projectionist.

In a similar program, also in the 1940s, the New Lexington, Ohio, club sponsored vision tests for more than 1,000 high school and grade school children. An optometrist member, Dr. Richard R. Wilson, performed the tests. During the 1930s and 1940s, Berkeley, California, was perhaps prouder of its club-sponsored blind Boy Scout Troop than of anything else in town. The troop met in quarters built for them by the Lions. Every nail was personally driven by a club member. Lions took troop members on mountain hikes, taught them to swim, and became their friends.

In the mid-1940s, the Naples, Florida, club examined more than 600 children in the first month of operating its eye clinic. A member, Dr. Goodrich T. Smith, a retired eye, ear, nose, and throat specialist, spearheaded the effort, donating his time and necessary equipment. The club donated the facilities and picked up the tab for children who needed but could not afford treatment.

"The clinic fills a great need in Collier County, as medical care is inadequate. We Lions feel we contributed to our community welfare in a manner not equalled by any other Lions Club in Florida, or, for that matter in the United States," Paul Cooke, the club's secretary, reported.

The Daytona Beach, Florida, club set a blind man up in a business of his own—a vending kiosk in a U.S. Post Office, which became a moneymaker after only two weeks. Secretary Lester C. Huffman wrote of the blind entrepreneur that "he has done, and is doing, a remarkable business. We are very proud of this undertaking."

In 1945, in Waynesville, North Carolina, a two-day eye clinic in which 107 children and young adults were examined turned up 17 cases where surgery was indicated and 43 children were given glasses. All costs were picked up by the Waynesville club.

In addition to sweat and dollars, member efforts could also be extremely creative.

An old time minstrel show mounted by the Canton, North Carolina, club turned out to be a standing room only attraction—and brought in $360, enough money to finance a county-wide eye clinic.

"We used ordinary window cards, newspaper ads and other programs to publicize the show, but our best advertising came from the 51 Lions who went out and sold the tickets. The work was so well done that before curtain time even the standing room in the auditorium was filled and it holds 800," reported secretary James B. Williamson.

Bridgeport, Connecticut, got a permanent home for its blind in July 1945, when its Lions club leased and furnished a facility. On the basis of a report by Jack Sweeney, chairman of the club's Blind Work Committee, it vowed to support it, as well. The club raised over $2,000 in cooperation with the area's blind association, secretary Ernest M. Butler, said.

The first corneal eye bank outside of New York was set up in the mid-1940s by the Louisville, Kentucky, club. The club gave the go-ahead for the project after the chairman of its Sight Conservation Committee, P. F. Stockler, visited eastern hospitals as a club representative.

Stockler recommended that the bank operate as a clearing house for those who wanted to donate corneas after their deaths. Blind persons awaiting corneas could register with the bank. Hundreds received new corneas as a result. The project became so large that other organizations joined in support and the bank became a separate, not-for-profit organization.

Also in 1945, twin teenage boys with a reputation as lazy students received vision tests sponsored by the Winston-Salem, North Carolina, club. The exam revealed each boy had a rare disease of the cornea not correctable with eye glasses. Contact lenses, then a brand new innovation, restored much of the boys' sight. Follow-up eye exercises brought almost perfect vision. All the services were paid for by the Winston-Salem club.

There are countless other stories of individual members and clubs, from big towns and little towns, who worked hard, with vision and enthusiasm to turn Helen Keller's beacon into a bonfire.

As 1945 ended, Lions and millions of other men, women, and children around the globe looked ahead with optimism. World War II was over and it was time to rebuild. Lions moved forward on many fronts; including a broadened commitment to the visually handicapped.

CHAPTER FIVE

A Global Vision for the Sightless

DOG GUIDE SCHOOLS

IN 1946, Lionism's principles began to heal the wounds left by the war. Through education, research, and vigorous action, Lions everywhere helped to dispel the myths, stereotypes, and fables that had so often restricted the lives of the blind. Speaking the international language of service, Lions' programs for the visually handicapped brought mobility and opportunity to the sightless in many corners of the world.

In Italy, Maurizio Galimberti had been a pilot in the Italian Air Force during World War II. He worked as a commercial pilot after the war and was blinded in a plane crash in 1948. Today, he travels with the help of a dog provided by the Lions Guide Dog Service in Limbiate, near Milan in northern Italy.

He said, "With the aid of guide dogs I've covered more than 200,000 miles by plane. I've been able to attend nine international conventions, including Tokyo, and four multiple district conventions in Europe. That's in addition to traveling all over Italy. My family is me and my dog, Liz, and thanks to her I'm free. My dog works 24 hours a day, in good weather and bad. She never takes a holiday and she's always happy."

Olga Baldassi is another person whose life has been enlarged by the Lions. Olga received her first dog from the Lions Guide Dog Service in 1971 when she was 15. She works as a translator for IBM in Milan and, along with her native Italian, is fluent in English, French, Spanish, German, Russian, Hebrew, and Finnish.

"At the time I got my first guide dog I was the youngest person to be given one by the Lions facility," Olga said. "Guide dogs can go anywhere and suddenly a new life opened up for me. I can travel around Milan or just about anywhere in the world with a highly trained companion that never deserts me.

"It has made an immense difference in my job because my guide dog has increased my mobility and freedom. If IBM needs a job done somewhere else, now I can go and do it where before it might have been impossible. Here in Italy the Lions Guide Dog Service is widely recognized for its continuing help for the sightless. I've learned to communicate in a number of different languages. My dog and I communicate in a language that has no words but is the language of love and companionship. Every day when I get up I'm grateful for him."

Olga's enthusiasm is shared by many other blind men and women who have experienced new lives as a result of guide dogs from the Lions center. The center is supported by 73 Lions clubs in the Milan area and has grown steadily. Today it occupies 25,000 square meters. Lions support a similar facility in Giugliano, near Naples in southern Italy.

The dogs are carefully selected and then trained extensively to function as the eyes of their masters. Each dog learns to guide his master around holes, to avoid objects that are too low to walk under, to function in traffic, to follow traffic signals correctly; and all the other activities required for living safely.

Cats and rabbits are among the Limbiate guide dog service's employees. "We want to make sure that when a dog sees a cat or a rabbit he won't run off and leave his master," explained Guido Giampi, a Lion and technical manager of the school. "We have three kinds of cats: those who are shy and run away, tough cats who attack, and we have friendly, playful cats. Each dog who graduates from the training must pass an extensive range of training exercises and cats and rabbits are just one phase of it."

"These dogs are rigorously screened for precisely the traits that will make them perform according to our standards," explained Lion Maurizio Galimberti who is secretary and treasurer of the facility. "As a consequence, about 95 percent of those who begin training complete it successfully."

"Being involved with this gives a feeling like that of a doctor who heals patients," Galimberti continued. "Yesterday a blind man from Bologna stopped in to say how grateful he was for the dog we provided for him. He works as a telephone operator and can get around with far greater ease and confidence. We invariably see personality changes in the blind men and women after they get a guide dog. They become more cheerful and outgoing."

"I've been working on this project since it began," said another Lion, Alessandro Pasquali. "I've seen so many lives changed. One woman, Bruna Calcagno, was born blind. After we gave her a guide dog she got married and today has two children. Every time she comes back to visit we feel like we're all part of the family."

Added a woman from Ravenna, who is in her 30s, "I've been blind since birth and my dog is one of the family. When I dance with my husband, the dog is dancing too. The dog is so well trained that I have complete confidence in going anywhere with him. I have a freedom that would be impossible without the beautiful four-footed friend the Lions gave me."

David Kolb of Columbus, Ohio, works for the state as a program analyst. Each working day, he commutes to his office on the 38th floor of the state's new office building, and each evening, he returns to his home in Whitehall. Nothing remarkable about that, except that David Kolb is blind and is guided during his two-way commute by Tatum, the second dog he has received from Lions Pilot Dogs, Inc., of Columbus.

While a sophomore at Ohio State, David received his first dog, Babe, from Pilot Dogs. Babe, a German shepherd, recently retired after 13 years of service and was replaced by Tatum. "The Pilot Dog changed my life," Kolb explains. "I have confidence, I have freedom, I have opportunities that I would never have had without my Pilot Dog."

The organization's founding and growth is an exciting chapter in the Lions' history of working with the blind. Now a not-for-profit organization, it has a single purpose: "To train the finest of guide dogs and present them as a gift to the blind." However, the Pilot Dogs program stumbled along from 1947 until 1950 when three men stepped in. They were Charles W. Medick, a Columbus automobile dealer, and two Lions, Stanley Doran and Everett Steece. They incorporated the program, defined its purpose, and enlisted the help of other Ohio clubs.

Over the next eight years, several clubs made substantial donations. In 1958, the Tri-Village Lions gave a donation of $1,500 which represented the cost of training a dog and four weeks of residence training for the blind person who would own the dog. The club stipulated that Pilot Dogs, Inc., must always have a Lion on its board, a condition which has been honored ever since. The Tri-Village club in 1960 requested support from Lions clubs in Multiple District 13 at the 1960 Ohio State Lions Convention. Pilot Dogs, Inc., was adopted as a state project and Ohio clubs raised nearly $3 million from 1960 to 1988.

The beneficiaries of Ohio Lions' generosity and drive have been legion. Jim Wilson of Ironton, Ohio, is a veteran who lost the sight in his right eye in 1942 and in his left in 1947. Today, he gets around with the help of a Pilot Dog named Em, whom Wilson describes as "one beautiful animal." "I can't imagine what my life would have been without the dog that Pilot Dogs gave me."

For Jean Olivieri, a 36-year-old Marseilles, France, factory worker blinded in an industrial accident, independence was the gift of ten Lions clubs on the Riviera who saw a need for a guide dog program in 1964 and set out to meet it.

After his accident, Olivieri was unable to work and totally dependent on his wife and mother. After three weeks of intensive training at the Training Center of Dogs for Blind People near Nice, Jean walks the streets of Marseilles confidently with his German shepherd dog guide.

The training center at Nice and several other centers supported by the Federation of Guide Dogs for Blind People that provide dogs and training to blind people trace their origins to the ten Riviera clubs and to the late Louis Berneux, a member of the Roquebrune/Cap Martin club who unified them in an effort to start a guide dog school. Together with private individuals, the clubs raised $25,000 and were given a tract of land for a training center in Sospel. Only ten dogs were trained in 1964 and 1965. But in 1966, newspapers and radio stations got behind the effort and spearheaded a campaign that brought in $125,000.

A driving force in the center's development was Pierre Aicard, a civil engineer and a member of the Cannes Mimosa Lions Club. In 1972, Aicard was instrumental in organizing the first International Congress of Guide Dogs for Blind people. Held in Cannes, the Congress attracted delegates from 15 guide schools in Europe and Australia. It galvanized civic leaders throughout the country to form the Federation of Guide Dogs for Blind People.

Aicard and the Federation worked to solve new problems which arose from the very success of the guide dog movement in France. As Aicard put it in 1973: "There is discrimination against the blind man with a dog in terms of housing, employment, and in public places." Aicard and the Federation fought in the years after 1973 for legislation which expanded the legal rights of the blind person and his guide dog.

In Canada, a group of Lions dreamed another big dream—to build and administer a school to train dogs to guide blind people to independence. They called their dream Canine Vision Canada. Before Canine Vision became a reality in 1985, a blind Canadian who wanted a guide dog had no choice but to go to a school in the United States. Today Canine Vision Canada is a rousing success story and a continuing project of another foundation, The Lions Foundation of Canada.

Founded in February 1983, the Foundation built the dog guide school on the site of an old school house in Oakville, Ontario. Over the next two years, Lions, Lionesses, companies, individuals, and dog clubs came forward with labor and funds for the project. A major fund-raising event, the 1985 Walk-A-Dog-A-Thon was held in Oakville, an event that continues today as Canada's national October Walk-A-Dog-A-Thon.

More than 1,000 people attended the Grand Opening, including representatives of many U.S. clubs. Initially, the emphasis was on training dogs for Canadians who had previously owned dog guides. In January 1986, seven people arrived to begin training with dogs who had been trained by Canine Vision Canada. Today, the school can train up to 120 dog/person teams a year. Students pay nothing. The cost of dog, training, equipment, room and board, and necessary transportation—about $6,000 per team—comes from Lions clubs and other supporters.

Breeders donate Labrador, Golden Retriever, and German shepherd pups. Some dogs come from Canine Vision's own breeding stock program. First the pups go to a previously selected foster family where they learn the skills of being a good house dog for 12 months. Then they return to the school for tests of temperament and physical well being. If they pass, the dogs get three months of intensive training before being matched up with their new masters. Dog and master work and live together for four weeks learning to cross streets, board buses, ride elevators, and, most importantly, trust one another.

EYE BANKS, CORNEAL TRANSPLANTS, AND EYE RESEARCH

Since Helen Keller spoke to the Lions at their convention in 1925 they have helped the blind on many fronts. Encouraging advances in research and treatment, the association supports eye banks and research centers in many parts of the world. As a result, four-year-old Eric Jones received the gift of sight. Eric, who was born blind, lives on a farm in northern Georgia.

"Eric had a corneal transplant on his right eye when he was four months old," said his father, Clyde Jones. "We were a little bit afraid of the first operation but everything went just fine and his recovery was excellent. He never had any problems and everything went so well that when Eric was 14 months old he had a corneal transplant on his left eye and we didn't have any problems with that either.

"You can't put a price on sight, especially with a little fellow as small as he is who's never seen anything. To have the windows opened in his eyes so that he can see things that we take for granted is really something. If it hadn't been for the work of the Lions and the Lions Eye Bank our son would be blind today."

Another Georgian, Jerry Hall, is a middle-aged businessman and a recipient of two transplants. "My vision is tremendously important," he said. "I didn't realize that I had become a person who was not competing in life anymore. Through my corneal transplants and being able to see again, I can see not only visually, but I can see where my life had gone. As a result, I was able to become a competitor. Once again I can participate in staff meetings because I can see the visuals that are used. I can take part in my family life again because I can become enthusiastic about games and other things they are interested in. Receiving a corneal transplant not only renews your sight, it gives you a whole new life."

Eric Jones and Jerry Hall moved from darkness into light because of the wide-ranging program sponsored by the Lions and implemented by the Georgia Lions Eye Bank, Inc., at Emory University in Atlanta. Their physical sight reflects the vision the Georgia Lions translated into practical help.

All of the elements: patient, donor, doctor come together through the awareness and generosity of residents in a community—linked with the actions and dedication of the Lions. The Lions are the catalyst for the process.

Corneal transplants are not new. The first successful human to human transplant was performed in 1911. In 1934 eye tissue from a deceased person was employed for the first time. However, corneal transplantation as a routine procedure is a relatively recent development.

Located in the front of the eye, the cornea is the clear window through which light passes. It may become clouded through injury, disease, infection, or congenital defects. Varying degrees of blindness can result. A corneal transplant replaces the damaged cornea with a new cornea taken from a donated eye. This process restores sight in more than 90 percent of the cases in which it is performed. In *every* instance it transforms the life of a person who had been living in darkness.

In the United States, some 500,000 persons suffer from blindness and at least 30,000 of them could be helped with a corneal transplant. Unfortunately, only a limited number of corneas are available.

To meet this challenge, the New York City Lions played a key role in founding the first eye bank in the mid-1940s. Today, more than 150 eye banks are operating throughout the world. The great majority of these are sponsored by Lions.

There are Lions eye banks functioning in Brazil, Australia, Canada, China, India, and Japan, as well as many states in the United States. For example, in Texas alone the Lions support eye banks in ten different cities.

In March 1986, the International Board of Directors adopted a policy titled The Lions Clubs International Eye Bank Program. It was designed to standardize policy and assure that all Lions Eye Banks operate in harmony with the policies of Lions Clubs International.

The program will help in establishing new Lions Eye Banks throughout the world. Objectives include extending Lions Eye Banking internationally so that quality eye tissue will be available for corneal transplants, research, and other medical purposes.

All eye banks recognized under this program will be called Lions Eye Banks. The majority of the Board of Directors of each Lions Eye Bank are to be Lions club members in good standing.

Throughout the world, local Lions are the starting point in most eye bank programs. With eye donor drives and public information projects the Lions secure pledges for donation of eyes after death.

When people sign the pledge card they help assure the success of research to preserve sight. Tissue is used by eye banks to investigate glaucoma, cataracts, and other eye diseases in studies that are often implemented with modern equipment supplied by the Lions. Since many eye diseases are hereditary, the research may ultimately benefit unborn generations.

A special card is issued declaring an individual's decision to be a donor. A file is maintained at a central location and upon the donor's death the attending physician or next of kin notifies the eye bank.

This begins a process that will ultimately bring the miracle of sight to another human being. Eye tissue must be removed within six hours after death and the eye bank sends a member of its technical team to perform the procedure. If the tissue is suitable for a transplant, the cornea is carefully removed and placed in a solution that allows corneas to be stored up to five days.

The eye bank calls the surgeon next on the waiting list. He accepts responsibility for informing his patient that the gift of sight is now available. Transportation of the tissue to the location where the operation will occur is handled by the eye bank. If necessary, state patrols, helicopters, and airlines all cooperate to guarantee that the transport will be as expeditious as possible. Often corneal tissue is transported from one nation to another when needed.

Recipients echo the words of Mrs. Shirley Blankenship of Joplin, Missouri. A homemaker with three children, she exclaimed, "I'm a new person. I received the transplant for my right eye in April 1961, and a transplant for my left eye in 1965. I am able to pass my driver's test now. I do needlepoint and make some of my daughter's and my own clothes.

"I'm a notary public and notarize eye donor cards without charge to anyone I can persuade to donate their eyes to the Missouri Lions Eye

Tissue Bank. If a person dies without donating his eyes he is literally throwing away the most precious and priceless gift he can bestow."

"I would agree with that," said Joe Scott, executive director of the Lions of District 22-C Eye Bank and Research Foundation. Located in Seabrook, Maryland, the facility was incorporated in May 1957.

"We're totally run and governed by the Lions from District 22-C," Scott continued. "We have a mobile health van that we send out to the community approximately 100 times a year to give free glaucoma, hearing, and vision screening to the community residents. We do as many as 20,000 tests each year. We also collect eyeglasses from the community, ship them to an organization in New Jersey which processes them and then distributes them around the world. Our budget is about $250,000 a year and we are completely supported by the 65 Lions clubs and 29 Lioness clubs of District 22-C."

The Eye Bank and Research Foundation began in December 1955, with a speech by Dr. J. Harry King to the Georgetown Lions Club in Washington, D.C. A U.S. Army ophthalmologist, Dr. King described the need for an eye bank in the Washington area. His speech excited the members and Stanton Kolb, program chairman of the club, was asked to explore the feasibility of starting an eye bank.

After discussing the question with officials of the Schenectady, New York, Eye Bank and learning what would be required for starting the project, Kolb reported to the Georgetown Lions Club at their meeting in January 1956. The members felt it would be too large a job for a single club.

The proposal was submitted to the clubs of District 22-C for adoption as a district project at a cabinet meeting in 1956. The newly-elected district governor, Lewis Hopfenmaier, had been present at the club meeting and enthusiastically supported the idea. A resolution was passed to organize an eye bank as a district project.

Through the years the research unit has made extensive contributions to ocular surgery, including development of new methods of preserving tissue, testing, and developing new suture materials and surgical instruments, devising new containers for shipping fresh eyes, and much more.

A youngster named Francisco Valente de Almedia came to the eye bank from Portugal for a corneal transplant. He went home with eyesight restored. Mrs. Miriam Haidar-Akbar, an Arab lady, received corneal transplants and went home able to see. A young girl from Bolivia was given a successful corneal transplant and the gift of sight. A little girl from Nicaragua was treated at the facility for a cataract in one eye and a corneal transplant for the other. Although most of its patients are from the United States, the eye bank's service is international.

By 1988, the eye bank had restored sight to more than 8,000 men, women, and children. The product of Dr. Harry King's dream and the efforts of District 22-C Lions and Lionesses, the eye bank continues to grow.

Through education and research Lions' programs have sparked advances in diagnosis and treatment of myriad eye problems. For example, when a cataract causes enough loss of vision that it interferes with a person's daily activities, the lens should be removed surgically. When faced with this operation, patients often react as one man did. He said, "I really want to avoid wearing those thick glasses that people have to wear after cataract surgery."

Until recently there would not have been much choice. However, today a plastic intraocular lens is implanted at the time the cataract is removed. A permanent implant made of purified plastic, the lens gives the patient eyesight that closely approximates the vision he had before cataracts. It avoids the distortion and reduced visual field usually associated with cataract glasses and the inconvenience of contact lenses. The technique has a 98 percent success rate.

Lions' screening programs have preserved vision for millions around the globe. In glaucoma, for instance, the fluid that nourishes the cornea and lens drains at a reduced rate. This causes increased pressure in the eye. The condition may be compared to an air conditioner that needs a filter change. If untreated, the pressure in the eye destroys the optic nerve.

The damage from glaucoma, which usually progresses slowly and without symptoms, can be prevented by periodic examinations and treatment. The screening process for detecting glaucoma is extremely fast and simple and can easily be performed on children. The condition is commonly treated by eye drops and occasionally by pills taken orally. Recently, lasers have been used for making microscopic holes through the plugged drainage meshwork in the angle of the eye. This is effective in at least 75 percent of glaucoma cases. Early detection is critical for treatment of glaucoma or it can cause blindness.

The laser's first medical use was in treating retinal detachment. If the retina tears loose from the eyeball, blindness can result. A laser beam, focusing through the lens of the eye, reattaches the retina by fusing it to the underlying tissue. It takes a thousandth of a second, while conventional surgery may take as long as several hours.

Blending inspiration with planning and hard work, Lions principles transform the world for the visually handicapped.

Reaching across thousands of miles, they heal the afflicted. In Soon Chun, Korea, 19-year-old Kim Chang Ehi lived with her parents, three brothers, and a sister in a two-room clapboard house. She was born cross-eyed. The best time to correct the condition is between the ages of four and six but, unfortunately, her father could not afford the operation.

Chang Ehi was overjoyed when she learned that a team of eye doctors sponsored by the Nam San Lions Club of Seoul would be coming to Soon Chun to perform free operations. After a careful examination, the visiting physician operated to correct the crossed eyes. Both of Chang Ehi's eyes were bandaged and her father led her down the steps and into a jeep waiting to take her home. When the bandages were removed Chang Ehi laughed delightedly as she looked at the world with normal vision for the first time in her life.

Dr. Kim Hi Joon, a charter member of the Nam San Lions Club, originated the idea of providing free eye operations for poor people in outlying areas. Dr. Kim was one of the founders of the Korean Ophthalmological Society in 1964. He initiated the Lions eye project in the same year and it has become an annual event.

Usually four or five doctors volunteer their time for a week. A different section of the country is selected each year and Lions clubs in various parts of the country help with local details. Sixty to 90 operations are performed in the week. Doctors also diagnose and treat a wide range of other eye problems.

In Caracas, Venezuela, Mrs. Maria Delgado de Alvarez can see because of the Lions. A 43-year-old widow with four children, Mrs. Delgado said she felt fine when a friend asked her to go along to the Lions-supported eye clinic in Caracas.

"What for?" asked Mrs. Alvarez. "I can see perfectly well and I don't have any problems with my vision."

"It won't hurt to have an examination," replied her friend.

"It's a good thing I listened to her and had my eyes checked," Mrs. Alvarez said later. "They found that I had undetected glaucoma and required emergency treatment. I was rushed to the hospital for further tests that same day and the doctor prescribed medication that reduced the pressure within the eyeball. Without the glaucoma test and prompt treatment I would have had serious problems and perhaps permanent damage to my sight."

Mrs. Alvarez is just one of countless Venezuelans who have benefited from the Lions-supported Venezuela Association Against Visual Handicaps and Eye Bank. Although accidents account for a sizable percentage of vision loss in Venezuela, glaucoma is the leading cause of preventable blindness. It is estimated that at least 100,000 Venezuelans have undetected glaucoma.

Early diagnosis is important and the key to saving sight. In Venezuela, as in other parts of the world, Lions are active in preserving sight. One of every four children in Venezuela suffers some form of visual impairment. To meet this problem, the clinic carries on a year-round program of education and eye examinations.

"We find a number of the children suffering from amblyopia, or lazy eye, and treat them immediately," said Dr. Sylvia Salinas, a member of the clinic staff. "If found and treated when the child is young, it can generally be corrected by placing a patch over the good eye to force the child to use the weaker eye."

Diabetes is often a cause of blindness in older persons and blood sugar evaluations are used in the clinic's testing approach. Appropriate measures are then prescribed for these patients with further testing when needed.

The clinic provides thorough examinations for cataracts, another leading cause of blindness in old age. If surgery is required, the patient pays whatever he can. If he is unable to pay, the operation is performed at no charge.

Education in eye safety is another facet in safeguarding the vision of Venezuelans of all ages. "We're trying to alert the public to the fact that

90 percent of all eye accidents are preventable," said Enrique Meza, a Caracas Lion.

In Melbourne, Australia, the Lions Research Unit of the Royal Victorian Eye and Ear Hospital has spearheaded studies designed to wipe out trachoma. This disease has been the scourge of the desert aborigines of Australia.

The work on trachoma in the 1960s was directed by the pathologist in charge, Dr. H. Courtenay Greer, who came to Australia from London.

Extremely contagious, the trachoma virus attacks the lining of the eyelid and outer coat of the eye. The mucous membrane covering the inner surface of the eyelids in front of the eyeball become severely inflamed. They develop a "sandy" surface leading to scarring and deformity of the lids. The eventual result may be total blindness.

After exhaustive investigation, the western Australian form of the virus was isolated in Perth in the early 1960s by Professor Ira Mann, who had done previous work at Oxford. The virus was brought to the Lions National Research Unit and introduced into the blind eye of a volunteer. It was then studied by Dr. Greer and his assistant.

The experiment produced an effective form of treatment with antibiotics. As a result, countless residents of Australia's desert areas have been saved from blindness. The trachoma research has been only one facet of the Royal Victorian Eye and Ear Hospital's wide-ranging research and treatment activities, made possible by the Lions-sponsored unit.

In 1955, the hospital had no eye research unit and the Lions stepped in to fill the need. A suitable building was found near the hospital. To buy and renovate the structure would cost about $55,000. Moving quickly, the Melbourne Lions Club provided a bank draft for $11,000. This enabled the hospital to begin the work and hire Dr. Greer. At that time he was one of only five ophthalmologists in the world specializing in pathology.

In 1956, at the District 201 Convention, Melbourne Lions Club president Viv Martyn and two other delegates presented the project to the members and it was adopted. At that time all of Australia was one district.

The Lions raised the money in three years. The building was purchased and remodeled for $40,000. The surplus of $15,000 was invested to create scholarships for medical research into the causes of blindness and to refine techniques for treating eye diseases.

In July 1963, the Lions National Research Unit funded the Ringland Anderson Chair of Ophthalmology. Among other programs, the department created the largest retinal investigation unit in the southern hemisphere.

Whether it's a dog guide, a white cane, a corneal transplant, or a high technology treatment center, the Lions find a way to supply it.

The Lions of Illinois Foundation proved that it could make big dreams happen fast after deciding at its May 1977 Annual Meeting to adopt research into the restoration of sight as its top priority. The Foundation set as its goal the establishment of an Eye Research Institute in the Chicago area where it would be accessible to a vast population. The West Side Medical Center of the University of Illinois at Chicago was selected as the site of the institute for several reasons. These included a convenient location, access to top eye researchers and a pressing need for modern research facilities at the university. Figuring large in the calculations, were the excellence of its Ophthalmology Department and its longtime history of working with the Illinois Lions.

Feasibility studies had shown that the Lions could generate the funds needed to establish a research facility. A blue ribbon committee under the direction of a past district governor was set up to plan and direct the campaign. At the beginning of the drive, a popular button worn by Lions read: "I feel good, let's make it happen." And make it happen they did. In 1981, the Lions of Illinois Foundation took over direction of the campaign and by September of 1982, more than $4.1 million had been subscribed in outright pledges or contributions.

Ultimately, the campaign raised $5 million to erect a new building for the Institute. It was dedicated in 1985. More than 95 percent of the state's clubs backed the campaign. At the dedication, International President Joseph L. Wroblewski delivered the keynote address and asked the Illinois Lions about the buttons. "What do you feel good about?" he asked. And hundreds of voices answered as one: "We're doing something good for humanity."

Today, a team of 30 researchers, clinicians, and teachers are seeking to unlock some of the secrets which will lead to better diagnosis and treatment of such major causes of eye diseases as diabetic retinopathy, glaucoma, macular degeneration, and cataracts.

"We believe that discoveries made in the Lions of Illinois Eye Research Institute will be of tremendous value, not just to the people of Illinois, but to people at risk of blindness wherever they are on this earth," is the evaluation of Dr. Morton I. Goldberg, former head of the university's Department of Ophthalmology. "The institute will hopefully do away with much of the blindness that now exists. We believe our team of outstanding scientists and eye doctors, working together, will conquer many of the eye diseases affecting our families, friends, and people across the earth."

Surgery, research, buildings, and technology are the tools that build new lives for the sightless. Fun is another factor in the Lions' commitment. The joy of discovery, the thrill of new experiences, the excitement of the outdoors . . . they all figure large in Lionism's equation.

CAMPS FOR THE VISUALLY HANDICAPPED

Lions clubs have worked to create unique summer camps that work to build confidence and skills. Many Lions vacation camps are founded initially for a single purpose—to help blind youth, or deaf young people, or those with some other physical disability. Often the clubs operating these single-purpose camps have found it an easy and natural step to expand their operations to include various disabilities. This has been true with some of the earliest camps. The Wisconsin Lions Camp opened in 1956 and started out helping the blind and then expanded its mission, according to Tony Omernik, secretary of the Rosholt Lions Club and a Lion for 16 years.

"The camp is owned and operated by the Wisconsin Lions Foundation," Omernik said. "The foundation itself is owned by almost 500 Wisconsin Lions clubs that, along with private individuals, donate around half a million dollars a year to keep the camp going."

"Campers between the ages of six and 18 enjoy a one-week camping experience during the camp's 12-week season," Omernik said, "and blind and deaf adults come at the end of the season." When the camp is going full blast, there are 60 counselors who handle 140 different campers a week. "So more than 1,700 people enjoy our camp every year." The campers pay no fees though the cost is about $200 a week per camper.

The Wisconsin camp's variety of activities for campers is typical of many. There is instruction in canoeing, boating, fishing, swimming, camping out, outdoor living skills, and handicrafts. There is also an "adventure" program for teenagers that involves biking, canoeing, and backpack trips which develop teamwork and self confidence of campers.

The 500 individual clubs that support the camp are enthusiastic. In enclosing a $1,000 check from the Grand Chute Lions Club, club President William J. Maas wrote: "Each time we visit . . . we receive the payment we all were promised when we pledged ourselves to serve."

And those who use the camp are equally enthusiastic. An adult couple from Wauwatosa, Wisconsin, wrote "We have renewed our faith in the goodness of people. . . ."

For many young people the camp experience has been almost mystical. Children and their parents write again and again of gaining new experience and confidence, of coming to the realization that despite a handicap, they are as important and worthwhile as any non-handicapped person.

"For some of these kids, there are life-changing things happening," is the way Omernik puts it.

A mother wrote: "Jenny has gained some wonderful experiences from her eight years at Lion's Camp. The increase in self-confidence has enriched her life and the friendships she has made are invaluable."

And a 61-year-old blind woman wrote: "I never had a chance to go to camp when I was a kid. I still can't believe how much fun I had. The staff achieved its goal. They gave me confidence and trust in myself and in them."

"We do not have the money to send our son to camp. With his problem, other camps don't want him. The Lions Camp has given him a chance to excel and be successful," the mother of a camper wrote.

Another parent wrote: "We feel our son is very special and so does the Lions Camp. We thank all of you."

"Lions Camp is the greatest thing to happen to our son. He has 51 weeks of not much 'winning' and then comes camp and he has one week of winning and being Number One."

Omernik, who worked at the camp for seven years before becoming a full-time employee, says, "The majority of camps like this one have been Lion-owned, Lion-operated, or heavily supported by Lions. The camp movement has been a logical extension of the traditional Lions' emphasis on help for the blind."

Wherever in the world they are found, Lions camps and projects for the blind are innovative and creative. They always seem a perfect fit for their time and place.

For instance, Norwegian Lions began holding cross country skiing meets for the visually handicapped in the mid-1960s despite the common belief that such an activity is suitable only for the sighted. So successful were the meets in Norway that, today, Lions in many areas of the world sponsor instruction and competition for blind skiers.

In 1975, a well-publicized "Race for Light" was sponsored jointly by the Lions of Colorado and Norwegian Lions clubs. It brought the best blind skiers in the world to Colorado and received international attention.

In Djakarta, Indonesia, a Lion-sponsored school helps young blind people to become independent and responsible adults by providing instruction in many subjects and in a variety of activities, including its highly acclaimed bamboo band. The program is unique, according to an Indonesian Lion spokesman, "because our goal is to work with the blind. We don't believe in telling them what to do. Instead, they tell us what they require and then we try and figure out a way to meet those needs."

Blind students in England are benefiting from that uniquely Lions way of finding a need and then filling it. Lions of the Shrewsbury Shropshire club noticed that blind students were losing the gains they had made in school because of unhappy home environments. The Lions thought a summer camp where blind youngsters—and some sighted children— could spend free time together would be the logical solution. The club began corrresponding with schools for the blind to identify students who might benefit from a summer camp program. They rented a former school in North Wales. The club wrote Lions clubs located near the homes of possible students asking if the clubs could provide or pay for transportation to the camp. The clubs could and did.

"The interaction of the blind and sighted students and the friendships which were made in camp gave the whole experience a new dimension," one Shrewsbury club member commented.

The day was threatening and the water rough, but the friends were warm and the fishing great for 12 blind men in the Yorktown, Virginia, area who spent the day on a fishing boat and caught no less than 105 fish. The happy fishermen were guests of the Yorktown Lions Club. Six of them came on the trip by themselves. Lunch, tackle, and boat rental were all provided by the club. "I don't think any of us even noticed the rough water, we were hauling in fish so fast," one Lion commented. "And afterwards, we sat around for a long time telling fish stories to each other."

The Lions have even made sailors out of blind and visually handicapped people. The Seattle (Waterfront), Washington, Lions Club participates in an ongoing sailing school for blind and visually handicapped students, many of whom have never been aboard a boat before. These neophytes are turned into helmsmen who can actually sail a 14-foot sailboat over a prescribed course.

An instructor, himself an experienced sailboat racer, marvelled at how quickly his students learned the techniques and arcane language of the sailor. "Several students—after a single time around the boat—identified every part of the hull and rigging by its proper name," he said. "I know sighted sailors who can't do that after a year's experience."

There was the experience of 12-year-old Bonnie who held a feather for the first time. She had never heard of one before. Carefully stroking the soft edges, Bonnie kept repeating, "Feather, feather, feather."

"I can see why they named it feather," she smiled. "It feels just like it sounds." A pretty girl with long, dark braids, Bonnie has been blind since birth but her world is growing larger.

Nearby, another 12-year-old girl caressed a baby chick and said wonderingly, "It smells soft." She, too, is blind. Other youngsters played with lambs, fawns, rabbits, and baby raccoons.

Bonnie and hundreds of other blind and physically handicapped boys and girls were enjoying the fun and adventure at Camp Courage, made possible to a large extent by the Minnesota Lions. Fifty miles northwest of Minneapolis, Camp Courage's 191 acres overlook Cedar Lake. Since 1954, it has been one of the main service projects of the District 5-M Lions. During the two-week camping session boys and girls discover abilities they never dreamed they possessed. As their world grows, their opinions of themselves improve as well. The camp is available to any Minnesota resident over the age of eight.

A speech and hearing clinic was added in 1966 and this four-week session is designed for children from eight to 16.

Campers romp with lambs, ride ponies, laugh at baby pigs, play with calves and ducklings, and feed little goats and baby chicks. Specially trained counselors selected for patience and understanding guide the youngsters through the two weeks. Joy, laughter, a sense of wonder— campers enjoy them all during the exhilarating experiences provided by the Minnesota Lions.

One of the earliest, and perhaps *the* earliest, Lions Camp was organized by the Casper, Wyoming, Lions Club. Named for the late Allen H. Stewart, former district governor, it opened in the mid-1930s.

"It was started as a milk-camp during the Depression," explained Frank Stewart (no relation to Allen), a member of the Casper Lions Club since 1957 and a past president. "The milk camp was there to provide milk and food for underprivileged children who were not getting a proper diet. It became a camp for the blind in 1939 and was supported by our club until about six years ago when it became a statewide project. For years it was known simply as the Lions Blind Camp on Casper Mountain. Some years ago Allen Stewart was caught in a blizzard while going to a Lions Club program in Ten Sleep, Wyoming, close to the Bighorn Mountains. He died in the blizzard. Our club decided that, because of his devotion to Lionism and the fact that he died while serving Lionism, it was appropriate to rename our blind camp after him."

The facility houses 130 campers at a time. The blind learn communication skills, walking skills, receive tips on personal care, and even study computer operation.

Instruction in piano and other musical instruments launched a number of blind campers on new careers. Completely blind, they found the music lessons at the camp so enjoyable they pursued them during high school and majored in music in college. At least two have become concert pianists as a result of their experiences at the camp.

"The camp for the blind is one of the reasons I joined the Lions," said Frank Stewart. "It's the glue that held us together and kept us working. It's given us a lot of motivation. We have three weeks in the summer when the camp is reserved for the blind. At other times we have hearing impaired groups and church groups. We have a retarded group. In the wintertime the camp is used only for day activities like ski groups or snowmobiling."

While some of the camps for the blind have branched into other areas of service to the handicapped, many like the camp for the blind founded by the Waycross (Okefenokee), Georgia, Lions Club have held to a single purpose.

In 1972, under the leadership of Dr. C. M. Blanton, a past governor of District 18-B, the club recognized the need for safe recreation for blind children in the state of Georgia. The Okefenokee Lions Club sponsored a one week summer camp for blind children in Laura S. Walker State Park near Waycross.

In July 1974, other Lions clubs in south Georgia asked District Governor Dan Anderson to create a committee that would organize a camp for the blind in the state of Georgia. Lion Anderson presented the idea to the Georgia Lions Council of Governors. After considering the proposal the Council of Governors voted to support the effort throughout the state.

In November 1974, a delegation of Georgia Lions met with Governor (and Lion) Jimmy Carter with a plan to secure 61 acres of land adjoining Laura S. Walker State Park to be used for a camp for the visually handicapped. Plans were approved and the Georgia Lions Camp for the Blind, Inc., was chartered as a non-profit organization on September 12, 1975.

The camp is designed to give an enjoyable outdoor experience without roughing it. Most buildings are air-conditioned and there are many shaded areas to take advantage of the breezes. The camping program is extensive.

"What I like best is the horseback riding," said 12-year- old Billy from nearby Valdosta. "I've never ridden a horse before and was a little nervous but my instructor was right there to look after me and that gave me confidence. I can't wait to get back next year."

Most campers echo Billy's enthusiasm. They enjoy backpacking, drama, dance, swimming, boating, games, music, and crafts of all kinds. Staff members include a specially trained dietitian and medical personnel.

Olympics for the Blind is a project of the camp. A number of campers from Georgia Lions Camp for the Blind have gone on to win silver and gold medals for Georgia in the national Olympics.

TRAINING AND SPECIAL DEVICES FOR THE BLIND

Giving the blind the skills they need to make a living and become self-supporting is typified by a Lions-sponsored school that uses a multi-disciplinary approach to restore pride. Audelino Castillo of Bogota, Colombia, seemed doomed to a life of dependency when he was blinded at the age of 26. Now 28, he can look forward to a life on his own. As a trainee at the Center for Rehabilitation of Blind Adults (CRAC) in Bogota, Castillo reported, "I've learned to travel by myself, to read and write in braille, to type, use the abacus, and a whole range of wood-working skills. This is in addition to the arts and crafts that have been taught me."

CRAC has been supported by the Bogota (Niza) Lions Club since 1970. It teaches its trainees basic techniques of daily living, like washing, dressing, and home management, as well as the skills they will need to communicate and earn a living. In 1971, Robert Uplinger, then international president, laid the cornerstone for a modern, new CRAC facility to replace the hodgepodge of old buildings. Many lives have been dramatically changed within the walls of the new center.

"For me, this training means that I can once again work and support my family," says Audelino Castillo.

Another graduate is Carlos, blind and hampered by a hand coordination problem, who entered the program in 1971 near despair. "I was sure that I would never be able to work and support myself. My life had gone steadily downward after I lost my eyesight two years before entering CRAC." Four years later, Carlos was a valued and trusted employee in a Bogota mill processing plant with a salary a third larger than the national average.

"The first and most important thing I got in this program was hope,"

Carlos said. "The instructors convinced me that their approach would work and as time went by I could see this was true. Along with their teaching skills they gave me that most important of all qualities—understanding. They patiently worked with me until I gradually overcame my problems."

CRAC's multi-dimensional approach has restored many despairing men and women like Carlos to life's mainstream.

As World War II began to fade from memory, Lions everywhere sought ways to make life better for the sightless, and nearly sightless, like 83-year-old Ada from Independence, Kansas.

"Oh, praise the Lord, I can see," she exclaimed as she read slowly from a small Bible.

"I've been praying for this."

Although legally blind, Ada's sight was restored with the help of optical aids provided by the Kansas Lions Sight Foundation, Inc. She gained 20/20 vision. Ada and others throughout the American Midwest who are legally blind are enjoying normal sight after treatment at the Kansas Low Vision Clinic in Wichita's E. B. Allen Hospital.

"Some convenience is sacrificed," said Dr. Robert Whittaker, an optometrist and Augusta, Kansas, Lion who treated Ada. "But if people have any sight at all and if they are determined, we can help them."

"We don't actually cure anyone of disease, but we suggest medical treatment in some cases," Whittaker added. "We fit patients with aids which expand their visual abilities and help them to make the best use of what vision they have."

He pointed to the case of an Oklahoma woman, legally blind, who rode a bus to work. She could only see well enough to recognize people and avoid running into walls. Her eyeglasses were as strong as could be ground by ordinary opticians. However, Dr. Whittaker found that by fitting her with specially ground microscopic lenses she had 20/20 vision.

"I can't believe it," she cried. "I wish I had heard about you 30 years ago."

The clinic is supported by the Kansas Lions who underwrite charges for patients who cannot afford the treatment fee. Lions provide free transportation to those unable to reach the clinic on their own. Since opening in 1960 the facility has helped thousands of patients from Kansas and surrounding areas.

One of the happiest patients was an 11-year-old boy from Kansas City, Missouri, who suffered from nystagmus, a spasmodic movement of the eyeballs, and amblyopia. He and his father were devoted fans of the Kansas City Chiefs football team and attended most of their games.

The youngster always took a portable radio so he could follow play-by-play action since he couldn't see the field very well. He would stand up and cheer with his dad, but without the radio, he wasn't sure what he was cheering for.

Testing at the clinic revealed that his best vision was 20/200. At the clinic he was fitted with a ten power telescope and his sight improved to 20/20. A week later his jubilant father called to tell the doctor that with the telescope his son could read the players' names on their jerseys. At last, too, he could read the scoreboard at the end of the field.

"Boy," said the young man, "I really can see what's happening in the game now. That sure beats trying to figure out the plays from my radio."

Lions-supported research and development programs have expanded the frontiers of equipment designed for the visually handicapped. Lions around the world have helped to harness space age technology to transform life for the sightless.

Using speech synthesizers, a blind person can get readouts and information via computer from libraries; he can check bank statements; do the shopping as well as an extensive range of other activities. The information can also be printed in braille, but the speech synthesizer is faster and cheaper. It costs about $100 for a speech machine while a braille printer costs $4,000.

Many of the blind are learning to use the computer as a prosthesis in the same way an amputee would use an artificial leg. A blind person learns to transmit information from a computer whose readout is auditory or tactile, rather than visual. Speech synthesizers take all the phonetic rules of the English language to create an unlimited vocabulary, something made possible by microchips.

Personal sensory aid computers are being tied to the big, mainframe computers used by business and industry to permit blind people to work at home. Eventually, experts predict, human brain waves, picked up by receivers tied to personal computers will allow a blind person to turn on the radio or coffee pot, or activate alarm systems.

Some of the other devices designed to make life easier for the blind: talking currency identifiers that tell the denomination of paper money; laser canes that beep within a ten or 15 foot range of objects; drinking glasses that beep when liquid is poured into them and the liquid reaches the correct level. Another significant advance is street signs with an electrical device implanted in them that activates a receiver carried by a blind person. The receiver, with a speech synthesizer, tells him the name of the street.

For blind people with normal hearing the tape recorder opens up wonderful possibilities. The blind student can now take a small recorder into the classroom and tape record the teacher's lecture. There is no need for the rattle and clatter of taking braille notes. Later the student can replay the lecture or simply save it for reviewing or listen again and put condensed notes or comments on another tape. Lions in many nations routinely provide tape recorders for the blind.

Whether it's a self-threading needle, a carpenter's level that beeps an appropriate signal, a slide rule with notched measurements, or brailled playing cards; each such device has meant another step enabling the blind to compete on even terms with the sighted.

––––––––––––

The year 1959 marked a major step forward in expanding the world of the visually handicapped. The first "talking books" were produced by the American Printing House for the Blind in Louisville, Kentucky. Articles from *Newsweek* magazine were recorded on tape for blind persons. These tapes were then purchased by Lions clubs and other civic and service groups for distribution to blind individuals and circulating libraries.

In the years that followed, *Talking Books* have become a major service for the blind. The development of the small tape recorder has created an important new tool for this activity. As a consequence, the visually handicapped have gained an opportunity for heightened awareness of world events and the chance to read for relaxation and enjoyment. Lions clubs are among the largest supporters of this service.

Another popular publication, the *Juvenile Braille Monthly,* is available to young blind individuals around the world. Begun in 1922, as a project of the Cincinnati, Ohio, Lions Club, the magazine is published at Clovernook Home and School for the Blind near Cincinnati. In 1925 the International Board of Directors adopted it for worldwide distribution, and ever since has paid the full cost of its publication.

The most recent of this group of publications, *Dialogue*, was chartered in 1961 and began publishing in Berwyn, Illinois, in January 1962, with a $1,000 grant from the Central Lions Club in Chicago. Originally called the *Talking Lion*, the publication's name was changed to *Dialogue* in 1964.

Begun by Don Nold, a member of the Berwyn Lions Club and a journalist who had lost his sight, it was published quarterly on 45 RPM phonograph records. The first year's budget of about $110,000 had grown to nearly $400,000 by 1988.

Today *Dialogue* is available in four different forms: on records, in braille, in large print, and on tapes. About 60 percent of its financial support comes from Lions clubs in various parts of the world. Widely recognized for its work for the visually handicapped, *Dialogue* is endorsed by the United States Library of Congress and affiliated libraries in the United States and Canada. A school for the blind in Japan uses its braille edition to assist in teaching English braille.

Dialogue is mailed to readers in five different countries in South America, nine in Europe, 15 in Asia, 12 in Africa, as well as to Australia, New Zealand, and all of Canada. With more than 200 pages in each issue, it offers a broad selection of articles to inform and entertain its readers.

The explosion of new technology and advanced teaching methods enable the blind to grasp opportunities and succeed in new fields that were only a dream a few years ago. Lions clubs everywhere have built and continue to support projects offering training for profitable careers.

In Little Rock, Arkansas, the Lions began a project in 1947 to provide employment for the blind. Today it is one of the largest in the world. Lion Roy Kumpe, a legally blind attorney, is generally considered the catalyst who made it happen. He lost his eyesight as a result of contracting trachoma when he was eight. Later trachoma was easily treated with sulfa drugs and then antibiotics, but in 1918 it meant either blindness or severe eye damage. Bitter experience with the problems of living with the handicap turned him into a lifelong crusader for opportunities for the blind.

A graduate of the Arkansas School for the Blind, Kumpe earned a degree from the University of Arkansas and then graduated from the University of Arkansas Law School. Very soon he saw the need for training for the visually handicapped that would fit them to compete in the job market.

As a result of Kumpe's appeal to his home club, the Little Rock Founders Lions Club, the members raised $10,000 to start the Arkansas Enterprises for the Blind (AEB). In 1949, two years after it opened, the Arkansas Lions voted to make it a statewide project.

Roy Kumpe served as executive director from 1947 to 1978. He died in 1987. Under his inspired leadership the AEB pioneered many advances to enlarge the lives of its students. Two future international presidents, Edward Barry and Finis Davis, worked closely with Kumpe to get the project moving.

Reflecting on the philosophy of AEB, Kumpe said, "The most important thing about a rehabilitation center is not the title on the door, but rather the daily activities to aid the blind that go on inside."

The record bears out his thoughts. Designed for the complete rehabilitation of the adult blind, AEB has served more than 6,000 visually handicapped individuals, with students coming from 54 different nations and all 50 of the United States. AEB offers dormitory facilities for its students; and when a blind person finishes training, he or she is ready to go to work.

In 1989, AEB changed its name to Lions World Services for the Blind to honor more than 40 years of Lions' support.

Jim Cordell is a Lion and executive director. He said, "During the 1980s vocational opportunities for blind and visually impaired persons have expanded at a rapid pace. We have people functioning as computer programmers, tax accountants with our federal government, medical transcribers, switchboard operators, small engine mechanics, teachers, lawyers, and in countless other vocational positions."

The emphasis is on performance. Becky Henry Darnell spent nine months studying computer programming. She said, "I really believe my whole perception of life—what I can do and what I can't do—changed because of AEB. I had three college degrees when I came to AEB, but I couldn't get a job. AEB was a turning point in my life. AEB made me realize if there's something out there that you really want, you can reach out and it is there."

Becky Henry Darnell is now a data base analyst for Walt Disney Productions in Lake Buena Vista, Florida. She's the first blind programmer they ever hired.

Another graduate of the program works as an operator for the Little Rock telephone company. Still enthusiastic about her training, she said, "I started here in 1975 working a board connecting departments to individuals. I do exactly the same job as other operators. My training helped me tremendously, especially in gaining a feeling of independence. My husband and I have a little boy who's five and a half months old. We have a house and I have a great job."

Lions World Services for the Blind provides training in one of the more dramatic developments for the visually handicapped, the Optacon. Using advanced electronics, the Optacon converts the image of an ordinary printed letter into a vibrating tactile form that a blind person can feel with one finger. Different printing styles and languages can be read with the Optacon because it reproduces exactly what is printed.

To read with the Optacon the blind person moves a miniature camera across a line of print with one hand. The index finger of the other hand is placed on the Optacon's tactile array. Approximately one inch long and one half inch wide, the tactile array consists of 144 miniature rods or stimulators in 24 rows and six columns.

As the camera is moved across a letter, the image is simultaneously reproduced on the tactile array by the tiny vibrating rods. The reading finger feels the enlarged letter as it passes across the tactile screen. The reader feels whatever image is seen by the camera's lens. For example, as the camera is moved across an upper case "E," the reader feels a distinct vertical line and three horizontal lines moving beneath the finger.

The miniature camera is the size of a small pocket knife and is equipped with a zoom lens to adjust magnification of the camera image to compensate for differences in print size. Designed with solid state circuitry and miniaturized components, the entire unit weighs only four pounds and is easily portable.

Training is essential for mastering skills needed to read with the Optacon. After completing Optacon training, users can read their own bank statements, follow recipes in printed cookbooks, and read storybooks to children. The Optacon has been especially important to blind students in advanced mathematics because it enables them to read complex equations directly without relying on cumbersome braille transcriptions.

Many visually handicapped persons have some sight but may be classed as "legally blind." Legal blindness was defined in a formula adopted in 1934 by the American Medical Association. In 1935 this was included in the Aid to the Blind Social Security Act. Legal blindness is defined as:

"Central visual acuity of 20/200 or less in the better eye with corrective glasses, or central visual acuity of more than 20/200 if there is a visual field defect in which the peripheral field is contracted to such an extent that the widest diameter of the visual field subtends an angular distance no greater than 20 degrees in the better eye."

In other words, a person is considered legally blind if even with perfectly fitted eyeglasses his better eye can see no more at a distance of 20 feet than a person with normal vision can see at a distance of 200 feet and/or if his central visual field is so restricted that he can only see objects within a 20 degree arc, in contrast with the visually normal person's ability to see objects in a much wider arc above, below and on each side of the line of sight.

Lions-sponsored research has sparked development of equipment enabling the legally blind to use the sight they have. This includes such machines as a closed circuit television set. Used primarily for reading, it magnifies what is being read up to 16 times its actual size. One model offers a split screen that allows the user to use two different texts on the same screen, or the user can read under one camera and write under the other camera. This enables a person to have the image from both texts on the screen at the same time.

EYE CAMPS AND DR. MODI

The word "heal" means to "make whole." Lionism's success has been its ability to translate noble principles into practical actions. In nearly every part of the world shattered, despairing human beings have found health and wholeness through the help of local Lions clubs.

Lionism's success, too, has been its capacity to enlist remarkable men and women to carry its healing message. In India, Dr. Muragapa Chenavirapa Modi has restored vision to countless thousands of his fellow men since graduating from medical school in 1943.

Although extensive opportunities for a lucrative practice were available to Dr. Modi, he remained unswerving in his devotion to helping the poor. Blindness in India often results from cataracts and they are the most common eye problem. Most surgeons take an hour or more to remove a cataract. Dr. Modi performs the operation in several minutes.

Penniless when he began his medical career, Dr. Modi rented a small building in the village of Patan after medical college and opened a tiny clinic. A few patients came to him, then more and soon they poured in for treatment from this amazing practitioner who performed scores of cataract operations every day.

Men and women who had been blind or visually handicapped for years suddenly could see. Dr. Modi's fame grew and he became known throughout India, and then the world. He organized a touring eye clinic that served the most remote sections of the country.

The Lions of India and their wives set to work and helped him with arranging trips, clinic sites, and patient care. Lions clubs provided funds for his activities. Gradually, as his reputation became worldwide, Lions clubs in the United States, Europe, and Asia provided equipment, vehicles, and other needed items.

Tireless in his zeal, Dr. Modi continues to work nonstop for the visually handicapped. As another example, during an eye operation camp organized by the Lions Club of Chirala, India, for poor people, Dr. Modi examined some 10,000 patients and performed 42 operations. Traveling by jeep, Lions spread the news of the camp to 80 villages on less than one week's notice.

In eight days Dr. Modi performed 350 eye operations in Bangalore City, India, as a result of more than 15,000 examinations. Another 1,351 persons were treated without surgery for a variety of eye disorders. In addition to the medical treatment, all of the patients and more than 8,000 persons who accompanied them were fed during the event. It was sponsored and financed by the Bangalore City Lions Club.

In 1962, International President Per Stahl of Sweden visited Dr. Modi in India. Lion Stahl presented Dr. Modi with his International President's Award for his "deep devotion to others in the field of sight conservation." In 1989, the association gave him its highest award, the Humanitarian Award, which included a $200,000 grant to expand his facilities.

Eye camps are a major Lions activity in the developing countries. Hundreds of eye camps are organized each year and provide surgery and treatment for men, women, and children who are blind. In nearly all cases they only need correct diagnosis and the services of a skilled specialist. In India, the nation most heavily afflicted with blindness, surgeons perform more cataract operations than anywhere else in the world.

Many Lions clubs underwrite these camps with contributions of food, manpower, and the services of a surgeon who is often a Lion. The eye camps move from village to village. The clinic is usually a school or public building that is used as a hospital and operating room during the ten to 15 day camp. Villagers and relatives of patients cook meals, carry stretchers, and serve as hospital assistants during post-operative care.

Everything is free. Eyeglasses, surgery, and medicines are provided at no charge. The surgeon performs as many as 50 cataract operations in one day and may treat more than 2,000 patients during one eye camp. Cost of the cataract surgery that restores vision to a blind person may be as little as five dollars.

LIONS MANOR

Lions' help for the blind has evolved with an ever-widening scope. When it opened in November 1979, Lions Manor in Windsor, Ontario, was believed to be the largest single club project in the world of Lionism.

Lions Manor was built and is operated by the Windsor (Downtown) Lions Club which was founded in 1920 as the first Lions club in Canada. The Lions spent more than $422,000 for recreational facilities and undertook a 50 year commitment for a $4.1 million mortgage for the rest of the building.*

Forty of the 150 apartments are reserved for the legally blind. The other 110 apartments are occupied by those over 60, and rents are

---

* The figures in this section refer to Canadian dollars.

adjusted according to ability to pay. The eight-story building blends in with the surrounding high rises. It is an ultra modern home for the blind and the elderly who are sighted. Members of each group help one another.

One of the happiest tenants is 39-year-old Bill Prentice. Bill has less than 10 percent vision and can barely decipher newspaper headlines with the help of a magnifying glass. "I lived with my parents and in several homes for the blind before coming to Lions Manor," he said. "Now I do my own cooking and have my own place where I can have visitors. My niece, Kim, who's seven and my nephew, Korey, who's three, come here all the time. I don't know what I'd do without them."

A relatively new concept when it opened in 1979, Lions Manor is proving highly successful. Its roots stretch back to 1950. In that year the Windsor (Downtown) Lions Club bought valuable riverfront land from the city for an assessed value of $5,000. With the aid of a $200,000 mortgage, they built Alexander Hall, a combined residential, recreational, and administrative building operated by the Canadian National Institute for the Blind. In the 1970s a survey of the blind revealed they wanted a new home and the Lions bought back Alexander Hall from the CNIB for $250,000.

The Lions study, at the start headed by the late Robert Whetstone, decided on an apartment complex that would offer recreation and housing for the blind and the sighted elderly. Ground for Lions Manor was broken in April 1978.

Elton Plant, past president of his club and past secretary-treasurer of Multiple District A, was named campaign chairman to raise $325,000 for the project. Plant, a Lion for 52 years, appointed a 15-member committee. All 85 members of the Windsor (Downtown) Lions Club collaborated on a mailing to 86,400 homes and businesses.

Lions were interviewed on radio, TV, and in the newspapers, and the publicity pulled in more receipts. Lions sponsored a walk-a-thon for the blind and generated $6,500 from sponsors of 75 blind walkers. Three Sunday afternoon concerts earned another $3,000.

The Lions hit their target of $325,000 by August 1978, but found they would need more money because of cost overruns. They extended the drive and by the end of 1979 they had collected $422,759. Half the amount came from the CNIB and the government-sponsored Wintario

Lottery. The other half of the donations came from the public, including $10,000 from the Lioness Club.

Residents echo the words of Alma LaLonde. Born blind, she was raised on a farm with her brother and sister who were also blind. She and her husband, Aurel, lived in Windsor and Alma ran the CNIB Canteen at Metropolitan Hospital for 35 years. Aurel died in 1978.

Smiling, Alma said, "We had lived in the same house since 1941 and I stayed there for a year after my husband died. But being blind and alone, that's no life. When I heard about Lions Manor I knew it was where I wanted to be. I have a real home again and I have new friends."

Norman Lloyd added, "In Lions Manor I can run my own life. I do my own shopping. I cook for myself and guests. I like living with people who can talk about something other than what it's like to be blind." An electrical engineer, Norman is 66 and lost his sight to glaucoma in 1962.

The Windsor (Downtown) Lions Club observed its 60th anniversary in April 1980, with International President Lloyd Morgan as the honored guest. The International Tri-District banquet entertained 600 Lions and friends from Districts A-1 (Ontario) and 11 A-1 and 11 A-2 (Michigan). The gathering was an occasion for reviewing the the previous six decades and a look at future goals.

While they were not among the evening's speakers, Bill Prentice, Alma LaLonde, Norman Lloyd, and the other residents of Lions Manor are eloquent witnesses to the effectiveness of Lions Clubs International.

SEE

Other Lions' programs send eye surgeons and technicians to many places in the world to help those who would never be able to pay for such care. Lions' generosity multiplies scenes like this one which took place in a temporary operating tent set up in a tiny Mexican town in the state of Jalisco.

Under generator-powered lights, a surgeon deftly removed the cataract-clouded lens from the eye of 52-year-old Juan Juarez, a farmer, and replaced it with a plastic lens. A few days later, the bandages came off. "I can see again," Juan exclaimed to the surgeon. Juan paid nothing for the operation.

SEE is a program which sends volunteer ophthalmologists and nurse/ technicians around the world to treat eye diseases and do eye surgery. Many of the patients live in underdeveloped countries where eye care is limited or nonexistent. Many of the SEE clinics are sponsored entirely by local Lions clubs.

The driving force behind SEE is a member of the Malibu, California, Lions Club, Dr. Harry S. Brown, an ophthalmologist. Brown completed a three-year residency at the Jules Stein Eye Institute, UCLA, and then went around the world, working with foreign ophthalmologists to learn the special needs and problems facing eye doctors in other countries. SEE began in 1972 and today more than 25 percent of the organization's board of directors are Lions. Funding has come from many different Lions clubs and the Lions Clubs International Foundation. The Lion Sight and Hearing Conservation Center at St. Francis Hospital in Santa Barbara, California, has also played an important role in supporting SEE International.

In 1987 alone, the value of donated medical and surgical services was close to $4 million. More than 90 physicians and 55 nurses and technicians performed 907 major eye surgeries and treated nearly 8,000 patients in Jordan, Colombia, Panama, New Guinea, Mexico, Malaysia, Jamaica, and the United States.

JOURNEY FOR SIGHT

Nowhere does Lions creativity show more graphically than in its fund-raising projects for sight-related enterprises. For instance, the Lions Journey for Sight—an annual event since 1983—attracts tens of thousands of participants throughout the world. Individual clubs or districts solicit pledges from individuals and businesses for each mile or kilometer traveled. Usually, the journeys involve running, jogging, walking, or cycling, but Lions, Lionesses, and Leos have come up with some startling variations on the journey theme.

For example, in Alberta, Canada, more than 70 vehicles displayed the Lions Journey for Sight banner while traveling the highways to the capital city of Edmonton as part of Lions Cavalcade '86. Lions in Montana, likewise, held a cavalcade with vehicles traveling to Billings.

The Chubby Challenge of the Exeter Township, Pennsylvania, Lions Club saw members passing a slice of strudel in a relay race instead of a baton. In Mutare, Zimbabwe, the Lions went on a motorized scavenger hunt.

Bancroft, Wisconsin, Lions journeyed in an antique auto parade and a team of Bedford, Ohio, Lions ran 357 miles from International Headquarters in Oak Brook, Illinois, back to their hometown. Two members of the Wellington (Host), New Zealand, Club rode horses on a ten-day, 300 kilometer trek from Wellington to Napier. The Glenavon and District Club in Saskatchewan, Canada, paddled in a canoe-a-thon. Bethlehem, Republic of South Africa, Lions pushed a fellow member around town in a wheelbarrow to raise funds. In a tremendous individual effort, Lion Norbert Peiker of the Mansfield (Evening), Ohio, Lions Club ran 4,000 miles cross-country for his personal journey, a commitment that included, as part of the journey, participation in the 1984 Boston Marathon.

These journeys have raised millions of dollars, with many clubs returning 25 percent of the proceeds to LCIF. This is then applied to sight-related activities such as grants for research into diabetic retinopathy, one of the leading causes of blindness in the world. Clubs and districts apply the remaining proceeds to projects in their respective areas—eye exams and eyeglasses for the indigent, vocational training for the blind, corneal transplants, research, sponsorship of summer camps for visually impaired and blind children, mobility aids; whatever the needs may be.

International Headquarters makes available to Lions a special journey kit with tips on how to organize successful events. Also available to help clubs promote journeys in the community are radio spot announcements made by former all-pro football lineman and television and movie star, Alex Karras. Sound-slide releases for TV also assist Lions in bringing news of this important fund-raiser to the attention of the general public from whom the funds will be generated.

Lions have a history of dreaming big dreams and then turning those dreams into happy realities.

Camps, schools, research facilities, institutes, and foundations, all inspired by Lions, have helped bring out the talent and individuality in those who suffer the handicap of blindness.

Many men and women have become prodigious achievers. Witness Dr. Richard Kinney, who was both blind and deaf. President of Hadley School for the Blind when he died in 1979, Dr. Kinney wrote four books of poetry, one textbook for the deaf blind, visited 40 foreign countries, published articles in many leading magazines, and received countless awards.

Living with joyous courage in a world he could neither see nor hear, he summed up his philosophy in the phrase, "To love and help live."

"If we shoot for the stars," said Kinney, "we may at least touch a rainbow."

Finding needs and meeting them on many different fronts each day, members of Lions Clubs International transform the reality of the sightless. Lives change, opportunities are created, and hope is generated as Lions make the possible happen. Taking the hands of the visually handicapped, Lions say, "Come with us. We'll help you shoot for the stars and we'll both touch a rainbow."

CHAPTER SIX

Hearing

"LIONS and my Hearing Dog, Ginger, have given my flagging spirit a great lift. They've ended the nightmare of isolation and my inability to communicate effectively. It's priceless," exclaimed Sylvia Wholohan of Sydney, Australia.

Australia's Hearing Ear Dog Program that brought Sylvia and Ginger together began with a conversation between Past District Governors Bob Allen and Brian Carter in 1980. They were on their way home from the international convention in Chicago. Both had heard of the Hearing Ear Dog Center in Denver, Colorado, and Allen had visited the facility.

When they arrived home in Australia the two Lions created a steering committee to study the problem of deafness and learned that between 800,000 and one million Australians suffer from some degree of hearing impairment.

In 1981, at the multiple district convention in Canberra, the delegates passed a motion to establish the Lions Hearing Dog Program. A trainer was hired from the Hearing Ear Dog Center in Denver. Her duties included training staff members as well as dogs.

The program has flourished with constant care from Australian Lions. Twenty kennels were built during 1982 along with offices and a house. By April 1986, 74 dogs had been trained and placed in the community and there were applications for other dogs in training.

Lions Hearing Dogs, Inc., was invited to join the Australian Deafness

Council, the coordinating body of many different groups serving the hearing impaired in Australia. The council of governors voted approval to join.

Hearing Dogs help the hearing impaired by alerting them to common sounds like a doorbell, telephone, smoke, burglar and clock alarms, a baby's cry. Hearing Dogs look after their owners every minute of the day. They tap them on the body when the tea kettle whistles, the doorbell rings, or it's time to wake for work. Hearing Dogs are "ears" for the deaf.

Sylvia Wholohan and Ginger go to college together. "The Epping-Eastwood Lions changed my life," Sylvia smiled. "I've started the second semester with confidence and a trouble-free mind thanks to Ginger and the Lions."

There is no legal definition of deafness and experts do not completely agree on when to use the term. Hearing specialists generally distinguish between deafness and hearing impairment. People with impaired hearing can usually hear and understand some speech, especially when it is loud enough. However, they may be unable to hear some other sounds such as doorbells or high musical notes.

Deaf children and youngsters with severe hearing impairments have great difficulty learning to speak. Normally children learn to speak by imitating the speech of others. Since deaf children cannot hear speech, many deaf people never learn to speak well enough to be understood. They use sign language and other special techniques to communicate. Education for the hearing impaired becomes a painful challenge.

For Ann Billington, however, it was a challenge to be met and mastered. Ann can't hear but she's a former beauty queen and a college graduate. Ann was crowned Miss Deaf America some years ago after she had first been named Miss Gallaudet at Gallaudet College in Washington, D.C. Gallaudet is the only accredited liberal arts college in the world for deaf students.

For many years Lions clubs in Virginia, Maryland, and Washington, D.C., have provided financial and emotional support for the school. Much of the money raised and donated by the Lions is designated for teaching students from other countries enrolled at Gallaudet.

"The education I received at Gallaudet 15 years ago gives me benefits every day of my life," said a French businessman. "The quality of instruction is high and the teachers are superbly trained to help each student perform up to his capacity. I met a number of Lions while I was attending the college and they took a personal interest in me and other students. They gave money but they also took time to make sure that we had what we needed. Being deaf isn't easy, but what I learned at Gallaudet changed my life."

As part of their support of the college, Lions finance numerous projects to send members of the college faculty abroad to study schools and programs for the deaf in other parts of the world.

Ever since it was founded in 1864 by an act of Congress, Gallaudet College has been sending young men and women out into the working world equipped to handle their handicaps. Thousands have graduated and led successful lives as a result. The college offers education in major fields of study along with an extensive sports program and social activities.

In Bhilai, India, hearing impaired boys and girls gained an opportunity for self-sufficiency with the help of a grant from the Lions Clubs International Foundation. Sponsored by the Bhilai Lions Club, an institute for the training of these youngsters doubled its enrollment with a $5,000 grant from LCIF in 1976 combined with substantial donations from the Bhilai Lions and local citizens. Youngsters in District 323-C who attend the school learn basic literacy skills and receive vocational training. The $5,000 donation was "seed money" to help the Bhilai Lions expand their program.

Hearing conservation and work with the deaf became a major activity of Lions Clubs International in October 1971. In 1977, the name was changed to "Hearing and Speech Action and Work with the Deaf." The change was made to mirror the Lions' concern and respect for the dignity and independence of men, women, and children with impaired communication skills.

While Ralph A. Lynam was 1978–79 international president, he named hearing and speech work with the deaf as his major program.

Lions' help for the deaf takes myriad forms. For 13-year-old Nicole it was a teletype (TTY) machine she could use at home. "Now," said Nicole, "I can call up my friends after school. I can hardly wait."

She had never been able to telephone her friends before. Nicole is deaf. She was a member of a class for hearing impaired sixth to eighth graders at Kent Middle School in Kenfield, California, near San Francisco.

The teletype machine, long used in newspaper offices before the advent of computers, was one of five TTYs with special accoustic couplers donated to Nicole's class by the Lions of nearby Corte Madera. The square, boxlike couplers convert typed messages into sound which can be sent by an ordinary telephone to another coupler and TTY at the other end.

Lyn Merritt, who was president of the Corte Madera Lions Club in 1978, presented the TTYs to the Marin County Schools for use in Nicole's class at the March 1978 executive cabinet meeting of northern California Lions clubs in Santa Rosa.

"The TTY is a valuable tool for teaching language as well," said teacher Grant Grover. "Before people with normal hearing learn to read they learn to speak. They learn vocabulary and grammar from hearing words, phrases, and sentences, and from copying what they hear.

"Deaf children are denied that experience. In many cases they remain non-readers. They often fail to grasp the basics of grammar.

"But the students are highly motivated to learn to use the TTY," Grover continued. "Now they can practice language by telephoning anyone in the country who has a TTY, or anyone in the world for that matter."

The Corte Madera Lions Club collected $2,300 to buy the TTYs and couplers. Most of the money was raised at a crab cioppino dinner. Lion Ernie Russo, dinner chairman, had a special interest in the project. His daughter, Cindy, was born deaf and is a former pupil of Grover's.

Lions club projects for the hearing impaired cover five major areas: 1) screening programs to identify those with hearing problems; 2) public information to heighten general understanding of the disorder and what can be done about it; 3) providing hearing aids, diagnostic services, and support of dogs for the deaf; 4) funding research on prevention and treatment and supporting temporal bone banks; and, 5) urging those with ear disorders to will their inner ear bones to the Deafness Research Foundation Temporal Bone Banks Program for Ear Research.

There are two main types of hearing disorders: *conductive disorders* and *sensorineural disorders*. Some people suffer a combination of these conditions called a mixed hearing loss.

Conductive disorders are caused by interference with the transmission of sound through the outer ear or the middle ear.

Sensorineural disorders result from a defect in the inner ear or in the auditory nerve, which leads from the inner ear to the brain. The inner ear contains the actual organ of hearing, called the organ of Corti.

Diseases cause most cases of conductive hearing loss. Birth defects account for many cases of sensorineural deafness or hearing impairment. Accidents or continuing exposure to loud noise can damage hearing. And hearing loss is often linked with aging.

Surgery and advanced technology have been highly effective in helping the hearing impaired. In California, a surgeon has used laser microsurgery to restore hearing. Dr. Rodney Perkins of Palo Alto uses an Argon laser to vaporize defective stapes, which are the bones in the inner ear. The stapes is one of a group of bones that transmit vibrations to the inner ear. When the bones harden they create severe hearing loss.

Dr. Perkins vaporizes a section of the bone with a laser beam. He then removes the rest with tweezers. Along with avoiding damage to the inner ear, the laser reduces bleeding because it requires a smaller surgical opening than other methods. It cauterizes the wound at the same time.

Another surgical technique, cochlear implants, may be the most exciting advance for the hearing impaired in history. With these, the totally deaf person can understand speech without reading lips.

Since 1981, the Iowa Lions have been supporting the cochlear implant program at the University of Iowa. In that year Dr. Brian McCabe requested help from the Iowa Lions Sight and Hearing Foundation to establish a cochlear implant center where profoundly deaf adults could obtain implants and where the research staff could study the six different cochlear inner ear implants currently available. This was of great importance because no one knew if the prevalent implant, the single channel model, was as good as the new multichannel devices or how the multichannel devices compared.

Because each medical center developed its own tests of hearing reception in implant users (tests that have to be quite different from those for patients who have hearing), comparison among reported groups of implant users was impossible; different standards were used. The study supported by Iowa Lions was the first in the world to clearly establish the difference in performance between single and multichannel implants. It is cited world wide.

The Lions Clubs International Foundation awarded the Department of Otolaryngology $30,000 that was matched by the Iowa Lions, who have continued to commit approximately $30,000 to $35,000 annually to the cochlear implant program.

Equipment bought with Lions' funds enabled scientists at the University of Iowa to gather enough information to write a grant proposal seeking funding as a major center for the comparison of implants.

"The Lions provided us with the initial support to collect data and begin our adult cochlear implant program," Dr. Tyler explained. "On the basis of that we applied for and got a five-year grant of $2.6 million from the National Institutes of Health (NIH)."

The NIH grant and continued Lions support have provided the base for the implant program, which has become world-renowned. "Before the cochlear implant there was no treatment at all for people with sensorineural deafness—and they are the majority of the profoundly deaf," Ruth Severson said.

Drs. McCabe and Gantz say that work at the University of Iowa has led to improvements in preoperative testing and in postoperative rehabilitation. Because of the testing, they are learning more about the fine differences among implants.

Gantz stressed that the implants don't replace hearing. Even multi-channel devices fall far short of the thousands of channels processed by a normal ear. So, considerable training is necessary for a patient to recognize variations in volume in a meaningful way. People with an implant first hear what Dr. McCabe calls "Star Wars sounds"—pops, whizzes, crackling, and buzzes. Over time, they come to associate these sounds with sounds in the environment and with words. Almost all patients improve in their ability to communicate after an implant because the sounds they hear enhance their ability to lip-read. Some patients improve so dramatically that they can converse over a telephone. The strange sounds heard through the implant in the early weeks are gradually correlated by the brain to the source: telephone ring, door bell, foot shuffle, a voice, a car engine. Finally, words, then phrases and sentences are heard by many patients (depending upon how many auditory nerve fibers are functioning).

How does it happen that a deaf person can hear sounds processed by the implant? The brain is the key. It sends collateral fibers (no regeneration of nerves occurs in the brain or the inner ear) to other brain centers to accommodate these new signals. The new signals become, finally, words. This adaptive response to new stimuli is a most marvelous example of the "plasticity" of the brain.

Cochlear implant units provide electrical stimulation to the auditory nerve, which sends impulses to the brain as recognizable sounds. The implanted electrode is placed beneath the skin behind one ear. It is connected to the external components, which include a microphone to detect sound, a speech processor to break sound into signals, and a transmitter coil to send the message to the internal electrode. Simply put, electrodes stimulate the active nerve fibers in the ear to transmit signals.

Learning to interpret those buzzes and beeps is Cassie Fuller of Muscatine, Iowa, who had a cochlear implant at the University of Iowa in October 1987, when she was 15 years old. Deaf from birth, Cassie is the daughter of Connie and Michael Fuller. (Michael is a member of the Muscatine, Iowa, Lions Club.) Three years after the operation, Cassie is still learning to recognize new sounds.

"It will be a learning experience for her that will go on and on," her father explained. "The main thing it will do is make her aware of her environment—the things around her, like telephones and cars." Her teacher said Cassie is starting to describe sounds she hears instead of the vibrations she feels. Cassie is excited about what she will gain from the implant.

By the end of 1986, 23 implants had been performed at the University of Iowa, all on adults. In August 1987, a major breakthrough was achieved. Tim Brandau, at the age of three, became the first child in Iowa to receive a cochlear implant. The Brandaus, who farm 300 acres of corn and beans near Rudd, Iowa, first suspected something was wrong in 1985. Their infant son, Tim, "didn't even flinch" when Sue Brandau banged pots and pans around the kitchen. There were other troubling signs. "He just wasn't babbling like his older brother had been at that age."

Eventually, the Brandaus found their way to the University of Iowa Hospitals and Clinics and to Dr. Gantz. Intrigued by the possible benefits of cochlear implant surgery, they consented to a series of hearing, psychological, and developmental tests. Tim passed with flying colors and a multichannel cochlear implant operation was performed by Dr. Gantz on August 21, 1987.

No one would know for sure whether Tim could hear until the anxiously awaited "hook-up day." Then the implant would be connected to a speech processor, the external device that turns sounds into electrical signals. The big day for Tim and his parents came on September 28 when the connections were made and tests by audiologist Holly Fryauf were begun.

"It went well," Ms. Fryauf happily told the Brandaus after the first four days of testing. "Tim raised his eyebrows and tapped his fingers to the rhythm of sounds we produced. That's what we hoped for."

That same day, testing began for seven-year-old Toni Whitmore from Stockton, Iowa, the second Iowa child to receive a cochlear implant. Dr. Gantz performed Toni's surgery five days after Tim's operation. The tests indicated that Toni, too, could hear a variety of stimuli and could learn to interpret them as sounds.

For both youngsters, a lot of work remains to be done. Tim and Toni participate in special elementary school programs in which they are continuing to interpret different sounds they hear with the implant. They have learned, for example, that a certain buzz can be heard as someone's voice. Or a distinctive beep is the sound of an approaching car. From these beginnings they progress to more abstract vocabularies.

Both families and their doctors have seen changes in the children's behavior. Toni's mother, Tami Whitmore, notices how much more aware her daughter has become. Tim is increasingly intrigued by the sound of his own voice. One day, in sign language, he told his mother, "Timmy happy to hear sound."

"Until Tim, we had never known anyone who was deaf," Sue Brandau said. "It really opened our eyes. I think it's given us more compassion toward people with all types of handicaps."

Researchers suspect that better results from cochlear implants are being achieved with very young patients. In the beginning, the human brain is very receptive to change. As it matures, it becomes less able to synthesize new information. "One of several important issues is discovering the optimum age for implantation in the congenitally deaf," Dr. McCabe states. Dr. Gantz adds, "We are hoping to receive a grant to conduct the same kind of studies in children as we have done since 1980 in adults."

Iowa Lions made it happen. They contributed initial matching funds to establish the Cochlear Implant Center at the University of Iowa. Subsequent annual contributions have supplied training materials and equipment to design evaluation instruments for determining which children are appropriate candidates and for measuring the progress of children and adults with implants. Now the University of Iowa team will establish a program for other boys and girls like Tim and Toni.

"If we have any impact at all in the area of implants," said Dr. Gantz, "it will be with the profoundly deaf child. Without further help, these children, on the average, will reach the educational level of a sixth-grade student, as they do in the average state school for the deaf."

The future research that is needed and that will be carried out at Iowa is in two areas. The first area is the identification of patients who have enough of an auditory nerve to be able to stimulate with a cochlear electrode. New methods of stimulation are in progress but need funding. The second is implanting an electrode directly into the brain where nerve pulses from the hearing nerve first arrive. In this way the inner ear and the nerve can be bypassed when these structures are absent.

Early experiments by Dr. William House, the father of cochlear implant surgery, are promising in this regard. Researchers need to know a great deal more about the feasibility of multichannel placement before human implants can begin. It means the possible restoration of significant hearing to those who have *both* inner ear and nerve deafness.

Even before the Iowa Lions began their work with the deaf, Lions in Virginia were embarking on an extensive cooperative program with the University of Virginia Medical Center. The program includes research, cochlear implants, public education, and a temporal bone bank.

Virginia's ambitious program began officially in May 1979 at the state convention. There, a resolution to establish The Lions of Virginia Hearing Foundation and Temporal Bone Bank passed enthusiastically and unanimously.

The ink was barely dry on the Virginia resolution when Past District

Governor Kenneth S. Hitch, with permission from the council of governors, contacted Dr. Robert W. Cantrell, chairman of the Department of Otolaryngology at the University of Virginia Medical Center, Charlottesville, Virginia.

Currently Lions clubs and individuals support the foundation in the amount of $100,000 a year. Clubs which donate $1,000 or more or contribute $10 per member receive special "Grand Award" patches from the foundation.

In only a few short years Virginia has become another showcase for Lions' efforts to restore the hearing impaired to the community and to give them the dignity and independence they deserve.

As in Iowa, Lions efforts have changed lives in wondrous ways.

"You can't call it anything less than a miracle," says Paula Baldwin, a mother of three grown children, whose world of silence ended after her implant. "I can hear people talking on the telephone."

Paula who lives in Bedford, Virginia, lost her hearing at the age of 20, raised her family and in her mid-40s, received an implant at the University of Virginia. For husband Gary, who courted Paula while she was a music major in college and married her after she became deaf, "Paula is now like she was when I first met her. The operation has restored our life to the way it was when we were dating. I'm rediscovering Paula. It's wonderful."

Lions in several Virginia clubs have heard Rhoda Showalter, a petite woman in her mid-40s, describe in moving terms what she calls her "new life." "I can hear a pin drop thanks to the Lions of Virginia who helped make my cochlear implant possible," she told members of one club recently. Rhoda works in an assembly plant in Fisherville, Virginia, with several other hearing impaired people where she acts as an interpreter between management and those employees. "I love my job and I love my life. I feel that I am a new person."

Another implant recipient was Misty Dotson, who lost her hearing after an auto accident at the age of six. In October 1987, Misty became the first Virginia teenager to receive a cochlear implant. "Before my operation I felt alone and apart. You Lions have given me help and support. Now I feel accepted, like I am one of the girls. I don't feel isolated anymore."

Ask the Canadian Lions of District 37-B in Edmonton, Alberta, about cochlear implants and they are likely to discuss the "Bionic Ear." Technically titled the "Nucleus Multi-Channel Implantable Hearing Prosthesis," the device had been implanted in eight patients by mid-1987 through the joint efforts of the Lions, Edmonton oto-laryngologists, two Edmonton hospitals, and Alberta Medicare, the provincial health care insurance organization. The patients were not charged for the procedure.

"It's a whole new way of life," said one recipient, a 52-year-old Edmonton man. "I can hear. I can enjoy movies, TV, and just visiting with friends; activities that hadn't been possible for years. The Bionic Ear took a little getting used to but now it's great."

Cochlear implants were done as early as 1972, but first generation models did not permit speech to be understood. They only restored a sensation of sound.

The Bionic Ear, as it's now called, provides the wearer with word fragments. In order to benefit from the unit, the person must have learned to speak before becoming deaf.

The Bionic Ear consists of four essential elements. The first of these is a directional microphone which picks up sounds and converts them into electrical impulses. The electrical impulses are transmitted to a speech processor which is about the size of a pocket cassette player. The processor is programmed to select and code the most useful sounds. The coded sounds then go to a transmitter which sends a coded signal through the skin to the cochlear implant.

The implant combines a receiver and a 22-channel electrode array which extends into the inner ear. The signals stimulate hearing nerve fibers and are in turn picked up by the brain. The microchip and transmitter are combined in a small headset worn behind the ear.

When the first Edmonton implant was done, the processor could handle words of only one or two syllables, each relayed to the user's ear in abbreviated form. Shortly afterwards, a microchip with a three sylla-ble capacity became available.

J. A. Kostiuk, M.D., told the Lions of northern Alberta about the Bionic Ear in May 1985. He asked for funding for a project to bring sound to the profoundly deaf and the Lions quickly agreed. The Cana-dian Lions raised $60,000 and LCIF made a grant of $30,000 toward this project.

The Edmonton (Host) Lions Club was the first to support the project with a commitment of $30,000. Other Lions and Lioness clubs quickly joined in. They included St. Albert (Host) and Sherwood Park (Breakfast) Lions clubs. Golden Gate North East, Northgate, South Edmonton, Southgate, and Westmount Lions clubs, all of Edmonton, contributed, too. Lioness clubs of Edmonton (Prairie Gold) and Legal also took part.

By the summer of 1987 more than 200 cochlear implants had been performed worldwide. About one-third of the recipients can distinguish speech. The remainder use their improved hearing as an aid to lip reading. Research funded by the Lions continues to improve the technology and effectiveness of this major breakthrough for the hearing impaired.

Unsparing in their efforts to help the handicapped, Lions inspire governments and private organizations in many nations to join in these activities. As one example, the Telephone Pioneers of America have opened up a sports arena for the disabled. By burying an electrical amplifier inside softballs, basketballs, or bowling balls it's possible for thousands of blind men, women, and children to enjoy these sports for the first time in their lives.

"The Telephone Pioneers of America is a group of more than 500,000 retired and active Bell System employees in the United States and Canada," explained Don Schroeder. A resident of LaGrange Park, Illinois, Schroeder retired from Illinois Bell in 1986. "We have 94 chapters and have developed hundreds of electrical and electronic helps for persons with speech and hearing problems. This is all done on our own time."

Schroeder continued, "The Pioneers have invented 'talking dolls' which are stuffed animals and other toys that enable the therapist to stay out of sight and still communicate with deaf or stuttering children. There's a blinking rabbit that inspires children to talk. It rewards speech sounds with a wink of its eyes. We're always looking for ways to harness technology to create objects that will help the handicapped. Many of the Pioneers are Lions who encourage us to develop these kinds of devices."

Technology, coupled with courage and determination, mean expanded opportunities for the disabled. Lions clubs around the world have heightened awareness of the needs of the handicapped. That has sparked increased funding that is translated into products they can use.

Kathy Schieferstein is a child who benefits from this. Special equipment enables Kathy to hear. Born with severely limited hearing, the two-and-a-half-year-old girl used a powerful hearing aid but still could distinguish only 10 to 20 percent of the sounds audible with normal hearing. An auditory trainer would help her achieve normal hearing but her parents, William and Betty Schieferstein, could not afford it.

When the Clinton, Maine, Lions Club heard about Kathy, her life began to change. Lion Jordan Williams and the 60 members of the club planned a benefit supper and alerted the community to Kathy's situation.

The Lions' enthusiasm excited the whole town and it seemed that nearly everyone in Clinton wanted to help. The Lions and other community members quickly raised the complete cost of the Telex Auditory Trainer. Today, Kathy hears her parents' voices at a normal level thanks to an FM radio unit she wears on a strap around her neck. Her mother wears a transmitting unit on her belt and a microphone pinned on her collar.

"The change in Kathy is phenomenal," said a neighbor. "She's in touch with everything now and her personality has developed quickly, along with her ability to speak. She's growing and maturing in ways that wouldn't have been possible without the auditory trainer. It's added an entirely new dimension to her life and future."

The handicapped person constantly runs into barriers. For the deaf, barriers include films and TV without captions, classes without interpreters, and a lack of telephone communication devices. For the blind, unbrailled menus in restaurants and unraised letters in public elevators are barriers. For the person in a wheel chair curved stairs, turnstiles, revolving doors, or narrow doors, all create architectural barriers.

Lions clubs throughout the world spearheaded information programs calculated to remove barriers for the handicapped; whatever they are. Projects include closed captioning equipment for TV viewing.

For the more than 14 million who are deaf or hearing impaired, "television is as silent as an old Charlie Chaplin movie," John E. D. Ball wrote in an article in *The Lion*. Television, from which most of us get hours of weekly entertainment, news, and sometimes even vital information, is closed to the deaf even though most of them have TV sets. "Even now, while hearing impaired viewers derive comparatively little meaning from television, they still own TV sets and watch television

1

2

3

Since its founding, Lions Clubs International has been headquartered at four locations: (*1*) Insurance Exchange Building, (*2*) McCormick Building, and (*3*) 209 North Michigan Building, all in downtown Chicago. In *1971*, the association moved to the modern and recently expanded headquarters in Oak Brook (*4*).

4

Until the hotel was razed a number of years ago, this plaque told guests of the important meeting held there in 1917. It now adorns the lobby of International Headquarters in Oak Brook.

This is the only known photo taken of the historic first convention at the Adolphus Hotel in Dallas, Texas. Melvin Jones is seated on the far left at the head table.

Members of the Chicago (Central) Lions Club pose for a 1919 group photo in front of one of the lions guarding the entrance to the Art Institute of Chicago. Melvin Jones is shown in the center.

There was something of a Spartan atmosphere in 1927 at THE LION Magazine offices in the McCormick Building.

Melvin Jones (lower right, aboard float) leads the parade down Chicago's Michigan Avenue during the 41st International Convention in 1958.

Sight restoring operations by the thousands are provided annually at Lions eye camps. This, in India, is typical of the projects that will be funded by SightFirst.

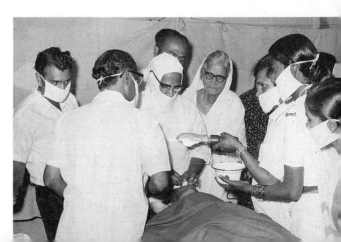

Lions in a number of nations sponsor dog guide schools. Here, visitors observe training at the school in Limbiate, Italy.

Personally escorting the physically disabled on outings is one of the many ways Lions give of themselves on behalf of others.

In many parts of the world, blind persons are given skiing instruction.

This home for the less fortunate is supported by the Lions of Benin City, Nigeria.

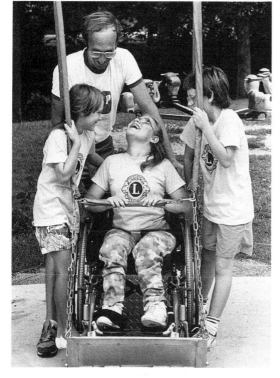

Many recreational facilities for the physically disabled have been built by Lions.

Lions provide educational opportunities to enable disadvantaged youngsters to gain knowledge in a variety of fields.

In Wisconsin, children thrill to a variety of special camping activities.

Worldwide, the Lions Journey for Sight has made the association's emblem more visible and respected among the public.

A session for children with diabetes is offered at the Texas Lions Camp.

Hearing screening clinics are offered by Lions worldwide.

The Lions-Quest "Skills" programs are gaining in popularity in schools worldwide.

International Youth Camps are sponsored by Lions in scores of countries.

The familiar White Canes have become popular fundraising items for many Lions clubs.

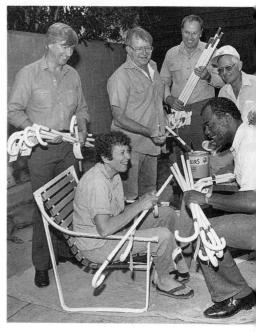

Thanks to Lions around the world, trained hands are able to read material printed in braille.

programs as frequently as the adult population," Ball wrote. Most deaf adults own at least one TV set and watch TV around three hours on weekdays and even more on the weekend.

Lions clubs throughout the country are supporting a recent technology which allows many of the hearing impaired to enjoy the full impact of their favorite sit-com, soap, or national newscaster. The system is called "closed-captioned television" and, in the words of Helen Keller, it helps the deaf to "remain in the intellectual company of men."

In the TV captioning process, the audio portion of the program is translated into phrases of dialogue which look much like the subtitles in a foreign movie. Open captioning—where the captions can be read by all viewers, both deaf and hearing—has been around for a long time, but general viewers complained that the captions were distracting. In the newer technique of closed captioning, the captions can be seen only on TV sets equipped with a special decoder.

"It sure helps when you can see what they're saying. I can really watch TV and enjoy it now," said 75-year-old Velma Patterson of the Four Seasons Nursing Center in Santa Fe, New Mexico. "I got tired of guessing what the main characters on the daytime serials were saying."

"In November 1980, members of the Santa Fe (Capital City) Lions Club donated a TeleCaption adapter to the Center," said Lion Gunther A. Werner. "It's attached to a TV set at the Four Seasons Center and displays printed subtitles on programs. Many other Lions clubs are taking part in this and donating equipment to organizations and families."

"About half of the Center's 120 residents are hearing impaired," added Patti Salopek, director of nursing. "With the new device they don't have to turn up the TV volume any more which is another benefit. It's not unusual to see 10 or 20 people in our TV room now where there used to be only two or three."

Today, countless hearing impaired human beings enjoy a dramatically broadened understanding of the world through closed captioned television. Sports, drama, comedy, news, classroom courses, and other TV programs are instantly intelligible to them. Available technology brings the world into their living rooms and enlarges their lives. It's very simple. Now they can read what others hear.

To provide captioned programming, a not-for-profit organization called the National Captioning Institute was established in 1979. NCI creates and distributes captions for broadcasters' programs from two studios, one in Falls Church, Virginia, and the other in Los Angeles.

Because the basic mission of closed captioning—making television more understandable for hearing-impaired audiences—fits closely with the aims of Lions Clubs International, NIC asked for Lion support for the project. Indeed, Lions Clubs International was the only non-hearing-impaired service organization which NCI asked for help. At its June 1979 meeting the International Board of Directors approved Lions' involvement in activities designed "to heighten awareness, understanding and accessibility of the closed captioning system."

Shortly afterwards, International President Lloyd Morgan sent a letter to club presidents, district governors, and district hearing chairmen. He quoted Helen Keller in stressing the critical importance of the project: "Deafness is a much worse misfortune (than blindness). For it brings the loss of the most vital stimulus—the sound of voice that brings language, sets thoughts astir, and keeps us in the intellectual company of man."

In 1973, when Lions Clubs International named hearing conservation and work with the deaf a major activity, the 15 Lions clubs of Region 21, District A-12, pledged full support for the Ontario, Canada, Camp for the Deaf. By the next year all 55 Lions clubs in the district were energetically involved. Started by a group of deaf Canadians, the camp began in 1960.

As the Lions worked more closely in the camp activities, the facility experienced a complete facelift. Dormitories, cottages, two large docks, and a boathouse were all constructed or enlarged.

Excavating, pouring a foundation, building new floors and sills, the Lions completely restored an original log cabin. They renovated the main lodge, Progress Inn, stained and painted other camp buildings, built roads and a new electrical system, and installed a septic system.

Campers enjoy a full range of camping activities that are planned for the particular needs of the hearing impaired. Counselors are carefully trained for their jobs and are experienced with the problems of the campers. Campers echo the words of 12-year-old Jeff Chandler.

"I had a great time there last summer," smiled Jeff. "That's the first time I ever went camping. I guess fishing was the thing I liked the most. The counselors were always helpful but they gave me a chance to do what I wanted to do, too."

With certain limitations, deaf children can do whatever a child with hearing can do, and that includes Scouting. In 1974, the Redbud Lions Club in Lubbock, Texas, adopted an 11 member Girl Scout troop, all of whom were deaf.

The troop had been organized three years before by Frances Wester, who had learned sign language when her younger brother lost most of his hearing. Her husband, Mike, a member of the Redbud Lions Club, asked the club's board of directors to endorse the troop and the idea was enthusiastically accepted. Christened the Redbud Lions Girl Scout Troop No. 75, the youngsters bloomed under the Lions' sponsorship.

Members help the group with their annual cookie sale. They provide adult supervision when there is a community event and host three or four girls at their weekly meetings. They also contribute cash each week to the troop's get-togethers.

The girls work on merit badges like any other troop, have cookouts, go camping and attend the Girl Scout summer camps.

"We feel that we can do just about anything that any other troop can do," said Mrs. Wester. "And that includes Christmas caroling."

The girls received national publicity when United Press International carried a story on their Christmas singing. They spent more than a month learning to "sing" carols in sign language. Caroling at schools, nursing homes, and city parks, the young ladies were cheered by their audiences.

"Since most people don't understand sign language," said Mrs. Wester, "we were accompanied by another Girl Scout troop, No. 432, of which my daughter is a member. They sang the songs the usual way while the deaf Scouts 'signed' them."

Whether weaving, camping, making baskets, or hiking, the members of Girl Scout Troop 75 experience a larger world through the world of Lionism.

So do the youngsters who enjoy the Lions Wilderness Camp for Deaf Children, Inc., operated by the California-Nevada Multiple District 4 Lions. Designed especially for deaf children, it's a camp where they can learn outdoor skills and delight in nature's wonders.

Opened in 1980, the camp is available for all hearing impaired children or children of hearing impaired parents between the ages of seven and 16. A special Leaders In Training program is offered for youngsters over 16 who are hearing impaired. Trained in a variety of skills, they help group leaders with the campers.

Located in stunningly beautiful country in the Sierra Mountains, the camp is 75 miles east of Stockton next to the Big Trees National Forest.

There is a group leader for each six campers. All staff members must know sign language and be more than 18 years old. Since communication is dependent on visual communication, members of the staff are identified by special shirts and jackets.

Programs range from star gazing to swimming, canoeing, life-saving techniques, crafts, outdoor cooking, archery, compass reading, and knot tying.

Nearly anywhere in the world where the deaf need help, Lions are there. In Buena Ventura, Colombia, local Lions opened a full scale rehabilitation program for the hearing impaired in 1974.

It started when the Lions learned that the government school for the deaf in Cali, 75 miles away, could no longer accept enrollments. They found a young teacher who had been teaching a tiny group of deaf boys and girls to read and write. The Lions talked with the Catholic bishop about their idea for a school and he loaned them a floor of an abandoned building that had been a trade school.

The Lions named their first fund-raising project "March for the Deaf." Young men and women, wearing brightly-painted signs, were sponsored by local businessmen to walk a specific distance for a donation. The marchers collected more than $2,200. In the following two years the Buena Ventura Lions spent more than $10,000 on the project. That included government funds, donations from private groups and contributions through Lions Clubs activities.

As the school took shape, one Lion said, "We began with something small, with practically nothing. We always had the hope it would become something big."

Gradually the school grew. The Lions got in touch with Colombia's National Institute for the Deaf in Bogota for advice on equipment and staffing. An audiologist/speech therapist joined the teacher who now had 24 children in her class.

A major electronics company heard of the school's needs and sent a complete audio training laboratory. This included amplifiers, microphones, and individual headsets for training the youngsters to discriminate sounds.

In addition, another organization made a commitment to pay half of the speech therapist's salary. Good fortune continued as the Colombian government provided money for two more teachers plus a janitor and a watchman.

During the six hour school day the children receive individualized speech therapy and auditory training. They study reading, history, mathematics, geography, science, and other subjects taught in regular school. Teachers make a special effort to help the boys and girls gain confidence and become self-sufficient.

It works. Said nine-year-old Roberto, "I never thought I'd like school but I like it here. We play leap frog and other games. For the first time I'm able to understand when people try to teach me something. I'm learning all kinds of things that I never understood before. The teachers treat me real well and I've learned to read. I couldn't do that before. I've learned to speak so that people can understand me. They never could before. I want to be a plumber and earn a good living when I grow up."

The Lions have added vocational training to the curriculum so that Roberto and other students will learn trades and become self supporting. The project the Lions "began with something small" has, as they hoped, "become something big."

In 1981, there were approximately 15,000 deaf persons in Greece. Six special schools for deaf children were operating in Patras, Athens, Thessaloniki, Volos, Seres, and Crete. The schools are under the supervision of the Ministry of Social Welfare and are administered by committees comprised of civil servants and volunteers.

The Thessaloniki School for the Deaf has about 200 students ranging in age from six to 18. On December 12, 1981, the Lions of District 117 presented new equipment to the school bought with a grant from Lions Clubs International Foundation. Equipment supplied by the LCIF funds included 100 individual hearing aids, five voice indicators, 100 pairs of tuners used to measure hearing, ten tape recorders, ten amplifiers, high fidelity cassette decks, ten lighted volume indicators, and other special devices.

The specially-equipped classroom was built with double booths for hearing measurement, measurement units, a unit for measuring hearing resistance, and equipment for precision hearing evaluation.

Dr. Aris Tzimourakas was district governor of District 117 Greece-Cyprus during the fiscal year 1981-1982. He wrote LCIF Chairman William C. Chandler: "The value of the entire equipment presented was 2,700,000 drachmas out of which 1,050,000 ($27,000) was contributed by LCIF while the balance of 1,650,000 drachmas was made by contributions from Lions, Lioness, and Leo clubs of District 117.

"There was wide press coverage by the media, press, radio, television, etc., of the very helpful donation of the Lions and the importance of the LCIF involvement."

For the 200 boys and girls in the school, the new equipment created opportunity, skills, learning, understanding, and improved chances for self-support. Linked by a network of compassion, Lions pool their efforts and alter tomorrow for the hearing impaired.

The world of silence is a lonely place to live. Thousands of humans in many nations have joined the world of sound, song, laughter, and communication as Lions have put their ideals into action.

CHAPTER SEVEN

Lions Clubs International Foundation

LIONS clubs everywhere are linked with the world of Lionism. When disaster strikes they can reach out for help from clubs in every area of the globe . . . and from the Lions Clubs International Foundation. Swift assistance is always near.

It was there after an earthquake lasting 33 seconds completely destroyed the Children's Hospital of San Juan Zacatepeque in Guatemala. It struck at three o'clock in the morning on February 4, 1976. At the time of the disaster there were 48 Lions clubs in Guatemala, 12 of them in Guatemala City alone.

Originally designed to restore health to tubercular youngsters in the country, the hospital was founded by the Guatemala (Central) Lions Club of Guatemala City on September 15, 1943.

"Superior medical care wiped out the TB problem and in 1970 we changed the hospital's purpose to deal with malnourished youngsters," explained Past District Governor Eduardo Escobar.

"The 1976 earthquake displaced nearly three feet of earth and destroyed extensive areas of the country," he continued. "The hospital is in a rural area 18 miles from Guatemala City and the destruction in that city was especially bad. In what we can only believe was a miracle, none of the 98 children in the hospital that night was injured, even though the hospital was totally destroyed. When we looked at the hospital the next day we couldn't understand how any of them survived, let alone how all of them emerged unhurt."

There was one fatality, the director who died of a heart attack. Roman Cano, the janitor, was the hero of the disaster. He forced his way through the wreckage that had shattered the living quarters in the hospital. Working methodically, Cano began rescuing the terrified boys and girls who ranged in age from six months to seven years.

"I woke up in the night with the walls and ceiling falling down and frightened children screaming," said Cano. "Because of the design of the beds, their frames held off the debris from the children and kept them from being hurt. None of the youngsters could get out by themselves so I found a pair of wire cutters to cut the bedsprings and got them out from the bottom. My wife ran to the village nearby for help and three men came at once to give me a hand rescuing the boys and girls.

"As we took them out of the wrecked building we put them on mattresses in a field where the hospital had been. We made tents from blankets and then got some food from what used to be the hospital kitchen. We counted the children as we took them out of the hospital and were overcome at the good fortune when we saw that all 98 had been saved. Not one was hurt. We fed the youngsters during the day and comforted them at night. They spent two nights in makeshift tents and then real tents began to arrive. They were donated by the U.S. Air Force and the U.S. Embassy. They lived outside there for five months, until we could get enough of the hospital rebuilt so they could be inside again."

President of the hospital committee, Jaime Tabarini, was the first Lion to arrive. "I got to the hospital in a truck at eleven in the morning after the quake. Roman Cano had carefully checked to see that all the boys and girls were safe. He was the hero of the disaster. His prompt action prevented a possible tragedy."

Acting quickly, the Lions Clubs International Foundation gave $10,000 for immediate emergency help after the quake. The Lions used it to build shelters for the homeless because the rainy season was about to begin.

"Fifteen days after the earthquake we began to collect money and develop plans for a new hospital on the same site," said Eduardo

Escobar. "We raised $15,000 in a few days and then we contacted the Lions Clubs International Foundation for assistance with the project because we wanted to rebuild the hospital quickly and could not have raised enough money by ourselves to do it."

In June 1976 LCIF approved $125,000 in designated funds for rebuilding and work began. Some of the Lions are engineers and architects; others in the construction business. This dramatically reduced building costs.

"We spent a total of $164,000 to rebuild and equip the children's hospital," explained Dr. Milton Zapeda Nuila, past president of the Guatemala (Central) Lions Club. "The building is far better than the one destroyed in 1976. It's specially designed to resist the effects of earthquakes. That's important because last year alone we had about a thousand tremors in the country."

Lionism's international message was eloquently shown as help poured in from clubs in the United States, Germany, Spain, Mexico, Costa Rica, and other nations. Interested Guatemalans donated bricks, glass, supplies, and other products to help keep the rebuilding costs down. Today, the modern new hospital is equipped with 200 beds and complete diagnostic and treatment facilities.

"Funds from LCIF enabled us to rebuild the hospital quickly and get on with our work of helping malnourished children in our country," said Past District Governor Lorenzo Hasbun. The facility was finished on July 18, 1977, and was back in service just 18 months after the earthquake. LCIF helps local Lions clubs handle the big problems that are too much for clubs in one area to solve without assistance."

And that's not all. LCIF provided another $81,600 for construction of 34 school buildings, amounting to 60 percent of the total cost. The Guatemala Lions contributed the remaining 40 percent.

Since it was created in 1968, the Lions Clubs International Foundation has given life to an impressive range of humanitarian projects around the world. Hunger, inadequate housing, diabetes research, books, schools, utensils, wells, mobility devices for the handicapped, disaster relief: these are some of the critical needs met by the foundation. Originally called the Lions International Foundation (LIF), the name was changed to the Lions Clubs International Foundation in 1980.

Building on a solid base, LIF took more than five years to accumulate enough assets to give nearly $100,000 in 1972–73. The majority of the grants that year were under $10,000 and nearly all were for disaster relief.

One of LIF's early grants enabled Turkish Lions to buy a much-needed electroencephalograph to meet another long-standing need. At the time of the grant Turkey had an estimated 400,000 epileptics, and technology for diagnosis and treatment was limited. The equipment provided by the foundation grant meant that treatment could be provided at a level that had not been available before. Once again, Lion-to-Lion involvement working through International Headquarters saw a lack and quickly furnished a solution. Countless Turkish epileptics enjoy health because Lions everywhere contributed to LIF.

Today LCIF is a major source of funding for Lions programs that meet needs in every corner of the world. As contributions grew, grants kept pace.

In 1974–75, grant disbursements totaled $165,000. Two years later they reached nearly $300,000. By 1979–80, 104 grants totaling $801,000 helped relieve human misery worldwide.

In 1982–83, LCIF disbursements were more than a million dollars for the first time, with a total given of slightly more than $1.4 million.

The next year the LCIF grants climbed to $1,774,000.

In 1986–87, the Foundation approved grants totaling more than $2.5 million. By the end of 1987 the foundation had disbursed grants of more than $14 million in 83 countries.

Contributions reached $722,000 in 1976–77. Two years later, for the first time in the foundation's history, contributions rose to more than $1 million.

Contributions reached just over $2 million in 1982–83.

By 1985–86, that figure had more than doubled, with total contributions of $4,053,378.

Lions' generosity continued unabated and donations climbed to nearly $5.3 million in 1986–87, up 30 percent from the previous year.

At the 1988 International Convention in Denver, Colorado, Past International President Sten Akestam addressed the Melvin Jones Fellow luncheon. He said, "Your help has provided relief for thousands of people when natural disasters strike, or major medical needs arise. Because of people like you, contributions to the foundation this past year have reached an all-time high of $10 million. This nearly doubles last year's record-high contributions of $5,290,000."

LCIF has dramatically expanded the abilities of Lions to help others as it has also enhanced the name and good will of The International Association of Lions Clubs. The foundation consistently increases recognition of Lions Clubs International as an organization aimed at altruistic goals on every continent.

The Republic of Belau is an example. Formerly known as the Palau Islands, it is a country of about 240 islands to the south of Japan. Although the tiny nation is blessed with a good climate and has a history of agricultural success, it was spending half of its annual import budget on food.

Belau enjoys abundant resources. However, its population of 16,000 lacked the skills and experience to develop them. Granted independence in 1981, Belau had spent many years under outside management and economic control. Consequently, the country was without a solid agricultural framework for self-support. Belau's young people were moving to the towns, and those who were educated left the country entirely.

The Palau Islands Lions Club sent out a call for help to nearby Japan. The Lions of District 337-A responded immediately by sending a team of agricultural experts to the islands. After careful study they concluded that Belau could effectively strengthen its economy by building a vigorous agricultural industry. The second point was to educate the young people in the fundamentals of farming.

In their application to LCIF, the Lions of District 337-A said, "We felt that teaching skills to promote self-sufficiency would contribute most to the nation's strength. We expect not only to train the students as farmers and agricultural leaders, but to provide them with an education in general economics as well."

After examining the problem, the district constructed a twin-building facility known as the "Lions Micronesian Job Training Center" offering training in agriculture, forestry, and stock breeding.

Sparked by an LCIF grant of $30,000 and a major commitment by District 337-A that included donating more than 1,500 pieces of agricultural equipment, the school has attracted an enrollment of more than 60 students from Belau and the neighboring Micronesian islands. Its reputation for excellence has created a waiting list of nearly 1,000.

Operating expenses are met by the donations of local residents and by the sale of goods produced by the students.

Originally, there were six major objectives of the foundation: Vocational Assistance Abroad, Major Disaster and Emergency Relief, Eye Care and Research, Cancer, Hearing, and Humanitarian Services. Contributions could be earmarked for one of these objectives or sent undesignated for use at the discretion of the foundation. This latter alternative was and is still the preferred manner, for it gives the foundation greater latitude in which to disburse funds when and where most requested.

Disaster relief was designed to assist Lions in quickly helping the homeless, hungry, and destitute in the wake of natural calamities. Working with local Lions made it possible to administer relief programs at a minimum cost because Lions contribute their time and efforts without pay.

In June of 1985 the trustees earmarked $100,000 annually for Major Catastrophe Relief. With these funds instantly available LCIF can respond to large scale disasters immediately, when help is most necessary.

Only a few months after the trustees' decision, a massive earthquake devastated parts of Mexico City and other areas of the country. Soon after, a volcanic eruption and mud slide struck in Colombia. Aided by Major Catastrophe Grants, Lions built a new school in Mexico City and an orphanage in Colombia.

The Lions have provided funds for "in country" education, training, and vocational assistance for students in developing nations to help them to build up their homelands. In the area of hearing, the foundation has distributed information on deafness to parents, employers, and educators; explained the needs of hearing impaired persons; and enlisted the aid of the news media in penetrating the wall of misunderstanding surrounding the deaf.

The Lions have supported glaucoma screening and vision testing for children; established and supported eye banks, workshops, clinics, summer camps, and recreational facilities; and funded important eye research. In the field of cancer, the Lions have funded research, therapy, diagnosis, and public information.

In the area of Humanitarian Services, Lions have provided hunger relief, housing for those in need, health clinics, schools, and other services of help linked with the "We Serve" philosophy of Lionism.

Over the years, the objectives of LCIF were reduced to three: Vocational Assistance, Major Disaster Relief, and Humanitarian Services. As a result of recent actions, LCIF can now make grants to recipients of the Lions Humanitarian Award, and to support the association's major service initiatives (currently the SightFirst blindness prevention program).

At its inception, and during its early years, the foundation was administered by a five-member Board of Trustees, appointed from time to time by the international president. It consisted of two past international presidents, two past international directors, and a past district governor. Today, the LCIF Executive Committee consists of nine members, appointed by the international president. They serve one year terms and the immediate past international president always serves as chairman. The entire International Board of Directors, along with this committee, constitutes the foundation's Board of Trustees.

Upon LCIF's formation, Past International President Dr. Eugene Briggs, the first president of the foundation's Board of Trustees, advised it would provide a means whereby Lions and other philanthropically-minded people throughout the world can be assured their gifts and donations will receive the most careful administration.

The grant applicant is usually a Lions district. The district is required to develop a blueprint explaining precisely how it will use the money to improve existing conditions. The districts themselves are expected to make a generous financial contribution to the project, as well. Throughout, the local Lions provide a meticulous accounting for all funds received from LCIF.

The very first grant consisted of $5,000 to South Dakota District 5-SW for aid in flood relief, and soon thereafter thousands of dollars were forwarded to Lions in New York, Pennsylvania, Virginia, and Maryland for relief in the wake of Hurricane Agnes. A sight conservation program in Bangladesh received $10,000, and $20,000 was disbursed to Nicaragua to assist earthquake victims. The largest grant that year was $26,809 to districts in India to help bring relief to people caught in the grip of a severe drought. Lions' gifts from one part of the world were instantly directed to human needs in another area.

In 1976, International President Joao Fernando Sobral commented on LCIF's unique effectiveness: "In answering human needs by providing financial assistance, LCIF brings about action on a Lion-to-Lion basis. The Lions in the nations and the communities receiving the grants actually distribute the money where they deem it is most needed. They also plan and supervise any construction which needs to be done. This is a fine way to build international fellowship. The Lions in those nations receiving aid feel needed because they are charged with actually deciding on the precise use of the funds and the supplies they purchase, and the Lions around the world who contributed feel needed because they can see exactly how their money is put to use. Consequently, everyone becomes personally involved."

A young man in India is eloquent testimony to the way LCIF contributions can change a life. Sivamani was a resident of Goodwill Children's Village in India, a recipient of an LCIF grant. He wrote to LCIF: "It is a sad day for me. The time has arrived when I have come to the end of my school days. It also means my happy days at Goodwill must come to an end.

"When I was a poor boy four years ago, Goodwill Village came to my aid. I shall be grateful all my life through.

"I cannot leave this place without writing to some of the wonderful friends who have helped Goodwill and children like me.

"That is why I say with love in my heart, thank you everyone at Lions Clubs International Foundation."

The Goodwill Children's Village in India is a powerful example of the good that LCIF dollars can do. A most unusual orphanage, it was begun by a man named John Foster. The village combines a loving home atmosphere with a superior educational system. While the orphanage was progressive educationally, in other ways it remained very primitive. Youngsters had to carry water a mile and a half each way because the village had no well. A $5,000 grant from LCIF was enough to build a well and a pumphouse. With cool fresh water only a few steps away, the youngsters have even more time to learn and to play. Through LCIF, Lions everywhere share in the expanded lives of these children.

During his 1986–87 term International President Sten A. Akestam stressed the need for quality in living and pointed to LCIF as the ideal vehicle to accomplish this. In 1986, he observed: "Again, I must stress how important it is for all members to recognize themselves as *International Lions*—international in thought and in action. Support for LCIF is one of the most significant ways possible for Lions to demonstrate their commitment to the international concepts of Lionism. Your generosity will enhance the image of our international association by making it possible for foundation funds to *Bring Quality To Life* in communities spanning the globe."

Sivamani from India and the deaf-blind in Finland would give grateful assent to Lion Akestam's thoughtful message.

Because there are only about 450 people who are both deaf and blind in Finland, facilities aimed at their special needs were few. Communication, travel, work, and routine living are all especially difficult for human beings with this double handicap. Until recently, Finland had no organized program targeted specifically for them.

Recognizing the problem and eager to solve it, the Lions of District 107-E, cooperated with the Finnish Deaf-Blind Association to build a center designed to expand opportunities for the deaf-blind. Proceeding carefully, the Lions received land from the city for the building, worked with the architect on plans, negotiated funding, and took bids for the construction.

At the same time, Lions throughout Finland spearheaded an appeal for funds. The program ranged across the spectrum of fund-raising. It included a program on Finnish radio inviting listeners to request their favorite songs for a donation.

Once again, LCIF provided a major boost with a grant of $30,000. Administered judiciously, the money bought indoor and outdoor equipment to provide stimulation, enjoyment, education, and opportunity for the Finnish deaf-blind. For the first time they are living in a center equipped for individuals with neither sight nor hearing.

On December 12, 1984, Past District Governor Martti O. Hirvonen wrote LCIF Headquarters from Finland: "We want to thank you again for your grant for the multiple-use-service-building for the deaf and blind. We are enclosing a report of grant usage, different kinds of photos and copies of newspaper clippings as well as a copy of the report for the news media.

"The project in question, or actually the first phase of it, was extremely successful. I think that the participation of LCIF was very important. We have not only brought the plight of the deaf and blind people to people's attention, but also our Lions association and LCIF have become well known. In my opinion, the contributions of Finland and all of Scandinavia will significantly increase."

As in Finland, there have been countless other occasions when LCIF funding has gotten projects moving. In May 1983 the Eye and Ear Hospital in Pittsburgh, Pennsylvania, requested help from the Pennsylvania Sight Conservation and Eye Research Foundation to create a laser center in the hospital. At that time the hospital had only one laser—an Argon laser. Five more lasers were needed but the hospital did not have the money to buy them.

Laser is an acronym for *l*ight *a*mplification by *s*timulated *e*mission of *r*adiation—in other words a device that strengthens light. This remarkable beam is very different from other light sources, such as electric bulbs, flourescent lamps, and the sun, whose light travels in all directions. Laser light travels in a narrow beam and in only one direction.

The *Argon Laser* sends a very high electric charge through argon gas.

The *Carbon Dioxide Laser* is a superb, high-precision surgical "knife" when used with an operating microscope. The CO_2 is highly effective in operating on the brain and spinal cord. It is also used to treat cervical cancer, remove nodes from the larynx, and open up blocked fallopian tubes.

The *Nd:YAG Laser* is the newest of the group. It can penetrate deeply within tissue and can be used in fluid-filled cavities such as the eyeball, as it passes through clear liquid.

The use of the laser has created an entirely new treatment approach in eye, ear, nose, and throat medicine. In many instances it has totally changed care of disorders by allowing treatment where it had not been possible. In other cases it has enabled surgeons to operate with less risk and bleeding.

The Lions Laser Center provides surgery and other treatment, and trains physicians enrolled in the Eye and Ear Hospital's program in the newest laser techniques.

The generosity sparked by the Lions fundraising project generated a surplus, which is being spent on basic research in the the use of the Image Processor, a revolutionary new camera. Computer controlled, the camera is a major advance in ocular photography. The equipment is housed in the Pennsylvania Lions Image Processor Center within the Pennsylvania Lions Laser Center.

LCIF grants reach into lives all over the world. They bring new meaning to the word "International" in Lions Clubs International.

"Unquestionably," said Dr. Richard Tyler, "the role the Lions have played in our work has had a worldwide impact. I think there are very few centers in the world as heavily involved in cochlear implant research with both adults and children as we are."

An audiologist in the Department of Otolaryngology at University Hospital in Iowa City, Iowa, Dr. Tyler has seen the program grow since LCIF provided a $30,000 grant in 1982. The combination of funds raised by Iowa Lions and the money from LCIF-supported research enabled the center to successfully apply for a five-year grant of $2.6 million from the National Institutes of Health.

"The funding by Iowa Lions and LCIF created a ripple effect that is felt in Australia, Europe, and other parts of the world," said Dr. Tyler. "The reason others are becoming interested is because the data from our groups are showing that cochlear implants have the potential to be an enormous benefit to deaf people."

In its global sweep, Lions Clubs International has taken a leading role in two programs that concern people everywhere: Drug Awareness and Diabetes Education and Research. In 1982–83 the foundation's trustees created Major International Service Program grants to help Lions deal with these problems. The first of these grants for $250,000 for research in diabetic blindness was approved the same year.

Diabetic retinopathy is a form of blindness resulting from diabetes-related complications. Among the leading causes of vision loss, it is the Number One cause of new blindness in people between the ages of 20 and 74.

Figures provided by the World Health Organization in Geneva, Switzerland, point to more than 30 million diabetics in the world today. It is estimated that up to 60 percent of diabetes-related blindness could be prevented with proper treatment.

Through the support and interest of LCIF and the efforts of Lions clubs around the world the picture is growing brighter for those suffering with this condition.

In 1985–86, the LCIF Board of Trustees responded to urging from Lions clubs and raised the yearly ceiling for International Service Program funding to $500,000. By May 1988, LCIF had given a total of

$2.1 million to diabetes research. The foundation granted another $100,000 to produce a diabetes awareness film.

In the first five years of the program, 15 investigators in four different countries received LCIF awards. Supported by these generous grants, scientists in England, Ireland, Canada, and the United States were afforded the opportunity to study causes and design effective treatments for diabetic retinopathy. In addition, LCIF funding underwrites new research facilities in Connecticut and Illinois studying diabetic-related eye disease. LCIF enables Lions in every corner of the world to share in this critically important research.

Grants are made in three basic categories: 1) Research and Development Awards, to support the work of young investigators entering the fields of research in this area; 2) Feasibility Grants, which support the development of new ideas in diabetic retinopathy research; and, 3) Fellowships to support training physicians in this field of research.

Grant recipients are carefully selected after an exhaustive investigation. Lions who donate to LCIF are assured the association receives maximum value for each grant. Studies funded take many forms.

In 1985, Dr. Eva Kohner of the Hammersmith Hospital in London, England, was awarded a Feasibility Grant. Dr. Kohner is investigating the connection between changes in retinal blood flow and the development of retinopathy in diabetics who use the insulin pump. She has been closely following a group of patients who are using the insulin pump and who have shown signs of early retinopathy.

Meticulous control of blood glucose levels is critically important in treating diabetes. Nonetheless, some studies have shown that individuals with early retinopathy who maintained strict control with the insulin pump deteriorated and retinopathy worsened.

Dr. Kohner's initial findings have demonstrated that reduced retinal blood flow is linked with the progression of retinopathy. She hopes that her studies will show precisely how insulin pump therapy will prevent this.

Researchers at the Emory University Eye Center in Atlanta, Georgia, are working with an LCIF grant to study "Low Dose Radiation For Diabetic Traction Retinal Detachment." Paul Sternberg, Jr., M.D., is an assistant professor of ophthalmology at the Emory Eye Center.

"Diabetic traction retinal detachment is one of the leading causes of blindness," said Dr. Sternberg. "Retinal detachment occurs when the retina pulls loose from the inner wall of the eyeball. There are a number of different types of retinal detachment. In one kind, there is a tear in the retina and the fluid goes through a hole underneath the retina and blisters the retina like a blister on your skin. The second type occurs when scar tissue forms on the surface of the retina. The scar tissue pulls the retina from its normal position and creates a tent-like condition. We have found that by using low dose radiation with laboratory animals we can reduce the degree of retinal detachment.

"The second phase of the study has been to take the cells of the retina that detach and that are part of the scar tissue process and irradiate them in a test tube to see if the radiation can inhibit their growth. We have been able to demonstrate that this is also true.

"All of the funds for our work have come from the Lions Clubs International Foundation. I feel that the LCIF program is one of the few programs specifically designed to promote research toward preventing the blinding complications of diabetes. I think there is no question that it will spark significant advances in the fight against diabetic retinopathy."

At the Queen's University of Belfast in Northern Ireland, Dr. Keith D. Buchanan is supported by an LCIF Feasibility Grant. Dr. Buchanan is investigating the function of protein peptides in the retina. Protein peptides are chemical messengers and act as regulators. Their presence in the retina was only recently discovered. Dr. Buchanan found that peptides are frequently present close to the blood vessels in the retina. Alterations in these peptides could result in their failure to function correctly and cause diabetic retinopathy.

With an LCIF Feasibility Grant received in 1985, Dr. Patricia Harvey is seeking answers to the effects of pregnancy on the progression of diabetic retinopathy. A researcher at Toronto Western Hospital in Toronto, Ontario, Canada, Dr. Harvey carefully monitored a group of women with insulin-dependent diabetes before, during, and after their pregnancies.

Dr. Harvey has followed 23 patients and identified additional women for study. Her findings have shown that retinopathy progresses during pregnancy. She is correlating her findings with other events that occur during pregnancy. Dr. Harvey believes that the results of her research should spotlight ways to stop progression of retinopathy.

Diabetics with retinopathy often experience subtle changes in vision long before their ophthalmologists can detect the problem.

But if very sensitive measures are used, retinal disease *can* be revealed early, explained Gary L. Trick, Ph.D. Trick, an assistant professor of ophthalmology at the Washington University School of Medicine in St. Louis, Missouri, is studying the early changes in visual function that precede diagnosis of retinopathy. Trick uses a variety of tests to measure vision in diabetic patients. And, he says, at least 30 to 40 percent of diabetics may have subtle changes that an ophthalmologist would not detect during a general eye examination.

"That's important," Trick said, "because many diabetics come with complaints that their vision is not as good as it was previously, yet ophthalmologists have not been able to detect any change. And it's disturbing to patients that nobody has been able to say, 'Yes, your vision is changing because of your disease.' There are certainly changes in the visual system that are occurring, and that in many cases are occurring very early in the course of the disease."

"Typical ophthalmological examinations of the retina will not show changes until the microvascular disease is there," Trick said. "With these more sensitive measures, we're able to see functionally that the patients do different things. In some cases their color vision begins to deteriorate or their ability to detect fine detail goes down. Electrophysiologically, we're able to show that the responses of neurons both in the retina and in the brain are disturbed prior to any of the changes that are typically called retinopathy."

Dr. Trick's findings will not have an immediate impact on treatment. Although laser surgery and other therapies exist for more advanced stages of retinopathy, there currently is no generally accepted treatment for early diabetic retinopathy. However, a variety of drugs are being developed and studied for their effectiveness in preventing the onset or progression of retinopathy.

His research is partially funded by an LCIF grant.

"One of the nice things about a grant of this nature is that it allows you to proceed with pilot studies in various areas where you might not be able to get funding from major national sources," Trick noted. "The pilot study grants allow you to formulate new ideas, initiate testing relatively quickly, and accumulate enough data to support applications to federal sources for further studies."

Until treatments have been developed and adequately assessed, Trick says, his findings may provide ophthalmologists with a different way to evaluate their diabetic patients. "Knowing whether there are visual complications could help them determine whether these patients need to be followed more carefully—they may need to come in more frequently, to be examined for other complications, or have their insulin or blood sugar monitored more closely."

The Joslin Diabetes Center in Boston, Massachusetts, has been a world leader in studying and treating diabetes and its visual complications. For many years Massachusetts Lions have supported Joslin's programs. Joslin scientists have also been funded by an LCIF grant.

In the mid 1960s, Joslin researchers developed a technique using laser beams to treat diabetic retinopathy. Today, Joslin's eye unit uses lasers and surgery to remove blood and abnormal tissue from the retina. This helped many people with diabetes to regain some vision after being considered permanently blind. Joslin physicians are also conducting studies using new drugs that they believe may slow or halt the progression of diabetes related eye disease. At Joslin, LCIF funds play a critical role in this research.

By supporting skilled, highly motivated scientists, the Lions Clubs International Foundation seeks ways to safeguard eyesight. Lions, their spouses, and their children may be among those who benefit from this in the future.

In 1986, the foundation committed $500,000 to the international expansion of the Lions-Quest *Skills for Adolescence* program, the school curriculum for ten to 14-year-olds designed to build their self-esteem and confidence as a viable way to cope with peer pressure to experiment with drugs.

Skills for Adolescence was already successful in the United States and Canada. The $500,000, actually two $250,000 grants approved that year, was earmarked to help finance the expansion of the program into other parts of the world. This required translating the material along with other changes to comply with local customs.

Within two years of this international commitment, the Lions-Quest

Skills for Adolescence curriculum was firmly established and being offered in schools in Puerto Rico, Australia, New Zealand, the United Kingdom, the Republic of Ireland, Sweden, Iceland, Bermuda, and the Cayman Islands. Educators hail it as an important tool against drug use.

Experts like Michael Darcy, president of Gateway Foundation in Chicago, Illinois, concur. Recognized as a world leader in the field of addiction, Gateway Foundation has been working with drug and alcohol abusers since 1968. Gateway operates 350 in-patient beds and provides drug prevention programs to 3,000 children annually in Illinois. The organization is an active member in the World Federation of Therapeutic Communities.

"Prevention is viewed as a multi-strategy effort," Darcy explained. "If it's going to work it has to be aimed at younger children. The Lions-Quest program is particulary valuable because of the Lions' international leadership and worldwide reputation for effective service. The Lions reach many parts of the world with a consistent message. The drug problem is international and if we're going to beat it we have to approach it on a global level. I think prevention is the answer for the drug and alcohol problems we have. The Lions are especially well equipped to implement this kind of action. By funding the Quest program the Lions are making an international contribution to dealing with drug addiction."

"There's some very good news in the battle against drug addiction," Darcy continued. "Yearly research at the University of Michigan has shown that the high school senior classes that are surveyed are beginning to use fewer drugs. The trend is downward. That would be because of approaches like the Lions-Quest program. Those kinds of programs play a major role in reversing the drug problem."

In 1980, International President William C. Chandler discussed the ways to support Lions Clubs International Foundation. "The most effective ways," said President Chandler, "are the Melvin Jones Fellowship and the Contributing Membership Program. I challenge you to recognize outstanding Lions in your club or district by making them Melvin Jones Fellows. They are honored and the foundation can better meet critical human needs whenever they may occur in the world."

The Melvin Jones Fellowship was created in 1973 to honor individuals who have made outstanding contributions to humanitarian endeavors. It is presented to anyone who makes a donation—or in whose name a donation is made—of $1,000 or more.

Membership in the fellowship grew steadily. In 1986, at the international convention in New Orleans, Louisiana, the foundation's trustees challenged Lions around the world to increase the fellowship's size to 20,000 to celebrate LCIF's 20th anniversary in 1988.

The goal was actually exceeded, with 23,397 fellowships on record by year's end. Now a new goal has been set—75,000 fellows before the end of the association's 75th anniversary in 1992.

Melvin Jones Fellows receive an inscribed plaque and wear a special lapel pin. For each $1,000 donation beyond the original commitment—up to an additional $5,000—a diamond is added to a Lion's Melvin Jones Fellowship lapel pin.

Incidentally, the first Melvin Jones Fellows were William G. Clayton on November 4, 1973, a member of the Fort Lauderdale (Downtown), Florida, Lions Club and Dr. Luciano Nunziante, June 14, 1974, a member of the Barletta, Italy, Lions Club.

Still relatively young, the Lions Clubs International Foundation has been the catalyst for many hundreds of life-changing programs. When the goal of 75,000 Melvin Jones Fellowships is attained, LCIF's scope will be expanded many times over.

Each grant translates cash into hope. For instance, $10,000 grants helped construct a blood bank in India; expanded a vocational center in Uruguay; bought a microscope for an eye bank in Brazil; erected a primary school in Kenya; and purchased a wide-angle camera for eye research in Washington.

In India, men, women, and children enjoy clear, cool water because of Lions Clubs International Foundation. Clean water is hard to find in many parts of the nation. Vast numbers of the people live in villages where the primary industry is farming. Far too often the nearest water is more than a mile away. In many communities where there is water, it is frequently an open pond. Used for drinking, washing clothes, bathing, and other needs, it is often polluted. In summer the ponds may dry up completely.

The Lions of District 322-B recognized the need and began installing tubewells to provide safe drinking water. Tubewells are operated by hand and draw water from the ground. They provide clear water but are unable to supply enough for many sections of the country.

Studying the problem, the Lions decided to work with nature to bring water from the earth to storage above ground. The answer: to combine tubewells and windmills.

Windmills, once operating, run nearly without cost. In addition, wind velocity is highest when irrigation needs are greatest; from March through October.

A $30,000 LCIF grant made the project happen. District 322-B has built numerous windmills or tubewells in coastal agricultural areas. Each windmill lifts 100,000 liters of water to a height of 15 feet. As the water gushes to the surface it serves the needs of about 1,750 people each day.

Nothing is wasted. Extra water, and every drop is precious, is used for irrigating crops. This means a bonus of an extra crop; allowing three rather than two crops to be planted each year.

LCIF reaches around the globe and satisfies human thirsts for water, for opportunity, for education, for job skills, for health, and for mobility.

The assistance ranges from old-fashioned windmills to modern high-performance aircraft. In April 1987, LCIF gave a $50,000 check to the Swedish Lions of District 101-S to buy a plane for Lions International Air Relief. The grant paid for a used Cessna 206 Turbo aircraft named *The Helping Lion V*. Lions International Air Relief helped support the work of the late Count Carl Gustaf von Rosen.

Describing von Rosen's work, journalist Lars Braw wrote: "Earlier than most, Carl Gustaf von Rosen understood that air transport is indispensable in what we now call the Third World. One-fourth of the world's population lives in areas where there are no real roads. To travel 100 kilometers in a four-wheel drive car often takes a whole day. Sometimes it is simply impossible."

A skilled, courageous pilot, von Rosen flew and saved lives in Africa for nearly half a century. He was killed by guerillas in the Ethiopian-Somalian desert in 1977.

Von Rosen's aims were threefold: 1) To save starving people in countries with deficient roads; 2) To help prevent the creation of slums in large, third world cities, because once they start, they merely continue to grow; and, 3) To provide food, seeds, medicines, vaccines, and development-assistance-workers to people in need—encouraging farmers and villagers to stay in the countryside and not flock to the overcrowded cities.

Mission Aviation Fellowship (MAF) is completely responsible for the operating expenses of *The Helping Lion V*. MAF pays for maintenance, insurance, and salaries for pilots and engineers.

The planes are piloted by men like Peter Empson who began flying in the British Royal Air Force when he was 17. They bring food to Ethiopia, Kenya, Tanzania, Uganda, and Chad. Peter Empson and other pilots carry doctors, nurses, food, missionaries, and medical supplies wherever they are needed. As flying ambulances, the planes save countless lives.

The statistics are gruesome. In Tanzania every third child dies before its fifth birthday. In most other African nations the statistics are the same. Every fourth child suffers from severe malnutrition. The most common ills are respiratory infections, diarrhea, measles, whooping cough, malaria, and tuberculosis.

Swedish pilot Kjell Erik Arnlund lives in Chad with his wife Birgitta and their five children. In one letter home Birgitta wrote: "We have a very tight schedule with food flights and all the work receiving and organizing for those who arrive to participate in the flights. Right now we have four pilots and two engineers. During three weeks we have flown 390 tons of supplies but the need is still great. We're planning to add 13 dispensaries so that each will receive 25 to 30 tons of grain and other necessities. This seems to be a normal year as far as rain is concerned, but, unfortunately, many people have eaten their seeds, which means that next year will be difficult anyway."

A month later Birgitta and Kjell Erik reported that 580 tons of supplies and new seeds had been flown out. In addition, 16,000 children had been vaccinated. About their newest aircraft Birgitta wrote: "You have no idea how long we have been waiting and longing for it. We are very happy and grateful for your efforts and for the new possibilities it opens up."

"Without the LCIF grant it would have been impossible to purchase *The Helping Lion IV* and *The Helping Lion V*," said Past District Governor Ture B. Nydren, of Malmo, Sweden. "Both the public and Lion members now have a broader understanding of the scope of Lions Clubs International."

Africa remains in the spotlight with its continuing agony. In July 1985, LCIF Trustees authorized a $30,000 grant to Helen Keller International, Inc. That was in response to an appeal for funds for a nutritional blindness prevention program in Ethiopia and Sudan.

Earlier that year Helen Keller International had received an urgent request from the Ethiopian government for five million megadoses of Vitamin A to treat the large numbers of children at risk of nutritional blindness. A report from the emergency feeding camps estimated that nutritional blindness, trachoma, and other acute eye infections threatened the sight of half the children and many adults.

"Nutritional blindness is the most devastating side effect of hunger," explained John Costello, executive director of Helen Keller International. "It can be avoided with inexpensive doses of Vitamin A."

Xerophthalmia is the medical term for the condition. Symptoms generally move from night blindness to dry eyes and corneal ulcers. In the later stages the eye deteriorates until the cornea is completely destroyed and the patient becomes irreversibly blind.

Young children whose fast-growing tissues require protein and Vitamin A are especially vulnerable to nutritional blindness. They are also at greatest risk of infectious diseases that precipitate or aggravate xerophthalmia.

A therapeutic dose of Vitamin A is 200,000 international units packaged in a small capsule. Because Vitamin A is stored in the liver, a dose of this size lasts up to six months.

On August 20, 1985, John Costello wrote to Bert Mason, immediate past international president and chairman of the board of trustees of LCIF.

"Over the years," Costello said, "Helen Keller International has enjoyed a most productive partnership with your foundation, with The International Association of Lions Clubs, and with many districts and individual clubs. The generosity of Lions throughout the world has enabled us to help prevent blindness and to bring services to incurably blind individuals ever since our illustrious founder spoke to your annual meeting in 1925.

"The present grant marks a special relationship, however, since this is the first time that we have sought assistance for disaster relief. As we wrote to you in our proposal, we discovered that malnutrition and lack of vitamin A were leading to record high rates of nutritional blindness and xerophthalmia."

Costello went on to say, "Thanks to your grant, we are able to send additional personnel to save children from lifetimes of darkness."

As part of the solution to the problem, Helen Keller International generated a donation of $30,000 worth of Vitamin A from F. Hoffman-LaRoche & Company, the largest manufacturer of the nutrient.

The problems in Africa have no simple or quick answers. Working with organizations such as Helen Keller International, LCIF provided life-saving assistance for human beings trapped in a tragic moment of history.

Helen Keller's appeal to the Lions in 1925 continues to be answered with help for famine victims in Africa. The Lions School for Unsighted Girls sponsored by the Lions Club of Srinagar, India, is another facet of the answer.

Founded by the Srinagar Lions of District 321-D in 1976, the school needed a two-story building to properly carry out its mission. The government had donated an acre of land valued at $87,500 and the Lions had collected $7,500. Their aim was to expand the facility to educate 75 blind girls each year. Training would include reading, writing, arithmetic, and other basic subjects. In addition, the curriculum would cover arts, crafts, music, and mobility instruction. On July 15, 1980, LCIF issued a check for a $10,000 grant to enable them to achieve their goal.

"The grant from LCIF made it all possible," said one of the members of the Srinagar Lions Club. "At the time of the grant we only had a day school that was operating for the girls in the city of Srinagar only. However, a larger blind population of girls lived in villages. We felt that if they had the benefit of the school's program we could change their futures completely. They would gain valuable skills and be able to lead independent lives.

"Because of that we decided to build a fulltime boarding school. For that we needed a structure to house it along with classrooms and a small gymnasium with a playground attached. The LCIF grant, along with other money we raised, enabled us to do this. It dramatizes the strength of Lions working together through the Lions Clubs International Foundation."

Energy, goodwill, organization, and money combine through LCIF to expand Lionism's international mission. Noble aims find practical solutions for human needs.

In 1988, International President Judge Brian Stevenson described Lionism's international impact this way:

"In promoting the 'We Serve' imperative of Lionism, we are demonstrating our adherance to a humanitarian philosophy that for seven decades has personified the very best qualities of human nature. In reaching out to help others—the infirm, the indigent, the homeless— we are giving undeniable evidence that the spirit of volunteerism can be one of the most powerful forces in the world. The dedicated work of more than 1,350,000 Lions, along with our Lionesses and Leos is enhancing the image of our proud emblem in 162 lands worldwide. Our international program objectives of diabetes education and research and Lions-Quest 'Skills for Adolescence' in addition to the tens of thousands of service activities conducted each year define with utter clarity the essence of our motto.

"As I have underscored so very often, those two profound words, 'We Serve,' say *who* we are, *what* we are, and *why* we are. This year it has been my privilege to work with you in helping to assure this motto is understood and honored in communities spanning the earth."

CHAPTER EIGHT

Emphasis on Youth

INTERNATIONAL YOUTH EXCHANGE

MANY thousands of young people have experienced the joys of international youth exchange participation. Some express their feelings with unusual eloquence. During her visit to Japan in 1978 Melissa DeMartin wrote her hometown newspaper in Gustine, California:

"I would like to share with you some of the experiences I have had since leaving Gustine for Japan four weeks ago.

"I left San Francisco, July 16, on a chartered plane filled with 200 other youth exchange students and arrived in Tokyo, Japan the following day.

"I was met by my first host family, the Tanakas, whose home is in Kamagori. Mr. Tanaka is a surveyor. The family consists of the father, mother, and two sisters, ages 13 and 16. Mr. Tanaka's mother and father live with the family, which is very common in the Japanese culture.

"I have really enjoyed living with the Tanaka family as they are very warm and friendly people.

"They have a terrific sense of humor and have had a great many laughs at my 'strange ways.' They are amused at the way I eat, including the fact that I use soy sauce on my rice. I am enjoying my stay here very, very much. I can't say enough about the beauty and friendliness here. I am very grateful to the Gustine Lions Club for the opportunity to meet these gracious people and see their beautiful country.

"I am very anxious to tell you about many more and wonderful experiences when I return to the USA and Gustine."

The Lions Youth Exchange Program—which marked its 25th anniversary in 1986—has been a glowing success from the start. It allows young people to do what few adults get to do—live under one roof as part of a family with people of another country.

The genesis of the program came out of a Lions meeting held in 1960 in Kobe, Japan, according to Joseph Saito of Sacramento, California, past chairman of the Multiple District 4 Youth Exchange Committee.

He reports that the idea first surfaced in a casual conversation between the President of the Kobe East Lions Club and two Lions from California/Nevada Multiple District 4. They talked about an exchange of youths during the summer vacation period. The youths were to stay with Lions families in the host countries.

That summer, nine youths from Japan spent the summer with California families while 13 youths from California went to families in Japan. That exchange was apparently organized independently of the association program and arranged between Lions in California and Japan.

"This small exchange was so successful that the International Board of Directors decided to make it a worldwide Lions' activity," Saito said. "When the Lions Youth Exchange Program was adopted, the Board of Directors concluded that this program could contribute significantly to a greater understanding among people throughout the world."

The resolution to create the program was formally adopted at the international convention in Atlantic City, New Jersey, in June 1961. The first official exchange took place in 1961 when 16-year-old Lorenzo Calabrese, sponsored by the Bari, Italy, Lions Club, was hosted by the Sam C. Verdi family of Detroit, Michigan.

The idea spread swiftly among Lions. By April 1962, 457 Lions clubs and 89 district leaders had requested information. Eighty-six clubs said they would serve as host clubs, and 60 as sponsor clubs. Applications flooded in. They included 118 young French men and women and 85 students from Sweden who planned to visit Minnesota.

The Downtown Lions Club of Long Beach, California, set aside several thousand dollars to participate in the youth exchange program. They paid round-trip transportation costs for four area youths chosen from candidates selected from local high schools and colleges on the basis of an essay written on why each student felt he or she would best represent the United States and Lions ideals in other countries. Of the four winners, one went to Mexico, two to Germany, and one to Denmark.

The St. Petersburg, Florida, Lions Club arranged for a one-for-one exchange between their club and the Lions club in Arequipa, Peru. The Lions Club of Vandalia, Ohio, sponsored five young women. One went to France, one to Switzerland, and three to Canada.

From the very first—and there were 131 exchanges reported to the International Headquarters Office in the first year—the program has accomplished what Lions hoped it would.

Those objectives as expressed by Past International President Kaoru Murakami were "to bring young people of the world into contact with the youth and adults of other countries, to share family and community life of another culture, to promote international understanding and goodwill throughout the world of Lionism . . . and to contribute to the attainment of world peace."

The program has enjoyed spectacular growth.

By 1971 more than 1,500 young people from 36 countries were participating annually. Ten years later annual participation had more than doubled with 3,548 exchanges involving 53 countries reported in 1981. In 1988/89, reports showed there were 3,385 exchanges among 40 countries. During the Youth Exchange Program's first 25 years, more than 50,000 young people from 80 different countries shared their cultures and developed friendships with families in participating nations.

"I think the Youth Exchange Program of Lions clubs gives the world a chance to unite in friendship. It's the most beautiful thing anyone could experience," said one exchange youth from the United States.

Lori Gail Anderson, another exchange youth from the United States wrote that living abroad with a family is "an education that is impossible to get in any school."

For Pekka Salomaa of Finland, living with a family in the United States deepened her understanding of what Lions activities are all about. "I want to do my best so that one day in the future I can be a Lion, and be worthy of the kindness I experienced."

The Youth Exchange Program became highly sophisticated as the years passed, but its objectives have never changed.

Lion Masonori Akahoshi, Youth Exchange Chairman of Multiple

District 335, Japan, noted in *Youth Exchange News* that "Youth Exchange is not a program to give a free vacation or to have our young people have a good time. It is . . . much deeper than that. I like to interpret it as 'sowing seeds for the future.' We're hoping that people who are living in these countries can hold hands together saying that I have a brother in so-and-so country, or a son in so-and-so country, or I have a mother in so-and-so country. We want to be brothers ten, 20, 30 years from now, and now we are sowing the seeds for that."

While program goals remain simple and clear, methods and operations have become more highly organized than in the early days of the program. Lion Akahoshi said that today in his country, district youth exchange chairmen begin informal meetings every year in June. Chairmen continue to meet about once a month with one person from each zone attending.

"The important thing here is to get more people involved," he said. The district governor calls each club in September and asks for a representative to come to a meeting for a discussion of exchange plans for the following year.

Youth exchanges can be arranged between two Lions clubs or two districts. Usually they last from four to six weeks and the program is open to all young men and women between the ages of 15 and 21. Each young person should have a good reputation in the community and an above average academic record. Sometimes applicants are selected through essay or speaking contests conducted by the sponsoring Lions club or district.

At the first district screening, the district governor explains to the participants what the Youth Exchange Program is and what is expected of them as representatives of Japan. A language test and individual interviews follow. The committee interviewing young people evaluates health, character, motives, and knowledge of the Youth Exchange Program and Lionism. Even the parents' attitudes toward the exchanges are noted and weighed. When an applicant is found to be not prepared or suited for the exchange, the sponsor club is notified. It is up to the individual sponsor club to decide whether a youth will participate.

About six months before the actual exchange date, orientation begins for both the young people and their parents. During the following months the youths meet between once a month and once a week to learn about Lions Clubs International, the objectives of youth exchange and the customs and traditions of the country to be visited.

The young men and women participating are encouraged to study the country they are visiting. They are urged to learn about the host country's history, national heroes, sports and entertainment figures, educational system, geographic features, principal religions, and other information designed to give them an understanding of the nation's culture.

At the same time, it is suggested that they bring with them photographs and slides of their families, home, school, community, friends, and other material that will help the host family understand them better. Slides, in particular, are suggested because often the young men and women are asked to give a presentation to the host Lions club. Frequently, the sponsor club provides a banner, pin, or other memento to give the host club at that time.

While the sponsor country is preparing its young people for the experience of living in a foreign land, Lions of the host country are making careful and elaborate preparations to find and prepare host families. Lion Barry Crowther, Youth Exchange Chairman for Multiple District 14, Pennsylvania, explained that "the most important part of hosting is finding and preparing the host families."

To recruit the families, a form letter is sent to each district youth exchange chairman and district governor requesting a projected number of host families, a list of desired countries for exchanges, and suggestions for the program. Youth exchange chairmen from each Lions club and a representative from each Lioness club gather to review goals and share suggestions.

"It is important to build up a reserve list of host families," Crowther said, "in case an assigned family is forced to withdraw because of unexpected circumstances." Another practical tip: "Discourage phone calls from parents during the first week of a youth's visit because it complicates the young person's adjustment to his new family. Most calls from parents are not because their sons or daughters are homesick but because the parents miss their child."

The key to obtaining the families is "old-fashioned salesmanship," according to Crowther. "If the chairman believes in the Youth Exchange Program, has tried it, and can guarantee its performance, the selling will be easy."

Despite the endless hours the job requires, Lions continue to shoulder the job of youth exchange chairman, and find in it a great sense of contributing to international understanding.

"I have thoroughly enjoyed and am continuing to experience tremendous satisfaction from this portfolio, especially when I welcome youths on their return from their participation overseas," says Lion Eric Fernandez of District 201-S2, Australia.

An indication of how well the program works is watching young people who have finished their visits to Australia and are departing. "The tearful, unhappy faces of those bound for their native lands and who are unhappy to part with their hosts is a clear indication that the first Object of Lions Clubs International—'To create and foster a spirit of understanding among the peoples of the world'—has certainly been achieved."

Lions sponsoring and hosting a visitor are responsible for:
- All financial matters related to the exchange,
- Travel arrangements, passports, visas,
- Local transportation, arrivals, departures,
- Insurance,
- Supervision of the exchange,
- Liaison with parents and host families,
- Emergency situations.

Thorough preparation pays off in individual exchanges which are spectacularly successful right from the start—like the visit of Lai Hooi Yee of Malaysia to Australia. In her own words, "The 5th of December, 1986, marked a very important page in my life's history. It was the first time I had left Malaysia to travel to a country which sounded so familiar and yet so strange to me. At Melbourne Airport I walked through a door which closed me out from the customs I was used to. I was in a strange country, but not for long.

"Suddenly a hand reached out toward me. My heart missed a beat, and I looked up at three friendly faces. The next thing I knew I was in their arms and asking whether I could call them 'Mum and Dad'. My stay in Australia started from the moment they took my hand and led me home, sweet home."

Before long, this young Malaysian girl was a "farmer's daughter" on the farm of her host family: John Davies, youth exchange chairman in Benalla, Australia, and his wife, Enid. "We brought sheep home together, collected eggs together. Anywhere they went, I went with them. Anything they did, I joined in. I really felt a part of them and I still do."

For many young people, the Lions Youth Exchange Program has made dreams come true. As a child in Uusikaaupunki, Finland, Kristiina Kontu had always dreamed of visiting the United States. As a guest of the South Boston, Virginia, Lions Club, during the summer of 1987, Kikka was "always learning—picking up our slang and our expressions and making universal comments on life," as one Lion put it. Kikka's observations of the United States were not always totally favorable, "but they were always interesting and usually right on the mark," another Lion observed.

"The standard of living is so high here," Kikka told her hosts. "Perhaps it is too high." She pronounced American clothes as "sweet, but too cute." She loved hot dogs, French fries, popcorn, and, especially, peaches. When she was leaving for the return trip home she refused to say "Good-bye," preferring "See you later," one of the Americanisms she learned. "Because that means we will meet again sometime, I hope."

What many thousands of young people who have participated in the Lions Youth Exchange Program have learned was aptly expressed by Kikka: "I think people are people everywhere. I have more understanding of myself as well as others and I have learned to love life in a new way."

How was it possible for two young Japanese girls to wind up in Wrexham, North Wales, to be entertained by the Mayor and Mayoress of Wrexham at a Welsh tea ceremony as special guests during their stay in Great Britain? It happened to two Japanese guests of the Wrexham Lions Club on a visit to Great Britain sponsored by the Osaka and Tokyo Lions clubs. At the ceremony, Host Lion Ray Barlow and Club President Jack Manuel received club pennants from Yoko Kuishi and Sanomi Oishi. Under the Wrexham Lions Club's auspices, the young women also visited the National Garden Festival at Stoke on Trent, the City of Chester, Eaton Hall, the home of the Duke and Duchess of Westminster,

Chirk Castle, a Welsh slate mine, Cambridge University, London, and the Norfolk Coast.

One family in Mahomet, Illinois, has an authentic Japanese wardrobe as a result of the Lions Youth Exchange Program. It was brought as a gift by 20-year-old Masashi "Harry" Haruyama, a student at Tokyo University. The clothes came from Masashi's father's clothing shop and were given to Deanna and Duane Wagers of the Mahomet Lions Club. For his trip to the United States, Harry did a lot of homework, including reading *Tom Sawyer*, *Huckleberry Finn*, the Bill of Rights, and the U.S. Constitution. He was also a regular viewer of American television programs and movies. "I absorb American culture," he smiles. One of his explorations into American culture was a trip to St. Louis with Duane to watch a Cardinals baseball game. Other excursions were to Hannibal, Missouri, and the state capital in Springfield, Illinois, where Harry wanted to see Lincoln's home. There was also a visit to the Chicago area, which included a trip to the Sears Tower and Lions Clubs International headquarters.

Members of several Lions clubs in New Zealand learned a lot about the United States when Diane Hillman of Northwood, Iowa, was sent to that country under the Lions Youth Exchange Program. According to Lowell Gangstad, the Northwood club's exchange program chairman, Diane prepared a slide show about her life in Northwood which she showed to several New Zealand clubs. "The New Zealanders were amazed at the size of the tractors and other farm machinery we use in Iowa," Diane told the Northwood Lions Club when she returned.

Other surprises: "When Lions saw slides of my home they always remarked that the windows were smaller than in New Zealand. They didn't realize how cold Iowa winters were or that we heated our houses all winter long." The family of Lion Peter Ryan with whom she stayed at Gladfield, a tiny farm community on New Zealand's South Island, "heated only one room of their house and that only one month out of the year," she told the sponsoring club.

She liked the fact that New Zealand students, even those in high school, wore uniforms. "Here it would be unthinkable to wear the same clothes two days in a row or even twice in the same week. With uniforms you wouldn't have the pressure. It would be easier for families on a limited income."

How do successful exchanges come about? In the case of New Zealand, one Lion's efforts to follow the first Object of the association led to that country's extensive Youth Exchange Program. In 1987, 200 young people visited New Zealand as guests of 600 host families. But for a time, it looked like the only Lion in New Zealand interested in the exchanges was M. E. "Mike" Brooke, past youth exchange chairman, Multiple District 202.

"I was the charter president, a brand new Lion, surrounded by 30 new Lions in March of 1971—and none of us knew anything about being a Lion," Brooke recalled at a seminar during the Lions Clubs International Convention in Denver in 1988. "I thought a good place to start would be the first Object: 'To create and foster a spirit of understanding among the peoples of the world.' As I got more into the thing I found that the logical answer for an activity would be youth exchange. Being a good Lion, I tried to lead by example. I called for volunteer hosts and put my own hand up, but nobody else did."

Undaunted, Brooke and his club secretary ("I persuaded him," said Mike. "I'm quite a persuasive fellow and I was bigger than he was.") hosted two foreign youths and unexpectedly found their own lives transformed by the experience.

"We started doing simple things as a family that we had gotten out of the habit of doing. We began visiting art galleries in Plymouth where I live, going to the beach, stopping for ice cream cones, just doing all sorts of normal things which families should be doing. Suddenly we found we were doing the things we liked doing. Not only were the youths from overseas enjoying it, but we were, too. In two or three weeks our visitors had become part of our family. Our own kids never stopped talking about them for months and months."

For New Zealand, that was the beginning of a thriving exchange program. For Brooke, it was the beginning of what he calls a "long and enthusiastic career in the business." That career led to his selection as district youth exchange chairman and as multiple district youth exchange chairman."

When Brooke first raised his hand as the sole host volunteer, he encountered what he describes as still the "biggest problem to be overcome in any country's foreign exchange program—getting hosts."

Finding hosts in New Zealand is the job of the district youth exchange chairman, Brooke explained. He must be a "totally dedicated and totally enthusiastic youth exchange chairman who does not send letters. He makes personal visits and contacts.

"You simply have to make a personal appeal and go there yourself. If the area is too big, then you have to involve others."

Is it worth all the effort? Mike Brooke thinks so: "We all have heard that the Youth Exchange Program is tailor-made to assure the future of world peace. I've heard these statements many times and they do seem rather extravagant. But I'm sure I would sooner put my trust in many teenagers than in some of the political leaders of the world today."

However it begins, a country's Youth Exchange Program usually expands, both in numbers of youths involved and in scope. Lion Juan Weiss of Lima, Peru, said that Peru's youth exchanges were, until recently, almost always with the United States. In recent years, Lions in Lima, Peru, have begun working with Lions in Italy to set up an exchange program between the two countries. "It was a natural start," Weiss said. "Many of the Peruvian youths who went to Italy had grandfathers and great-grandfathers who came from that country and many of them had some knowledge of the Italian language."

Twelve Peruvian youths around the age of 16 went to Italy in 1987 where they spent one week with an Italian host-family in each of the seven districts of the country, giving the Peruvian youngsters "an unparalleled introduction to Italy." So that they would get the most benefit from the Italian experience, most of the boys and girls were selected because they knew some Italian, their family background, or because they attended Lima's Italian School.

"I believe that it is extremely important that youths participating in these exchanges should have at least the basics of the language of the country they visit," Weiss said. "The Lima Lions Club is now working with Lions clubs in Germany and France for exchange programs patterned on the successful exchanges with Italy."

The first Peruvian Lions club was established in Lima in 1944, and there are now about 180 Lions clubs in Peru. "Several Peruvian clubs send an average of 80 to 100 youths abroad and receive a like number from other countries each year," Weiss noted.

Reactions of the youths who have traveled to Italy have been "marvelous . . . extraordinary." Youths report universally that their foreign experience was more wonderful than they had imagined. They all particularly enjoy living on a day to day basis with the host families.

"The Youth Exchange Program is perhaps the biggest step that Lions Clubs International has taken to promote peace," Weiss concluded.

Sometimes, youth exchanges involve small dynamic packages—like Maki Agata, a 3-foot-1-inch, 20-year-old Japanese student who enjoyed a pleasant summer stay with a California family. Maki's visit to the United States was prompted by a sudden awareness on the part of Lion Bob Olson of Livingston, California, that he had never heard of an exchange involving a handicapped youth. Actually, many handicapped youths had participated in the Youth Exchange Program from the beginning.

Olson contacted Stockton Lion Vern Gogna, who was then the Lions Youth Exchange Chairman for the area. Gogna told him that no handicapped youth had ever asked about the exchange program, nor had any family volunteered to host such a youth. Gogna made a call to a Lion in Japan who received Maki's name from one of her college teachers.

Soon, Maki, who needs a Japanese-English dictionary and a little help to communicate in English, was living with the Olsons. They even arranged a visit for Maki with an unusually short couple who have learned to live successfully in the full-sized world. Maki's opinion of America? "It's so big," she told her new friends, "and the people are so friendly."

LOCAL YOUTH EXCHANGE

"The yellow school bus ground to a halt before the long, low building in the Arizona desert," wrote Eldonna Fisher in the March 1986 issue of The Lion. "A paper banner heralding 'Bienvenidos-Arizpe-Welcome!' which Palominas, Arizona, students made, broke in two as the bus drove through the entrance into the parking lot.

"As 60 Mexican students alighted from the bus, they were met with cheers of welcome by 400 friendly, excited American boys and girls.

"Many of the American children had visited Arizpe, Sonora, Mexico, on an earlier exchange, and were now ready to entertain their Mexican friends for two nights and three days. The students, a mixed group of fifth through eighth graders, were delighted to be among their American friends again—the result of the months of planning on both sides of the border."

A generous donation from the Sierra Vista, Arizona, Lions Club was a major factor in the activity between the two cities.

For both sides this was truly an exchange. The American students had been working three hours a week on their Spanish for months before the Mexican group of fifth through eighth graders had arrived. During their visit, the Mexicans learned how to use an Apple computer to play games, learn typing, and do arithmetic problems.

Unlike the international youth exchanges cited in the previous section, this exchange came to pass as a local arrangement between the two Lions clubs. Although different in that sense, it provides a similar dimension of international understanding created by the Youth Exchange Program.

The exchange came about because Lions Charles Pullen and Ray Willcox, both past presidents of the Sierra Vista Lions Club were aware of the importance of cultural understanding. Their homes and workplaces were only a few miles from the U.S.-Mexican border. When officials of the Palominas school district spoke to the club about a possible student exchange, Pullen, Willcox, and the club got behind the idea with donations. Willcox, an administrator of Cochise Community College, sent the college media specialist on some of the trips to Arizpe to make a videotaped record of the exchanges titled: "The School That Dared." Spanish-language versions were given to school officials in Sonora.

The first exchange has become many, allowing American and Mexican children to gain firsthand experience of one another's lifestyles, language, and customs. One Arizona school official summed it up this way: "Changes in attitudes have been enormous since the program began. We loaded up two buses with parents for a trip to Arizpe. They were delighted and completely positive about the experience."

International links are strongly forged and often very long lasting. Some of the long-standing exchanges between two clubs take some very creative turns, to the benefit of both home countries. For instance, after 10 years of twinning between the York Lions Club, England, and the Lions Club of Mulheim-Ruhr Hellweg near Dusseldorf, Germany, the clubs have added education as a purpose of their mutual exchanges—and have raised the age of students who participate.

In the first such exchange involving a university-age student, the York Lions Club sent Iain, a young English electronics student as a guest of the Mulheim club. The student was placed with a large industrial company and lived on the campus of the University of Essen. His company superiors were so impressed with his ability, they invited him, in September 1987, for a year of study and in-plant training. In an address to the sponsoring York Lions Club, Iain told the club what they had hoped to hear—that his visit to Germany had given him a much broader view of electronics applications.

As part of this English-German exchange, two girls from Bochum and Essen universities came to York and were placed in three-week intern programs with Barclay's Bank and with British Rail, the country's national rail service.

INTERNATIONAL YOUTH CAMPS

Working in concert with the concept of breaking down international barriers by having young people in dozens of countries participate in youth exchanges is participation in international youth camps.

These enable young people from several different nations to join together for several days or weeks in a camp supported by Lions clubs.

International Youth Camps are sponsored by Lions clubs and districts and held each year in France, Belgium, Denmark, England, Finland, India, the United States, Italy, Germany, Norway, Sweden, and dozens of other countries.

When they met in Calgary, Alberta, Canada, in October 1987, the International Board of Directors listed four points that define a Lions International Youth Camp. To be named a "Lions International Youth Camp" the project must:

1. Use the name "Lions" in its official title in compliance with the policy requirements established by the International Board of Directors.
2. Be at least one week long.
3. Involve participation of youths from different countries.
4. Provide a schedule of activities determined by the camp organizers, consistent with the program's objectives.

In 1988/89, young people enjoyed camping experiences in 76 Lions International Youth Camps in 23 different countries. Activities include sports, nature study, sightseeing, painting, seminars on drug and diabetes awareness, talent shows, and studying local culture.

Each camp is different in that the program varies from one camp to another. In another sense the camps are similar because they create strong bonds of friendship among the campers as they work and play together during the camping session.

Said an Australian youth who attended a Lions international camp in Texas, "I learned more than ever before to share, to participate, and to contribute. The time in the camp was the greatest in my life without a doubt. It taught me that we have to serve our neighbors and pursue worthwhile aims. I'm proud of the camp and my participation in it."

Some of the camps are organized for special purposes. In Multiple District 104, Norwegian Lions sponsor a camp for the handicapped between the ages of 18 and 30.

Swedish Lions of Multiple District 101 sponsor a Lions Folk Music Camp in Jamtland, Sweden, for boys and girls from 16 to 23 who can play the violin.

In August 1988, 16-year-old Anthony Millar traveled from his home in River Forest, Illinois, to Sweden to take part in the Lions International Camp for Diabetic Teenagers. A student at Oak Park-River Forest High School, Anthony enjoys lacrosse, water skiing, and snow skiing. He became a diabetic at the age of four.

"The camp is about an hour and a half from Stockholm and it was great," he smiled. "It really helped me with my diabetes. I used to eat candy even though my mother told me not to. These kids just amazed me because they wouldn't go near it. We had a doctor there who is an expert on diabetes, Dr. Johnny Ludvigsson. After breakfast we'd go to the conference room and discuss topics. He talked about self-control, fibers, diet, meal planning, alcohol, and other subjects that affect the diabetic. I learned a lot that I hadn't known before, including different types of insulin techniques."

"After the morning discussion we played games until lunch," Anthony continued. "The afternoon was free time and we'd spend it canoeing, swimming, or playing soccer or volleyball. I'd never traveled to a different country before. I flew from Chicago to Copenhagen and then to Stockholm and then took a train the rest of the way. They have great trains. I was sponsored by the Berwyn, Illinois, Lions Club. They filled out my application for the camp, sent it to Sweden, and I was accepted. It was an outstanding experience."

Anthony was the only American among the 30 boys and girls attending. Others came from England, Denmark, Germany, Switzerland, Austria, and Sweden. All the campers spoke English, the official language of the camp. Anthony spent two weeks before the camp visiting with District Governor Lars Lundstrom. "His family is really nice," said Anthony. "They went out of their way to be hospitable. They have a 17-year-old son and a 15-year-old daughter. Lars and the other Lions took us to see Stockholm and other points of interest in their country. They were very thoughtful hosts."

The aims of the camp are fourfold, explained Dr. Ludvigsson, the specialist in diabetes. "The camp is designed to: 1) reward and encourage diabetic teenagers; 2) stimulate international contacts between youngsters; 3) provide education about modern active treatment for diabetes; and, 4) spread ideas about active treatment of diabetes in different countries."

Rose Ann Millar, Anthony's mother, called his experience in Sweden "wonderful." She added, "I think seeing that there are so many other kids with diabetes gave him a feeling that he wasn't the only one who had to take shots on an outing and be careful of his diet. He met great kids that he really liked and learned a great deal about diabetes and its management. Finding out that he can travel by himself gave him confidence. He's happier and more outgoing than he was before going to Sweden. The experience has been very, very positive for him."

The Iowa Lions Youth Camp in Madrid, Iowa, is another example of how Lions as citizens of the world are promoting a world without borders and fostering international understanding among the future leaders of the world.

The camp is 100 percent supported by Iowa Lions clubs. Campers pay nothing for the time they spend in the camp's 1,100 acres of woods, river, meadow, lodge, and comfortable dormitory housing.

As campers, visitors from several countries participate in activities such as swimming, archery, skeet shooting, Frisbee, golf, volleyball, softball, soccer, canoeing, and dancing.

"It may be that ours is the only Lions camp in the world which offers campers the chance to soar into the air aboard a hot air balloon for a bird's-eye view of the countryside," Orlin E. Buck, the Iowa Lions Club youth coordinator points out. "Dedicated balloonists interested in our project frequently bring in their balloons and launching equipment and take our kids for a ride," Buck explains.

"Each of the nine districts in Iowa is asked to provide a boy or girl as a counselor, and all meal preparation and other work in the camp is handled by volunteer Lions, Lionesses, and spouses (or family members)," Buck continued. "We also assign two or three foreign youths to help campers having problems with language or cultural differences, so the camping experience usually goes very smoothly for every camper."

There is a drug abuse program where campers describe drug or alcohol problems in their home countries. There are also some strictly enforced rules. "No drinking or drugs, no boys in girls' quarters or vice versa, and we discourage smoking."

A highlight of the one-week camping experience is when foreign youths explain their flag and their country to other campers.

Does the camp really break down the barriers and bring youths from many different countries closer?

"You just have to believe it does on the last day of camp when you see how close these new-found friends have grown and how reluctant they are to part," Buck said. "Our camp motto is 'We met as strangers, but leave as friends,' and I can see the motto has become a reality. When those boys and girls leave us they are friends."

Another testament came from Kare of Denmark who attended the camp in Mount Brydges (Districts A-1/A-2 Lions Clubs International Friendship Youth Camp, Canada). "I came to the camp with quite a lot of fear and skepticism. I was afraid of being shy and not being a part of the group. Usually, I don't make friends easily.

"In this camp I met some wonderful human beings whom I am going to keep as my dearest friends forever. All 34 of us became friends in spite of culture, religion, and opinions. We took the first giant step toward the happy and absolutely necessary reunion of all the people on this earth. I have gained belief in a global understanding and peace; a peace growing out of happiness and joy, thanks to all Lions and Lionesses. I wish with all my heart that this was more than a one-time experience."

The Norwegian Lions camp is dual purpose in that it allows able-bodied youths to volunteer to assist the handicapped campers and learn camp management. The primary purpose, of course, is to help the handicapped young people develop their own possibilities and establish relationships with other handicapped people of their own age from many different countries.

In only a year of organizing, the Lions Club of Lofoten, Norway, with help from clubs in District 104-A, organized a very successful camp that promoted "international friendship north of the Arctic Circle."

"We definitely did not want it to be a vacation camp," explained Arne Christoffersen, club president. "The intention was to gather youths from around the world with an interest in international cooperation and understanding, culture, trade, and industry." In all, the two-week camp attracted 28 persons from Norway and 14 different countries in 1986, its first year. Participants also spent another week in the homes of host families.

Campers visited commercial and industrial companies, schools, and museums, heard presentations about one another's countries, and went fishing and climbed mountains.

"We got many reports later that many of the participants were getting together privately in several countries for discussions similar to those fostered in camp," said Christofferson. "That was proof that the camp was not a vacation camp and had achieved the objectives we had set for it."

LOCAL YOUTH ACTIVITIES

International youth exchanges and international youth camps are vivid examples of how Lions clubs all over the world work with our most precious resource—young people—in ways which promote peace, cultural understanding, and international friendship. That concern of Lions clubs for youth is also apparent in the creative and innovative programs developed in so many different countries to give deprived and disabled youths a chance at a decent future.

Robbie, a 17-year-old, is learning how to test and overcome his own limits at a unique Lions-run camp in Illinois.

With the help of another teenaged boy, Robbie strings two ropes across a river, one rope above the other. Then, feet perched precariously on the bottom rope and hands grasping the top rope, he begins fearfully to inch his way out over the river. Almost across, the young man's grip loosens and he falls with a great splash into the river. Other teenagers watching yell, "Yo! Robbie! Try it again! Try it again!"

The second try brings a successful crossing, a victorious smile, and excited cheers from the watchers.

Partially blind and totally deaf, Robbie has conquered a fear and taken a giant step toward self-reliance.

There is nothing like camping, hiking, and mountain climbing in the wilderness to develop muscles, initiative, and self-confidence.

Robbie is getting this important formative experience at a special program offered through Camp Lions which is funded and administered by the Lions clubs of Multiple District 1 through their charitable arm, the Lions of Illinois Foundation. Called CLAWS (for Camp Lions Adventure Wilderness School), the program is an offshoot of the Illinois Camping program which serves from 400 to 500 children each summer during regular camping programs at two sites: Camp Lions "Ravenswood" at Lake Villa in northern Illinois and in the southern part of the state at Camp Lions "Touch of Nature," in Carbondale.

Founded in 1980, CLAWS has become so successful that it was awarded the prestigious Eleanor P. Eells Award of the American Camping Association for "providing sensitive and thoughtful leadership which resulted in the enrichment of human growth through the outdoor experience."

In 1981, a more advanced CLAWS program, CLAWS II, was begun for graduates of CLAWS I. In CLAWS II, graduates of CLAWS learn to become full fledged counselors capable a teaching wilderness skills to other handicapped youngsters.

The setting is heavily wooded, with rock cliffs, lakes, and streams, an ideal environment to encourage teens to stretch themselves to their limits. Campers in the CLAWS I program participate with counselors in four "schools"—Pioneers, Mariners, Voyagers, and Mountaineers. Pioneers learn shelter building, fire starting, rope work, backpacking, land navigation, camp site selection, and bridge building. Mariners learn boat and raft building, swimming skills, and life saving. For Voyagers, it is canoeing, portaging, and navigation, while the Mountaineers concentrate on repelling, climbing, vertical rigging, and rescue.

Handicapped youngsters not only survive but thrive on the grueling wilderness tests. George B. Davis, Director of the Touch of Nature Camp in Carbondale, isn't surprised. "These kids are capable of a great deal. They are the determinants of their own limits if they can learn to ignore a society that has told them they are limited. Barriers have been erected by virtue of a child's difference; not by the child but by the world around him."

Some of the letters received from parents, and from the campers themselves, bear Davis out. "To see the happiness on his face and to listen to him while he told us what he got to do was tremendously rewarding," wrote parents from Vandalia, Illinois, about their son, Curt. "These are the children of our future and they can have a bright future if they are given a chance. Being handicapped makes them special, not different. Your support and interest has already made a big change in Curt's life."

Though the Lions take a world view, they can also focus on the practical "little" things such as a hearty breakfast for children in Palomas, Mexico, a regional Special Olympics in Leadville, Colorado, or the installation of physical education equipment for five- and six-year-old children in Shawnee, Oklahoma.

Palomas, Mexico, is a poor, dusty border town about two miles from Columbus, New Mexico, the site of Pancho Villa's 1916 raid. Its school children now eat a hearty breakfast in the form of fresh milk and "pan dulce," sweet bread, provided by Palomas-Columbus Lions and Lioness clubs. Dr. Ricardo Fierro, a Palomas dentist and president of the club, which is composed of two-thirds Americans and one-third Mexicans, said that since the program began, teachers report a marked improvement in class attention as well as improved attendance.

"The kids have been more alert in their classes and have advanced faster in their schoolwork. Prior to the program, the teachers noted that a large percentage of the children hadn't eaten before they came to school and some even fell asleep in class." Teachers estimate that at least a third of the students and probably many more came to school without eating breakfast, and stayed hungry all day long.

About 600 children in kindergarten through sixth grade attend the school in shifts, half in the morning and half in the evening. None of them turn down the milk and the bread. One of the young teachers in the school said: "In Mexico, a lot of families have trouble providing milk for their children. Even those who can afford to eat often, cannot afford milk. This is a great supplement to their diet."

The Shawnee, Oklahoma, Lions club invested $10,000 in time and money to provide playground and exercise equipment for kindergarten-age children of the Shawnee school system. The school district was unable to provide the equipment for its early childhood program, which includes both kindergarten children and children who have completed kindergarten but are not yet ready for first grade.

In Leadville, Colorado, the Lions club turned out to be the answer to the prayer of Neil Utz, coordinator of the Pikes Peak Area VI Special Olympics.

Special Olympics is the largest sports participation group of the mentally handicapped in the world, involving more than one million athletes from 60 countries.

Special Olympians, who must be over the age of eight and have physical handicaps, compete in 15 summer and winter sports. The games are conducted with true Olympic pomp and flair, including formal opening ceremonies, lighting of the Olympic flame, and awards presentations of ribbons or medals at the games' end.

Utz had contracted Ski Cooper in Leadville, a family resort with "the comfortable friendly atmosphere we needed for the Olympics," said Utz, "but it was not a destination resort and did not have the overnight accommodations needed for the 100 or more special athletes we were expecting to participate."

In order to handle the Special Olympics, Utz and Ski Cooper needed a co-sponsor—an active, enthusiastic group that could generate community-wide interest in the event. "The timing was perfect," recalls Lion Howard Hill, who with fellow club member Randy Wiges, served as co-chairmen of the Special Olympics project.

"Our club membership had been looking for a good, service-oriented project. Then Neil came along and we decided that the Special Olympics was that project."

The 44-member club funded the event, arranged for transportation, food, lodging, and ski lift tickets for 139 Special Olympians and their 45 coaches and chaperons from Colorado communities like Leadville, Buena Vista, Salida, Boulder, and Colorado Springs. Lions also scheduled two days of exciting events with an afternoon of qualifying runs, skiing for fun, a parade, a spaghetti dinner, a dance, a group breakfast, a race competition, and an awards presentation ceremony.

All of the projects that Lions the world over have created and supported help youth in myriad ways. They also contribute "to the image we project on the international level," as 1988-89 International President Austin P. Jennings said in his inaugural address in Denver, Colorado, in 1988.

Jennings went on to say, "The thousands of young people who have participated in these activities came away convinced that, in fact, differences in language, race, culture, and politics are really superficial matters that can be overcome—that what is truly important is a desire to extend the hand of friendship across the continents and seas, a willingness to enter into dialogue with others, and, of great consideration, a commitment to agree to disagree when necessary, but in so doing, not lose your respect for the other person's opinions.

"These young participants learn at an early age the critical value of understanding and appreciating the world community, and Lions should realize the importance of expanding these two programs which truly spread our ideals of peace and friendship into communities spanning the globe.

"Twenty-five years ago, my family cautiously entered into an exchange program involving our daughter and a student from Switzerland. This experience changed our lives and, I am sure, had a direct impact on my presence at this podium today."

CHAPTER NINE

Lionesses Make Things Happen

"I FOUND out that women have a good, firm hand all over the world," said Marjorie Tinkey of Bailey, Colorado. "I used to think that women in other parts of the world weren't allowed to do very much. However, here at the Lions Clubs International Convention I've talked with Lionesses from many other countries. I've met them from India, Nigeria, Japan, South America, the Philippines. They accomplish a great deal and command a great deal of respect. That was great to learn."

Exuberant and outgoing, Marjorie Tinkey has been a Lioness for six and a half years and was attending the International Convention in Denver, Colorado, in July 1988.

"We have 57 members and are the largest Lioness club in the state of Colorado," she continued. "My husband has been a Lion for 11 years and our club began in 1981. Now that women can become Lions I'm sure that some Lionesses will. However, I don't intend to. I think that we have our own separate jobs to do. Our club has a diabetes screening program, we help patients in nursing homes, bring them toothbrushes, slippers, other things that nursing homes require. Some of our members donate blood. We have a food basket program that runs all the time for any family that needs it. These are all separate from Lions club programs. We work with the Lions on the Health Fair. If they have a fundraiser we help with that, too.

"We get a chance to put our principles into action. When you see a smile on somebody's face for something you've done for them, it's a pretty good feeling. It helps to take my mind off my problems and put them in their real perspective."

Even the brutal realities of civil war don't keep Lioness clubs from their mission of uplifting the less fortunate. In war-ravaged Lebanon, 22 Lioness clubs work systematically to relieve the misery created by the nation's seemingly endless suffering.

"I've lived in Lebanon all my life," said Lioness Claire Chehab, of the Jounieh, Lebanon, Lioness Club. "My husband has been a Lion for ten years and I've been a Lioness since 1984. With the war we have terrible problems in our country. I live only 15 minutes by automobile from Beirut where the fighting goes on periodically. We have 27 members in our Lioness club and work closely with the Lions club which has about 40 members."

Claire Chehab, who served as president of the Jounieh Lioness Club in 1988–89, continued, "The civil war makes our Lioness work even more important for our country. Many children in Lebanon are orphaned and the first project we had this year was to send children to school and pay for everything from our club. We don't have any government schools. These are special Catholic schools. We support five girls who have no parents and send them to school. We pay for books, clothing, everything they need. Basically, our club adopts the children and sends them to school and they stay with the sisters while they're going to school.

"We raise money with ladies' nights and sell tickets for a dollar to raise money. Being a Lioness has given me more confidence and expanded my personality. It lets me do things for others. I've also made many friends in other clubs that we can call on when we need help for our war-torn nation. We can reach out to other parts of the world for assistance. For instance, the Lionesses in Paris send us medicine for the children."

The first Lioness club was formed during the term of International President Harry Aslan on December 24, 1975. It was the Mount Pleasant, North Carolina, Lioness Club and was the first to be certified in the Lioness Clubs program.

The ladies' auxiliaries had been in existence for 40 years before the

Lioness clubs program began and had created many highly effective service projects in that time. Most of them became Lioness clubs when the program was established. As one example, the Binghampton, New York, Lioness Club started as a ladies' auxiliary in 1944 and was famed for its wide range of services for the visually handicapped.

In its early years, the primary objective of the group was to help young people in Broome County's Sightsaving School. Glasses, large type books, transcribing services, and special help were supported by funds provided by the club. Equipment given in the late 1940s is still at work in the local school for the handicapped. In more recent years, Lionesses in Binghampton have stressed amblyopia vision screening. Other auxiliaries around the world moved their inititiative and sense of commitment into the Lioness Clubs program when it began.

Lioness membership soared from the start. Only 13 months after the program began, the Waterford, Ontario, Canada, Lioness Club, originally organized as a Lions auxiliary in April 1970, became the 1,000th club to be certified. After attending the Lioness Seminar at the Lions Clubs International Hawaii Convention in 1976, some members of the club urged official certification in the Lioness Clubs Program. The Waterford Lioness projects include a halfway house for alcoholics, donations toward construction of a community skating arena, assisting the local "White Cane Club" for the visually impaired, and helping their sponsoring Lions with the annual Bluegrass Music Festival.

On January 9, 1979, the Tochigi (Miyoka), Lioness club of District 33-B, Japan, became the 2,000th Lioness club certified in the program. This occurred just a little more than three years after the program began. By that time membership had grown to more than 50,000 in 54 nations.

Growth remained steady. In its first seven years, the Lioness Clubs program attracted 4,100 clubs with a membership of more than 103,000. Ten years after the first club was certified there were 5,362 Lioness clubs active in 92 countries. Total membership had reached 139,412.

I

In April 1980, the Lions Clubs International Board of Directors adopted a resolution permitting Lioness district and multiple district constitutions. Five years later, 62 Lioness districts had formed in ten countries representing 1,111 Lioness clubs and 24,792 Lionesses. Oregon formed the first Lioness multiple district. By 1985, it had 83 clubs in four districts with a membership of 2,158. In June 1985, Philippines Multiple District 301 was created from Lioness Districts 301-A1, B, C, and E.

To establish a Lioness district there must be at least 12 Lioness clubs in a Lions district and 75 percent of all Lioness clubs in the district must request formation of a Lioness district. The district cabinet of that Lions district may then approve formation of a corresponding Lioness district.

As of October 28, 1988, there were 5,863 Lioness clubs with more than 152,000 members in 101 countries, 79 Lioness districts, and four Lioness multiple districts.

At a meeting in Calgary, Alberta, Canada, in October 1987, the Lions Clubs International Board of Directors amended the standard Lioness Club Constitution to allow males to become Lionesses, thus making the Lioness clubs consistent with Lions clubs, which opened to women earlier in the year.

In 1976, Lioness Betty Schweiss of the Fox Lake, Illinois, Lioness Club was the first woman ever named a Melvin Jones Fellow by the Lions Clubs International Foundation. Her Lioness club made a $1,000 undesignated contribution to LCIF and asked that she be named a Melvin Jones Fellow. A past president of her club, Mrs. Schweiss had a lengthy background of effective service.

When he spoke to Lionesses of 4-C3 at their first Lioness district convention, Past International President Harry Aslan said, "You are one of the leaders, setting the pace for the other Lionesses to follow. We are impressed with your enthusiasm and dedication. Deep down, we always knew the ladies were important to Lions activities. So, in 1975, the Lioness Clubs program was born. Now, Lionesses are busy throughout the world, proud of their community spirit and compassion and the services they have to offer. We are proud of you, too, and your worldwide structure."

And a worldwide structure it has become. There seems to be a Lioness club everywhere, each supporting one or more imaginative projects.

In Milan, Italy, education for older people continues thanks to the Lionesses. They have helped people like Adriano, 84, now a local authority on the origins of opera, though he spent most of his life working as a machinist in a small factory outside of Milan. Adriano studies opera as a student at the University of the Third Age, a Lioness project that offers the elderly practical and cultural courses for mental growth. Instructors include 54 professors who give of their time and knowledge to an enrollment of 500 students. This fascinating educational experiment won a Top Ten service award in 1983–84 for the Milano (Duomo), Lioness Club and is enriching the lives of many older people.

The Jakarta (Shanti Sari), Lioness Club in Indonesia initiated another project for the elderly, a special ward built in the Jakarta Hospital compound. The club raised enough money to build the facility which includes three wards with 12 beds, a waiting room, kitchen facilities, and a medical examining room.

In Tanzania, a Lioness club is helping to fight a serious parasitic disease called bilharzia, which causes major epidemics from time to time in different parts of the country. The Dar Es Salaam Lioness Club implemented a program of testing for the parasite and provided medication for 2,000 Karume primary school children.

And in Singapore, the Lions and Lioness clubs of Kuching sponsored a Health Week. More than 10,000 people attended the event which featured health seminars, exhibitions, testing for diabetes, blood pressure readings, drug abuse information, vision screening, and first aid demonstrations along with health food suggestions and anti-smoking information.

II

A Lioness club is defined as a group of service-minded individuals sponsored by a Lions club for the purpose of providing service to the community while creating fellowship and mutual understanding within the club. Working with a Lions club, a Lioness club may co-sponsor a new Lioness club.

The Lioness Clubs program resulted from a desire of the Lions Clubs International Board of Directors to highlight the extensive and valuable contributions women make to the association and to expand their opportunities for community service.

Lioness clubs enjoy an extensive range of services from International Headquarters. Whatever the question, chances are it has been answered in readily available material. This includes new member kits, activity guides for service projects, publicity tips, aids for officers, suggestions for gaining and holding members, fund-raising tips, club supplies, and an international newsletter.

"Creative support" describes the relationship between a Lioness club and a Lions club. Since many members are the wives of Lions, the ties between the Lioness club and the Lions club are strong. Lioness clubs carry out innovative service activities they develop themselves. Energized by thoughtful cooperation, they enlarge the quantity and quality of services in their communities.

This dimension of Lioness participation, according to Joseph L. Wroblewski, president of Lions Clubs International in 1985–86 "is enhancing the image of Lionism in the community by providing a vehicle for women to become involved in service activities. These women are truly realizing the benefits, to themselves and to humanity, in uniting with us to promote association causes and I look forward to the humanitarian objectives of Lionism being pursued with even greater vigor because of the involvement of women dedicated to serving community and human needs."

Every Lioness club is sponsored by a Lions club. This strengthens the cooperative bonds. However, Lions sponsorship has a practical side as well. Legal responsibilities regarding tax returns and liability insurance are greatly helped for the women when the Lioness club operates as an extension of the Lions club. A Lioness club is organized and certified through the sponsorship of a Lions club and is considered a program of that Lions club. When a Lioness club is certified it receives a Certificate of Organization from Lions Clubs International. A Lioness club is not chartered.

To facilitate a direct channel of communications between the Lioness club and the Lions club, one Lions club member is appointed as liaison. The Lions club member is there to carry information and requests from one group to the other and be certain that the two clubs are working for common purposes. The Lion is also there to be ready to lend a helping hand.

However, it is not necessary for a Lioness to be related to a Lion.

"That's a good thing," smiled Lioness Messeret Woubshet. Unmarried, she lives in Addis Ababa, the capital of Ethiopia and became a Lioness in 1987. A graduate of St. Joseph's School in Nazareth, she speaks English and French in addition to her native language.

"I wanted to serve my community," she said. "I looked around at various ways I might do this and concluded that being a Lioness would accomplish most because they seemed to do a lot with a minimum amount of discussion. Our Lioness club was organized in 1986 and we have 20 members, most of whom are married to Lions."

She thought for a moment and then added, "Our club got into the construction business kind of by accident. We helped build a bridge and a school for orphans. About 50 of them attend the school where they live. The Lionesses pay for everything. The boys and girls go to school up to the sixth grade. Although I've only been a Lioness for a short time, it's helped me learn about the world. It has helped me grow as a human being and understand how I can help others."

Young women who have been Leo club members are able to continue their involvement with the Lions organization by joining a Lioness club. Now that women are becoming Lions that is yet another avenue for the female Leo to remain active in Lionism.

Although women often join a Lioness club because they are married to Lions, sometimes it works the other way around. Many times women have become Lionesses and inspired their husbands to become Lions. There is at least one Lioness club made up of women who are deaf and one composed of women who are blind. Truly international in scope, the Lioness Clubs program cuts across all boundaries around the world. Lionesses come from widely diverse backgrounds of culture, education, language and nationality. They are united by a profound desire to make the world better.

III

The synergism which results when Lions and Lionesses combine efforts has "made it possible for countless community needs to be met and increased the number of less fortunate people to be given the opportunity to lead healthful and fulfilling lives," echoes Past International President Bert Mason.

Joined in the family of Lionism, Lioness clubs dramatize the thoughts of Past International President Judge Brian Stevenson: "Building a happier world for our children to inherit is a goal we all share, because no matter in which part of the world we live—we live in it together."

Sometimes clubs do extensive research to determine which project will most benefit the community. For instance, in Malaysia, the Penang Lioness Club did a community analysis for a rural community of 20,000 people covering possible projects and decided that one of the most pressing social needs was help for children and old people dependent on others for care or financial support. The Ipoh, Malaysia, Lioness Club helped start the only drug treatment and rehabilitation center for women in the country.

Whatever the approach, it is individualized for that area of the world. In the People's Republic of Congo, the Brazzaville "Elika" Lisalisi Lioness Club gave 300 tsetse fly traps to the physician in charge of the Endemic Diseases Department of the local health services. The deadly bloodsucking fly is the cause of sleeping sickness and other trypanosome infections in human beings and animals.

Simple but cleverly-designed, the fly traps are constructed of a fabric covered oil lamp. The white, blue, and black colored lamps attract and destroy the flies.

In Zaire, the Likasi Lioness Club supports several institutions including a leprosy center, a center for the handicapped, a facility serving malnourished children, and clinics in distant rural areas. The club provides food, soap, medicines, clothing, brooms, buckets, and sewing machines . . . and gifts at Christmas.

Several years ago the Lioness club of Trang, Thailand, raised more than $2,500 by sponsoring a film showing, along with a concert by school children. Part of the money was used to finance education for needy youngsters. The rest was directed to building a pedestrian bus stop on a busy highway. Whatever the need, Lionesses transcend limitations and find a solution.

"I became a Lioness in 1980 because I saw that Lioness clubs spend much more time accomplishing things than talking about what to do," said Nieves M. Lingsangan, a member of City Metro Novaliches Lioness Club in Quezon City, Philippines. "We have six Lioness districts in the Philippines with 21 clubs and about 540 members in all. We work on joint projects with the Lions, in addition to our regular projects. One of our best activities is a feeding program for malnourished children. We've established four day care centers that opened in 1983. In these centers, trained workers attend to the children in the morning for working mothers.

"Our Lioness clubs are very active in providing medical care for those who can't afford it. That includes regular medical, dental, and eye examinations and supporting the eye banks. We have lady Lions in the Philippines now and I suspect that some of our Lionesses may become Lions. I've gained a great sense of fulfillment from the Lioness Clubs program. We expand as human beings and learn from other Lionesses around the world. We share in everyone's experience."

Concerned with the intrinsic worth of a human being of any age, the Canaan, New Hampshire, Lioness Club mounted a major attack on child abuse and neglect. The program began in 1986 and much of the motivation was provided by Anita M. Beloin, who was president of the club.

"We felt it was important to use existing sources. We didn't need to reinvent the wheel," said Lioness Beloin. "Our message was that we were concerned about this problem, that we were making efforts to establish, and in fact *would* establish, our own task force on child abuse and neglect."

Members were determined to make a positive impact on the problem. They began by giving out bumper stickers saying: "It shouldn't hurt to be a child." Using materials provided free by the New Hampshire Task Force on Child Abuse and Neglect they distributed informative literature on the problem. Each piece of literature was stamped: "Distributed by the Canaan Lioness Club."

The goal of the promotion was to hold a public meeting and then create a task force from those attending. They listed 90 key people they hoped would attend the meeting. These included doctors, nurses, state representatives, police, school officials, and social service workers. Members of the club made a personal phone call to each one, explaining the purpose of the task force.

"We wanted to educate the community about child abuse, increase awareness of it, and stimulate action to deal with it," one Lioness explained. "It turned out even better than we had hoped. Sixty people attended our meeting, including professionals in many fields. This sparked the first community task force in the state of New Hampshire to be chartered under and affiliated with the New Hampshire Task Force on Child Abuse and Neglect. The Enfield/Mascoma and Canaan Lioness clubs are members of the task force."

Starting with the spirited discussion in their public meeting, the Canaan Lioness Club created a ripple effect. As a result, the prevention of child abuse and neglect was adopted by New Hampshire's Lioness Districts 44-N and 44-H as a major project. Canaan, New Hampshire, incidentally, has a population of only 2,500 persons.

Since the start of the program, the focus has shifted to children between the ages of 9 and 16. It includes prevention of drug abuse and suicide as well as encouraging the formation of Leo clubs and building a diabetes camp with the Lions.

Both Lioness districts support the "Mile of Pennies" campaign devised by Cindy Hobbs of the Milford, New Hampshire, Lioness Club. Coffee cans wrapped with the project logo—two children, one with a black eye, and one smiling, with a link of pennies between them, are placed in public places to collect funds. It takes about 85,000 pennies to make a mile. Monies go for care of abused children. In District 44-N, with 100 percent of the clubs participating, they had already collected nearly two miles of pennies on the way to their goal of five miles, by mid-1988.

As a result of the experience of the Canaan Lioness Club, clubs in other parts of the world have been inspired to develop programs to fight child abuse. From California to Pakistan, from Peru to Japan, from Africa to the Arctic Circle, women are putting thought into action through a Lioness club. Good works are their best advertisement.

IV

Thirteen-year-old Mike of Big Lake, Alaska, has an almost insatiable interest in airplanes and wants to become an aeronautical engineer. According to his mother, he reads everything he can get his hands on about airplanes, from World War I Spads and Fokkers through World War II Thunderbolts and Lightnings right on up to the new Stealth bomber. He likes technical drawings, design details, and specifications.

Until 1986, Mike had a difficult time learning about airplanes because there was no public library in Big Lake. "I had already read everything in the school library about airplanes, and I didn't have any money to order books by mail or for magazine subscriptions."

To get some of the technical materials Mike wanted, his dad had to drive him 25 miles to another town for library service.

Since the Big Lake Community Library opened, Mike's life has changed radically. "I spent half of last Saturday in the library, just going through magazines on subjects I was interested in. And next to my bed are three unread new books on aeronautical science which the library got for me from larger technical libraries in the state."

Mike is not the only resident of Big Lake who is happy that Big Lake has its own library. In its first year after it opened, the library served more than 7,000 patrons.

There probably would still be no library in Big Lake if the Big Lake Lioness Club had not decided in 1982 that a healthy Lioness club backs long-term projects. The club surveyed the community and found that a majority of residents wanted a library.

Over the next four years, with the support of the Lions, the club raised two-thirds of the $15,000 needed to build the facility. They canvassed the community for materials and labor and gathered books. Lions excavated and built the library structure while the Lionesses sorted, repaired, and cataloged the books. Big Lake's library, unlike most, is not a public library supported by taxes. In every sense, it is a community library which operates on donations and volunteer help. What keeps the library going as a visible and needed community resource is the Big Lake Lioness Club.

"I'm going to work around airplanes one of these days," Mike says. "And I'm ready to give all of the credit to the Lionesses. They're great."

In California, the Martinez Lioness Club bought $30,000 worth of medical equipment including hospital beds, wheelchairs, walkers, commodes, trapezes, and crutches for its Hospital Equipment Lending Program (HELP). Residents can borrow the equipment free of charge. The club periodically runs publicity drives so that more and more people get to know about the program.

"I heard about the Lioness program from a friend of mine at church and I decided to join," said Lioness Cynthia Bailey of the San Fernando Lioness Club in Trinidad, West Indies. "Lionesses in Trinidad are well known for the good things they do and that's what attracted me. I've been a Lioness for two and a half years and have found a great deal of joy in being useful in my community. At this point in Trinidad we have 11 Lioness clubs and our club has 45 members. We do a lot of work with the poor and the needy and visit sick children in hospitals and take them toys. We raise money with barbecues, carnival dances, fashion shows, tea parties, and other activities of that kind. We've gotten some very effective service ideas from the *Lioness International Newsletter*. We learn from each other."

The Port Harcourt, Nigeria, Lioness Club raised $35,000 to build an oral rehydration treatment center for a local hospital which is designed to teach mothers living in rural areas how to fight malnutrition with soybean milk and inexpensively prepared soups.

In Taiwan, Republic of China, the Chiaya Lioness Club runs a sophisticated anti-drug educational program. The club designed and printed anti-drug abuse materials and distributes them wherever teens gather—in parks, at skating rinks, and in theaters. The club produced a film which moves from theater to theater where it is shown for a month at a time before moving on to the next theater.

In the 1970s, the Lioness club of Istanbul, Fatih, Turkey, instituted a program to aid juvenile offenders. In Turkey, juvenile offenders are generally imprisoned with adults and there are no probation officers.

"We visited a prison," said Lioness Secretary Nur Timurjan, "and obtained permission from the authorities to test the youngsters with the help of Lioness Gulsen Kozaci, a psychologist. We're trying to find ways to help these children live more productively and not return to delinquency. We're also helping them with their legal problems through our Lioness president who is a lawyer.

"We've bought them shirts, trousers, shoes, books, and snacks. We're trying to help those who are not lost. They're the most helpless in our country and no other club has been interested in doing anything for them."

According to prison authorities, the Istanbul (Fatih), Lioness Club is the first local group to ever recognize the acute needs of these young offenders and then deal with them. Lionesses write to prison officials urging them to separate young offenders from adults. They visit the youthful prisoners while they are in jail and help them find jobs or schooling after they are released.

V

Lionism puts words into action. During his term as international president, Joseph M. McLoughlin wrote: "I believe that activities on behalf of young people are among the most important in which Lioness clubs can participate. Children and young adults need our guidance, our assistance—our *care*. Peer group pressures and the numerous pitfalls presented by a complex society remain a constant hazard. Too many young lives are still blighted by poverty, ignorance, and disease."

Lionesses provide help for the helpless. They bring hope to those who have none. As with Lioness clubs in countless other nations, the Fatih Lionesses combined initiative and commitment to bring hope and help to those who had neither.

Age is no barrier. In Iola, Illinois, the Lioness club held a beauty contest for grandmothers in 1977. "There's always a young, pretty queen chosen to reign over Iola Appreciation Days," said Lioness Sam Shaw, "but honor should be given to others who also deserve it."

A grandchild or other relative was required to nominate the contestant, and to provide reasons for the nomination. "I'm nominating my grandmother because she put up with Grandpa for 49 years," wrote one grandchild. Grandmothers submitted a craft or performed in a talent show and were interviewed by the judges. The winner and runners-up received vigorous applause and the "Grandma Pageant" was the high point of the festival.

The Lioness club of West Ryde, New South Wales, Australia, in cooperation with the Lions club of West Ryde and the Leos, delivered a wheelchair bus worth $30,000 to the Royal Ryde Rehabilitation Hospital. The money was raised by the combined efforts of the Lions, Lionesses, and Leos of the area. Designed with a hydraulic lift, the new bus makes wheelchair accessibility far easier. Patients are more mobile and now enjoy outings, picnics, shows, and other activities.

Lionesses are everywhere. At the top of the world in Point Barrow, Alaska, they busily raise money for their projects with bingo games, fashion shows, pot luck suppers, bake sales, and carnivals. The northernmost point in the United States, Point Barrow is more than 400 miles north of the Arctic Circle. At 50 below zero Lionesses still find ways to help another human being, no matter how rugged the surroundings.

Appropriate technology blends with enthusiasm and vision and a young lady in Burnside, Australia, can "really talk with the world around her," for the first time.

Born with the Rh factor in her blood, Sandy had minimal coordination and little control of mouth and facial muscles, as well as other parts of her body. She never learned to speak.

"I used a black and white board with the alphabet grated on it," Sandy explained. "It was hard to use and drove people away from communicating with me."

One day Sandy's black and white board needed servicing. The service man realized the limitations the board imposed on Sandy. His thoughtful concern alerted the Burnside Lioness Club to Sandy's difficulty.

Now Sandy wears a Canon Communicator strapped to her wrist. Essentially a mini-typewriter, it acts as a mouthpiece for the delighted young woman. She types sentences that are printed on a tape and read by the person with whom she is speaking. Her isolation has ended.

Said Sandy, "When I was brought my beautiful new voice I couldn't believe, and still cannot, what a tremendous difference it has made— not only to my life but to the many people who now feel more at ease with me. It was so exciting to go into a shop and be able to ask for the things I wanted. My precious companion has opened so many doors for me. I hope others will be as fortunate as I in not being isolated anymore by muteness."

Ingenious fundraisers, members of the North Kamloops Lioness Club, British Columbia, Canada, invented a board game called "Game of Kamloops." They had 1,260 copies printed and sold more than 800 games to raise funds for the donation of two cutaneous oxygen monitors for the newborn intensive care unit at the Royal Inland Hospital. Income quickly outpaced their predictions. Members had expected to raise $20,000 for their project in the next five years. To their pleased amazement, they reached their goal in just over two years, and plans now include a "Game of Kamloops" tournament.

VI

More than 200 clubs participated in twinning during the first six years of the Lioness Clubs program. For the most part, these clubs twinned with one or two Lioness clubs in other nations. The Pontefract Lioness Club in England twinned with eight Lioness clubs in the United States and Canada. In Turkey, the Istanbul Lioness Club twinned with 15 Lioness clubs in six other countries. Members speak enthusiastically of the ways that twinning energizes the Lionistic objective of "creating a spirit of understanding among the peoples of the world." Said one Lioness from Atlanta, Georgia, "Twinning enables us to get to know Lionesses of various cultures and to understand each other better. We learn that we're all trying to accomplish the same things."

Invariably effective in their communities, sometimes Lionesses are literally life savers. The alertness of Lioness Saroj Ahluwalia, treasurer of the Lioness club of Dehra Dun, India, saved her village from a cholera epidemic. Recognizing three cases of cholera in the village of Badripur, she rushed them to a hospital for treatment. Then she and other members of her club notified the district magistrate who immediately sent medical technicians to vaccinate the villagers in Badripur. The members of the Lioness and Lions clubs provided support services for the medical teams.

The prompt intervention in Badripur would be no surprise to Jyoti Tharaney, a Lioness from Ajmer, India, District 323-E2. She has been a Lioness since 1982. Her husband, Prabhu, became a Lion in 1977.

"In India we have many medical projects," she said. "We sponsor medical checkup camps and eye camps and do extensive examinations for eye, ear, nose, and throat problems. We're also committed to improving education in our country. We raise money for schools. We supply books, supplies, and uniforms for students. In some cases we furnish food where it is needed. We also work with the handicapped by providing wheelchairs and other aids."

Lions-sponsored fairs are especially popular with children.

International Youth Exchange has proven successful in building global good will and understanding.

Throughout the world, Lions provide the necessities of life.

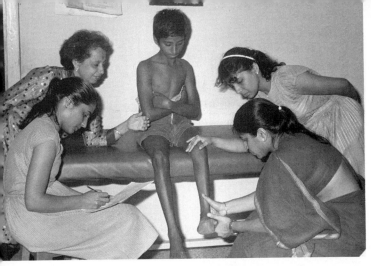

This Lioness club in India is one of hundreds around the world actively supporting medical facilities.

This Leo club in Portugal sponsored a radio program during which members spoke about Lionism and the activities of their club.

In Gdansk, Poland, Lions support a pre-school program for brain-damaged children.

Christmas parties for handicapped youngsters are popular annual activities.

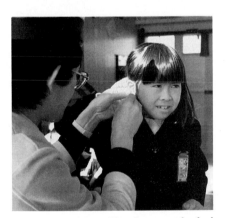

In Japan, a little girl has her ears checked at a Lions-sponsored screening.

In Ipswich, Queensland, Australia, Lions sponsor an outing for the disabled.

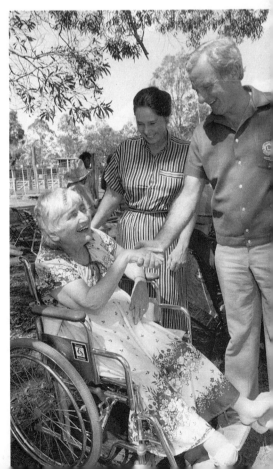

The pool table in a Lions-sponsored rehabilitation center in Calgary, Alberta, Canada, is a popular meeting place.

Lions clubs in many communities have purchased and donated modern operating room equipment for hospitals.

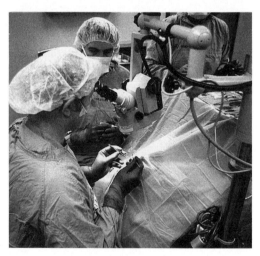

LCIF distributes millions of dollars each year. This facility, in India, was one of its early projects.

In Nairobi, Kenya, Mother Teresa accepts a check from Lions and Lionesses to support her humanitarian initiatives.

Very often, Lions will travel to local schools to instruct students in proper hygiene and dental care.

Constructing schools are ongoing activities among Hispanic Lions. This one, named after the association's founder, now offers quality education in Rafaela, Argentina.

Red Feather fundraising campaigns are popular among Scandinavian Lions.

The massed flags of the nations of Lions Clubs International lead an international convention parade.

Lions Day with the United Nations draws hundreds of Lions and Lionesses each year to U.N. Headquarters in New York City.

School teacher Christa McAuliffe, who was to perish in the Challenger space shuttle disaster, gives the thumbs up along with her children, in a Lions-sponsored parade in New Hampshire.

Environmental programs, such as planting trees, are popular among the Lions of Japan.

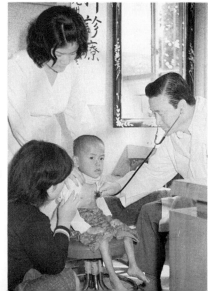

Free medical examinations for poor children were provided by this Korean Lions club.

These Lions help provide medical supplies in Mexico.

Mustafa Tahoukji, of Beirut, Lebanon, stands in United Nations Plaza proudly holding his grand prize winner in the first annual Lions International Peace Poster Contest in 1989. In the background is the sculpture "Non-Violence."

Indiana Lions have, for a number of years, driven caravans of donated ambulances, fire trucks, and other emergency vehicles to Lions in Guatemala for use in their communities.

Education is also a high priority item in the club Indu Sehgal belongs to. A Lioness since 1987, she is a member of Lioness Club Jalandar (Sewak), India. Her husband has been a Lion since 1970 and is a past president of the Jalandar (Sewak), Lions club.

"We go to downtrodden areas and look after some very poor schools," she explained. "We select the best students and if they have any health problems we see that they receive the proper treatment. We give the children textbooks, paper, pens, notebooks, and shoes and other clothing if they need it. Usually they do. We also work very hard on blood donation drives and eye examination camps."

Lionesses in India meet a broad range of needs. The Lioness club of Delhi East, India, for example, supplies woolen pullover sweaters for orphan children in their community. "We don't buy the sweaters," said one club member. "We make them with our own hands and feel that makes the gift something special."

The Mirzapur, India, Lioness Club created a children's library in a new school that had been established by the Lions. In addition, the Lionesses presented ten sets of crutches to youngsters enrolled in a school for crippled children.

In the Philippines, the Zamboanga City (Host), Lioness Club sponsored a free medical clinic for thousands of residents of a remote village. It provided free medical and dental treatment and also distributed milk, noodles, biscuits, and vegetables, and gave lectures on family planning.

Lionesses of Ferntree Gully, Australia, gave $100 to a drug rehabilitation center and another hundred to aid research into multiple sclerosis. In addition, club members purchased a piano for the enjoyment of residents of a home for senior citizens.

The Lioness club of Bandug Melati, Indonesia, sponsored a beauty care show for women which netted members enough funds to buy sheets for a local orphanage. The show featured the beauty makeovers of members of the audience.

Members of the Winner, South Dakota, Lioness Club were cooperative sponsors of a Health Day Clinic during which more than 200 persons participated.

Two dentists gave oral cancer checkups, a doctor screened for glaucoma, and a county nurse gave inoculations. Winner Lions also helped by running an eye screening booth. Eye donors were signed up and several eyesight and blood pressure problems were discovered in area citizens.

The Lioness club of Comilla, Bangladesh, gave a donation to its sponsoring Lions club to help pay costs of an eye operation and treatment camp. Each Lioness took an active role in making the camp a success. A total of 98 cataract patients underwent surgery and were supplied with eyeglasses.

VII

Teddy bears carry a message of hope and security to youngsters in northern California. The Santa Rosa Lioness Club voted to try this approach to help children cope with traumatic experiences. For boys and girls who have suffered child abuse, accidents, or shock, the little stuffed bears become warm friends in a crisis, friends the youngsters can love and trust.

The Santa Rosa Lionesses provide the teddy bears to the police and sheriff's department of Sonoma County. The individual policemen in turn give them to children they feel will benefit from a cuddly "friend."

The idea works beautifully. One of the first recipients was a little five-year-old boy who was struck by a car as he attempted to cross the street alone. He was lying frightened and in pain with a broken leg when a burly policeman approached and handed him Heart Throb, a little brown teddy bear with a big red heart embroidered on its chest.

"I don't think he thought much about the leg until the ambulance came," the officer said. "He just hugged that little bear as hard as he could."

Fran Weber, chairman of the teddy bear project, first took the idea to Captain James E. Kuskie of the Santa Rosa Police Department. Kuskie is in charge of the department's special services, which also investigates child abuse cases.

Kuskie was immediately intrigued. "I discussed the idea with the chief and we decided to take the Lionesses up on their generous offer and see what would happen." Though Kuskie, with his long experience with children, thought the idea would work, some of the patrol officers were a little leery of riding around with teddy bears in their patrol cars. "When the first shipment arrived," Kuskie recalled, "there was a lot of joking and wondering if I was serious."

When Detective Sergeant Mike Brown, in charge of the violent crimes division of the Sonoma County Sheriff's Department, first heard about Heart Throb, he too anticipated a lot of resistance from sheriff's deputies on patrol. But "the guys seem genuinely excited about it. I haven't heard a single negative comment."

While the two police organizations were trying out the teddy bear idea, the Lionesses wondered how many bears they would be called upon to produce. Initial results indicated that a lot of bears would be needed—more than even one very dedicated club could handle.

The word went out to other Gateway area Lioness clubs and the response was outstanding. The Coddington, Redwood Empire, Lazy L, Russian River, and Roaring 20s clubs donated enough money to buy the first 300 teddy bears which went to the police departments.

They did it by sponsoring a fundraising dinner that netted $3,600. An additional $2,000 was donated by the Dakin Company of San Francisco, the manufacturer of the teddy bears which sells them to the clubs at $4 apiece.

Kuskie said that the bear project got off to a quick start the very first night the bears were passed out to police officers. Two policemen responding to a report of a domestic dispute found a very frightened three-year-old boy watching his parents fighting over his custody. "You can imagine how fearful the boy was with his parents arguing and a uniformed policeman standing there with a gun. The officer was pleased to have the teddy bear at his disposal—and the mother was thankful because it turned out to be the child's first teddy bear."

The Sonoma County Lionesses have hit on a tremendously effective program in Heart Throb. It blends psychology, concern for the community, and the street smarts of an experienced police officer. After seeing Heart Throb in operation, Brown is unstinting in his praise. "It was Fran Weber who brought the project to our attention. She and the other Lionesses get all the credit as far as I'm concerned." Brown's sentiments are echoed by Kuskie: "With 20 years in this business, this program is one of the most positive I've ever seen."

Despite its proven value, law enforcement agencies cannot budget for the Heart Throb program themselves because it would be considered giving teddy bears to children with public funds. Both the Santa Rosa Police Department and the Sonoma County Sheriff's Department—as well as the highway patrol and fire departments who are also interested in the program—must depend on donations to keep the teddy bear program going.

Therefore, the Lionesses have assumed the heavy commitment of continuing to supply Heart Throb bears indefinitely.

VIII

"Lionesses quickly turn strangers into friends," said Jo Ann Veith. "When my husband and I moved up to Lake Wylie, South Carolina, from Florida in 1988, one of my new friends introduced me to the River Hills Lioness Club. We're a busy group and I found right away that it helped me to fit into the community and contribute in useful activities. The club was founded in June 1979, with 29 charter members and by October 1989, was up to 70. Action is the key.

"For instance, two years ago we received the Top Ten Lioness Club Service Award for amblyopia testing of pre-school children in our area. Our club is actively involved in the Leader Dog Program, Special Olympics, Hearing Dog Program for the Deaf, Camp for Diabetic Children, Teenagers Drug Abuse Retreat, The York County Literacy Association . . . and that's only part of it. I didn't know much about Lionesses until moving up here from Florida. However, now it's easy to understand why they continue to grow throughout the world. It dramatically expands a person's life and range of usefulness."

The future role of women in Lionism seems unlimited.

Past International Director Dr. Lawrence M. Newth expressed that future this way in an article in the June 1977 issue of *The Lion*.

"With the advent of the 21st Century, Lions worldwide can undoubtedly look forward to increased involvement on the part of women in the work of Lionism. Through their activities up to the present time, women have shown repeatedly that they have been and will continue to be a vital force in the global activities of the Lions movement.

"Decidedly, the role of women in Lionism, like the role of women in society, is one that will continue to expand as time progresses. Whether their involvement is work with the elderly, family counseling, health, agriculture or education, I am sure that these women will continue, as they have in the past, to prove themselves equal to the tasks ahead."

Lionesses everywhere, like those who conceived and support the teddy bear project in Sonoma County, have the heart and the will to make good things happen.

Energized by enduring principles, they create sweeping changes in all the lives they touch.

CHAPTER TEN

Leos Serve Around the World

LEO clubs attract talented, highly-motivated young people like Benita Fitzgerald-Brown. In 1978, she was elected president of the Gar-Field High School Leo Club in Dale City, Virginia.

Six years later, in the 1984 Olympics in Los Angeles she won a gold medal in the 100 meter hurdles. The first American to win this event in 52 years, her time of 12.84 was the second fastest in U.S. history. She set ten relay hurdle records in 1981, 1982, and 1983. In December 1983, she was ranked Number One in the United States and Number Ten in the world in hurdles. She is married to Laron Gregg Brown, who was a fellow student at the University of Tennessee.

Benita is an Honorary Member of the Dale City Lioness Club and in 1984 she was honored with the largest parade ever held in her community.

Leadership, Experience, Opportunity . . . put them all together and they spell LEO. Not all Leos are Olympic medalists, but they're *all* winners. Said one young woman, "Being a Leo teaches me things that life does not teach every day. The sense of service, for example." She is one of more than 100,000 Leos around the world. Nigel Packer is another.

"There was an old age pensioner," said Nigel Packer. "Her garden was a jungle. It hadn't been touched for years. So members of our Leo club got together with tools and the girls went inside and cleaned the house. Outside, the boys went to work cleaning up the garden, planted some flowers, dug the weeds out of the lawn and made it look like a lawn again. When the lady saw how nice everything looked she burst into tears."

A native of Swansea, Wales, 28-year-old Nigel Packer served as President of Leo Multiple District 105 during 1987-88. The district includes England, Scotland, Wales, Ireland, Jersey, Guernsey, and the Isle of Man. Multiple District 105 numbers more than 200 Leo clubs with nearly 5,000 members. He began helping his father with Lions clubs projects 20 years ago, and credits that with creating his interest in becoming a Leo.

"We're very successful with our fundraising and try to concentrate as much as possible on programs that really help those who need it," Nigel continued. "It's expanded my own life immensely. For instance, I was in Jersey for a holiday and I went to visit the Jersey Leo Club. They had a project for mentally and physically disabled people. I'd never worked with disabled people and had actually directed my own club projects away from them because they made me uneasy. Members of the Jersey club asked me to go with them. I spent three hours talking and playing with the children. I watched parapalegics disco dancing in wheelchairs. It changed my outlook completely. When I got home I got my own club active in working with the disabled.

"We do a lot of work with underprivileged youngsters in the area. There's one 10-year-old boy who lived no more than 10 miles from the ocean and had never been to the beach. He was one of a group we took there and for the first time in his life he felt sand running between his toes. One of our more successful projects is taking disadvantaged people from large cities and giving them a stay at the seaside for five to ten days. This project is worked out between clubs in the coastal areas and the inner city clubs."

Leo members of MD-105 perform about 700,000 hours of service work annually, Nigel Packer explained. Helping the visually handicapped and providing dog guides is the main project. Training a dog guide costs about $2,000. One member said, "There are so many dog guides named 'Leo' that it would be extremely confusing if they all got together at once."

"There's a great satisfaction in being a Leo; it expands a person's life immeasurably," Packer said. "We've had countless young men and women who join the club and they're shy and withdrawn. After a bit they begin to come out of themselves. They learn to speak in public. They take charge of activities. They become different human beings as a result of their experience. That's one reason the Leo program is developing so fast. It's very strong in Italy. The same in France. Finland is growing very well. In fact we have quite a good liaison between Finland and the United Kingdom.

"Leos help to make the world better. I'm reminded of a retired gentleman in his late 70s. He had been retired a long time and was alone. I didn't know him but was going around Swansea one Christmas with food parcels. I knocked at his door and asked if he would like to take the food parcel from the Swansea Leo Club. He excused himself and came back a moment later with his teeth. He asked how much he owed and I said it was a gift. He smiled and then invited me in. We sat and talked for over half an hour. Without us his Christmas would have been a tin of beans and some bread."

"Leoism changed me from a shy person concerned mostly about himself into someone who is interested in the rest of the world," Packer concluded. "It shows in many different aspects of my life. I'm more involved in my community, a better employee at work, and able to speak to 2,500 people, as I did at the last Multiple District Convention. When I first joined I couldn't talk in front of 50, let alone 2,500. We give and we grow."

The first Leo club was founded in 1957 by the Glenside, Pennsylvania, Lions Club. The program began as the Abington High School Leo Club. Co-founders Bill Ernst and James Graver and the other members of the Glenside Lions Club were looking for practical ways to introduce young people to service. The first Leo club was made up of members of the high school's baseball team, which was coached by James Graver. There were 26 members.

The Abington High School Leo Club began with four objectives:

- To serve the school by cooperating with the administration and faculty in the development of students for leadership, scholastic achievement, individual responsibility, honesty, and respect for others.

- To serve the community by responding to the needs of others.
- To serve the nation by promoting the ideals of democracy and the principles of good government and citizenship.
- To unite the members in bonds of friendship, fellowship, and mutual understanding.

From its 1957 beginning in Glenside, Pennsylvania, the Leo Program and its purposes have expanded on every continent. By the end of 1990, Leo clubs numbered 4,422 throughout the world with well over 110,000 members. India led with 750 clubs, the United States ranked second with 543, Brazil third with 258, followed by Japan with 235, and Italy with 202. With their global view of responsibility and service, Leo clubs change lives on every continent.

"In Jamaica, the Leos are active in giving vision tests, glaucoma screening, and working with the disabled," said Patsy Henry, a member of the Spanishtown Leo Club in St. Catherine, Jamaica. "We learn sign language so we can communicate with the speech and hearing impaired. We teach them mathematics, English language, sewing, and cooking. We also hold a Special Olympics for handicapped youngsters."

Twenty-four years old, Patsy Henry has been a Leo for three years. Her club has 15 members and is one of 18 Leo clubs in Jamaica. Average club size is 20 to 25, with one club of 46 members.

"We're working very hard to battle drug use in our area. We're active in schools, not only high schools but grammar schools and working with the four, five, and six year olds. We go to schools with little tots and tell them, 'Say no to drugs.' They draw pictures about it and then take this message home to their parents. We try to be consistent so at our Leo functions nobody smokes or uses alcohol. Being a Leo has made me a better human being. I thank God for making it possible for me to touch someone."

Does Patsy Henry plan to become a Lion when she grows too old for her Leo club? "No," she smiled, "I'm going to be a Lioness."

Concerned with the physical environment, Leos have planted thousands of trees in areas where soil conservation is crucial. Concerned with the moral environment, Leos sponsor lectures on drug identification, drug addiction, and the parents' role in preventing drug abuse. With films, exhibitions, speeches, workshops, poster contests, seminars, and public discussion, they increase public awareness of the problem and its solution.

The majority of Leo activities take place in their own communities. Members of the Leo Club of Pantnagar, India, worked four hours a day for two months distributing textbooks to needy students. More than 800 young men and women were provided with books at only 15 percent of the original price.

In England, the Halesworth Leo Club raised enough money through a disco to buy four mobile oxygen tanks for a local clinic. Club members helped an elderly woman in the town to beautify her home. They cut the grass, dug the garden, trimmed trees and hedges and then removed trash that had piled up around the house. "These wonderful young people made my home look like it did when I was younger," she exclaimed.

High-flying members of the Blackburn Leo Club in England parachuted from a plane to raise several hundred dollars for their club's service program. Five Leos jumped from an altitude of 3,000 feet and all landed unscathed.

Hot dogs raised $3,700 for the Rio de Janeiro, Brazil, Leo Club which took part in a Providence Fair. "I didn't realize people liked hot dogs that much," said one young lady who worked in the booth. "We'll be able to use the money for several different projects we sponsor."

In Bangladesh, the first Leo club was formed in 1973 by Lion Abdul Jabbar Khan. By 1988 this had grown to 88 Leo clubs with some 5,000 members.

Twenty-five-year-old Saiful Bari Khan, a Leo for six years, was president of Leo District Council 315-A in 1988–89. A graduate of the University of Bangladesh, he is working toward a master's degree in political science.

"I was looking for some way to help the people in my country," he said, "and a friend asked me to join the Leos. He said that I could learn something about leadership and serving the needs of my fellow men and women. My friend was right. There are more than 100 million people in Bangladesh and there's plenty to do to make life better for them.

"We raise money and make sure it goes to work where it's needed. For instance, we saw that a farmer who had been using his cow and plow to cultivate other people's land had been put nearly out of business because his cow died and he couldn't afford another one. He and his son began to play the role of the cow and pull the plow themselves. We saw this in the newspaper and contributed some money for another cow and then presented it to the farmer. I've never seen a more grateful human being when he saw the cow and realized it was a gift for him.

"More than 75 Leos became eye donors. We have a large eye hospital in Bangladesh and the number one eye specialist is a past district governor of Lions Clubs International. The death rate of children in our country is very high and we sponsor immunization programs against polio, along with general vaccination programs and dental camps.

A serious, thoughtful young man, Saiful Bari Kahn continued, "We had a big flood in Bangladesh a few months ago and during this time there was no food. Mothers sometimes could feed their children, but had no food for themselves. We'd find out about that and take food to the mothers, and anything else they needed. Our Leo district slogan is 'Drug Free Society' and we've been making a major effort in the fight against drug addiction. It's an ongoing activity with us and we can see progress, even though it's slow. Whether it's food for flood victims, buying a cow for a farmer, or donating corneas, we keep busy."

The Abington High School Leo Club chartering ceremony was held on December 5, 1957. The first president was William J. Graver, son of co-founder James Graver and now the son-in-law of Bill Ernst, the other co-founder. It is probable that none of the participants foresaw a day when there would be Leo clubs flourishing in more than 100 nations with new clubs organized at the rate of 40 a month.

The second Leo club, the Tamaqua, Pennsylvania, Leo Club was not organized until 1963. The Abington Leo Club presented a banner as a gift to the Tamaqua Leos.

Led by District Governor Clarence Templeton in 1964, the District 14-K Lions joined with the Glenside Lions and created Leo Clubs, Inc., of Pennsylvania. The Leo Program was made an official District 14-K project. Momentum grew as a number of other Leo clubs sprang up in larger high schools in the area. The publicity generated lively interest in other districts in the state and Leo clubs were organized throughout Pennsylvania.

As awareness grew of the program's accomplishments, the Leo Club idea spread rapidly. In the spring of 1967, Leo Clubs, Inc., held the first statewide Leo Clubs Convention. Lions who learned of the program returned home enthusiastic about the possibility of carrying the Lions service message to young people.

In the first 10 years of Leo clubs the concept grew steadily in effectiveness and popularity. In 1967 the Youth Committee of Lions Clubs International studied the possibilities of developing a Youth Club Program that would operate in conjunction with The International Association of Lions Clubs. At the October 1967 meeting of the International Board of Directors the members voted to implement the Leo Club Program.

By October 1968, 200 Leo clubs had been organized. By October 1969, there were 918 clubs in 48 countries. By 1974, there were 2,000 clubs, with 50,000 Leos hard at work in 68 countries. Today there are clubs in over 100 countries. Leo clubs continue to expand because they fill a need.

Club Twinning is a popular Leo activity. Members of Leo clubs correspond with each other and share their experiences with different kinds of projects. Sometimes members of Twinning Clubs visit each other in exchanges to learn first hand about the other's country.

Leos may form district and multiple district organizations. To form a Leo district there must be at least six certified Leo clubs within the Lions district. This also requires the approval of the district governor. When 10 certified Leo clubs, consisting of 100 members, are organized within a Lions multiple district, a Leo multiple distict may be formed with the approval of the council of governors or the multiple district. As of January 1989, there were 161 Leo districts and 21 Leo multiple districts that conducted conferences and other large-scale activities.

In 1986, International President Joseph L. Wroblewski observed, "Lions clubs sponsoring Leo clubs are united in their praise of the young people for their zeal and their commitment to pursuing an objective to its successful conclusion. They are tomorrow's leaders, and through their association with the sponsoring Lions, they are learning how to plan and conduct projects and realize the critical role volunteers play in the community.

"Together, Leos are giving evidence to the residents of their communities how young people, properly motivated, can channel their energy and enthusiasm to positive ends. They are demonstrating the importance of getting young people involved in community service, for once they come to understand and appreciate how much their time and skills are needed they will definitely be more inclined to become involved in voluntary service when they reach adulthood. The success of our Leo Club Program shows how responsible young people can be and how rewarding it is for Lions to be associated with them."

Leos make notable contributions in money and dedication. The Leo Club of San Fernando, Trinidad, took part in a food collection and distribution program called "Can It." They collected more than $12,000 worth of food and distributed it to needy families, homes for the aged and handicapped, and to a halfway house for women.

In Louisiana, the Avondale Leo Club donated more than $6,700 to various community organizations in a 12-week period. During that time club members donated a total of 244 volunteer hours of service activities.

The New Iberia Senior High Leo Club in Louisiana rocked to a profit. The club's annual Rockathon raised nearly $1,400 as members rocked in rocking chairs for 24 hours straight.

The Phytolacca-Monte Castro, Argentina, Leo Club contributed a total of $4,850 raised through an intensive fund-raising program. The money was directed to the Eye Bank Foundation, to toys for the Vocational Training School for the Deaf, the Argentine Home Foundation, and a geriatric institute.

Handicapped youngsters in Turkey enjoy their lives more because of the Kocaeli (Golcuk) Leo Club. The Leos helped furnish and decorate a room in a special home for handicapped children to make living conditions more attractive. In addition, they bought a variety of toys, including 30 bicycles and various games and some clothes for the boys and girls.

A Leo club may be associated with a school or be based in the community. Supervision of a school-affiliated Leo club by the sponsoring Lions club is carried out in cooperation with school authorities. Lions club guidance is exercised under the same regulations provided by the school for its other student organizations and activities.

A brochure published by Lions Clubs International titled, "Introduce Young People To Service—Sponsor a Leo Club," spells out the relationship between the Lions club and the Leo club.

"The Lions club has the responsibility of providing proper guidance and counsel to its Leo club and working with it closely to insure that it operates within the policies of Lions Clubs International.

"Because a Leo club is an activity of the Lions club, time, energy and dedication on the part of the Lion sponsors are essential to the vitality and long term success of the Leo club. Leos will have their own club officers and their own constitution. They will be responsible for planning and implementing their activities, financing their projects and maintaining the smooth operation of the club.

"A dedicated Lion or Lioness able to communicate with young people should be appointed as the Leo Club Advisor. The advisor offers constructive suggestions to the Leos, reports on their activities to the Lions club and helps promote cooperative working and social relationships between the two."

Membership is open to any male or female of good moral character between the ages of 14 and 28. There are two membership divisions: Alpha (or regular) members age 14 to 17 and Omega (or senior) members age 18 to 28. A Leo club may be made up of either or both age classifications, depending on local preference.

"I am a Leo because I intend to become a Lion, like my father," said one young man. "And, of course, having been a Leo, I'll be a more experienced Lion."

On the other hand, many Leos do not have parents who are members of Lions Clubs International.

Leos operate in the real world. They solve problems with courage and imagination. In Peru, the Leos in Tingo Maria are battling the drug scourge. A relatively small town of 25,000 persons on the edge of the jungle, Tingo Maria has a Leo club with between 20 and 25 girls and boys as members.

"Most of the Leos are young people around 16 or 17," explained a Lion from Lima. "They are very effective in programs opposing drug abuse. That includes drug education. That's a tough, dangerous job because there are many drug dealers and terrorists in that area. However, these Leos are fearless and are working tirelessly to combat the drug epidemic. They don't seem to be having any problems with the drug dealers or the terrorists.

"District T-3 in Chile also has a very strong and active Leo district. They work very closely with the Lions because Lionism is very active in

Chile. In Chile most of the Leo Clubs, especially the big ones, have clubhouses in which they also perform such activities as helping people with dental services, medicines, glaucoma screening, providing eye-glasses, and other health aids."

In District 306-B, in Sri Lanka, 12 Leo clubs cooperated to develop milk-feeding centers for undernourished children and a regular feeding program for 200 adults. The members sponsored a Leo Light Camp for 100 mentally and physically handicapped boys and girls. They are active in cleaning, painting, and decorating local hospitals. In addition, they promote seminars aimed at preventing crime and juvenile delinquency.

Jumping up and down to raise money, the Leo Club of Salisbury, Zimbabwe, sponsored a trampoline marathon, along with a copper collection and a "junk" sale. In a special presentation attended by the government's Minister of Home Affairs, a club representative presented checks for $100 each to a home for war victims, a suicide prevention center, a children's group, a facility for handicapped children, and a final check for animal protection.

Members of the Ernst-August, Germany, Leo Club are engaged in an on-going project of painting and renovating a local home for autistic children. The Leos continue their project 12 months a year and their persistent painting and decorating have created a cheerier and more homelike atmosphere for the residents. Their sponsoring Lions Club, Hanover-Tiergarten, supplies the Leos with funds for paint and other materials. The Leos plan to raise their own money with a series of fund-raisers.

The Chembur, India, Leo Club provided free vision screening for 7,000 school children. Members distributed slates, writing materials, and candy to children in a home for orphans.

In Trinidad, a man enjoys health and vigor furnished by the Port of Spain Leo Club. The Leos raised and contributed $2,000 to help buy a pacemaker for the man who had undergone heart surgery.

In Australia, the Leo Program has grown to 130 clubs averaging 20 to 25 members in each, with some clubs boasting memberships of 35 and more. One of the projects is an elderly citizen's house. An average of 30 elderly men and women occupy the accommodation center. At least one Sunday a month the Leos take them on a bus trip around Melbourne and arrange entertainment for them.

"We work hard at what we consider worthwhile activities," said

Andrew Wyllie, a Leo from Melbourne. He was discussing the Australian Leo Program while attending the Lions Clubs International Convention in Denver, Colorado, in July 1988.

"Another of our projects is a camp down in Victoria. It's run professionally with a camp manager, cooks, cleaners, and so forth. We raise money with raffles, picture nights, bus trips, and all kinds of things. We have bush dances which are quite successful. A bush dance is an Australian version of a barn dance and we have lots of fun with them. Our Leos are hard workers and we don't have any trouble raising money for our activities."

Even though Leo clubs are found in more than 100 countries and are increasing at the rate of about 500 a year, the program still has a recognition problem in some areas. Nevertheless, Leos everywhere blend energy and imagination to increase general awareness.

"In Jamaica," Patsy Henry said, "we've done massive campaigning to make people more conscious of our Leo clubs in Jamaica. It used to be when you said to somebody, 'I'm a Leo,' they would answer, 'Well, I'm a Virgo, or a Taurus.' We'd say, 'No, ours is a leadership experience and program of service.' Generally, when you tell them it's part of Lions Clubs International they immediately know what it is. To counteract this we've been on TV, radio, and in the newspapers a great deal in the past several years. The media exposure has dramatically increased understanding of Leoism."

"We've had a similar problem in Australia," said Andrew Wyllie. "My father is a Lion and after going to a few meetings with him I got interested in becoming a Leo. I hope to be a Lion when I get a bit older because this is certainly a good foundation for that. Surprisingly, at least it's surprising to me, we find that a lot of Lions aren't familiar with the Leo Program. I can go and talk to a Lions Club about Leo activities and many Lions there don't know what the Leo movement is. We're trying to change that condition."

Avoiding the temptation for narrow specialization, Leo Clubs move with bold steps into a broad range of human services. With keen eyes and sensitive hearts, Leos devise potent answers for those in need.

During disasters they furnish money, blankets, clothes, food, shelter, and comfort to victims of earthquakes, floods, fires, and other tragedies. Leos administer tests for diabetes, buy artificial limbs, find organ donors, and test for hypertension. Clubs may spend days picking up litter from parks and beaches. They may collect books and establish libraries.

Leos help those who need a hand: orphans, underprivileged children, the elderly. Leos sponsor picnics, holiday parties, campouts, sightseeing trips. Again for older citizens, Leos organize lunches, entertainment, and outings for residents of nursing and retirement homes. They serve in nearly every corner of the world.

In Germany, members of the Kiel Leo Club donated a control monitor to a local children's hospital. The control monitor alerts hospital personnel when a child is not breathing properly. Club members raised money to buy the monitor by selling firewood and organizing a refreshment stand during a week-long community celebration. The hospital matched funds the Leos collected to buy the device.

Another medical need was met when the Torrington Leo Club of Connecticut raised $2,000 by selling sandwiches. They manned a sandwich booth for three 12-hour days at a major Connecticut fair. Proceeds from the sale were used to buy a Life Pak 4 Unit. Installed in the emergency room of the Charlotte Hungerford Hospital, the portable cardiac defibrilator is used mainly for heart attacks. Speed is essential in these emergency cases. If left untreated after four to six minutes, cardiac arrest will cause brain damage and after that time is usually fatal.

Members of the Canelon, Chico, Uruguay, Leo Club reported that an eye screening of 553 school children found that a total of 29 of them suffered from serious visual defects. These Leos sponsored a football game in which strong legs ran to raise money to buy a pair of artificial legs for a youngster whose parents could not afford to buy them. Working with their sponsoring Lions Club, the Leos built a bus shelter for children at a local school.

In 1970, International President W. R. Bryan wrote, "For years, a rutted and often muddy path served the people in a small island village near Hong Kong. Today, 120 feet of pavement has replaced the ancient road. A group of boys from Hong Kong recently spent hours of their free time mixing and pouring cement for the path; their only reward— realization that they had accomplished something worthwhile for others in need. These young men are Leos. Their action typifies the community spirit that guides the worldwide Leo club movement of our association."

More than 100,000 Leos have fun while they serve. The Leo Club of Gauhati Girls in India presented a check for 1,000 rupees to a female Leo so she could go to England and take part in the "World Arm Wrestling" championships held in London. Obviously no weakling, she won third prize. The club is sponsored by the Lions Club of Gauhati, District 322-D. Versatile in their activities, the Gauhati Girls raised money for baby food, took part in a drug awareness seminar, helped support an eye camp, distributed food, toys, and clothes to a children's home, and took part with Lions and Lionesses in a blood donation drive at the Gauhati Medical College.

Young men and women become Leos so they can improve the quality of life for others. Said Joseph Perez, president of the Rouen, Beffroy, Leo Club in France, "I really found out what Lionism is, and I'm glad to be a Leo member today. I think there is a need to give young people of our world a chance to understand each other. Leo clubs are also a good way to create peace."

Eleven-year-old Cindy Evans had a short life but it was better because of the love and compassion of the Leo Club in Noble Park, Australia.

Cindy had cystic fibrosis. A hereditary disease, cystic fibrosis attacks the digestive system and lungs. It is characterized by the production of a thick mucus that obstructs the pancreatic ducts and bronchi. It leads to infection and development of excess fibrous connective tissue. Cindy's mother was plagued with severe financial problems because of the medical and hospital bills.

In August 1987, Lion George Carlton attended a meeting of the Noble Park Leos and explained Cindy's situation. Her brother had died of cystic fibrosis 14 months before. The Leos were unanimous in their decision to help, and help began immediately.

In *Leo World*, the Leo newsletter, Leo Sharon Hawley explained how it went:

"On August 11th, Cindy had her 11th birthday so we decided to take her out and since Red Rooster was her favorite, there's where we went. All of us met Cindy for the first time and didn't quite know what to expect. Was she going to be in pain? How would we treat her? What would we say? All of us had our questions, yet when we finally met her we found our questions useless. Cindy walked in and we had to smile. Obviously, she wasn't the healthiest of children, but she was the bravest little girl I ever met. Delighted by all of her presents, she smiled all night.

"From that day on we kept a close watch on her and through the Lions we helped in any way possible. Cindy had a few wishes in life and one of them was to see 'Dreamworld.' The Noble Park Lions made that possible.

"Before I heard of Cindy I was completely ignorant of such a disease as cystic fibrosis let alone able to pronounce it. So, as my interest grew I decided to study it. Through my research I found out just how brave that little girl really was. The information I gathered showed the pain and suffering she must have gone through and from understanding that you would have to salute her mother and everyone else who deals with this and other diseases through life.

"Eleven-year-old Cindy passed away on April 4th. To us it seemed so sudden and such a waste, but for Cindy it was over. She was now, for the first time, able to rest in peace, never to know such pain again.

"The funeral service was held on April 7th. Many people loved her, even those who came into contact with her just once or twice. It makes you really take a good look at life and realize just how lucky you are. Five of us at Noble Park Leos joined the Lions to say a sad farewell to Cindy Evans, the bravest little girl to enter my life."

In one of their major, and most important stands, Leos are in the forefront of battling drugs. Cutting through every strata of society and striking everywhere in the world, drugs are a cancer threatening disaster for millions.

Enrique Triminol is past district governor of District F-3 in Colombia. "The Leos have accomplished a great deal in my country. They held a conference against drug use that has dramatized the situation and energized the community to deal with it. Another positive point is their stand against smoking. They have a slogan: 'No thanks, I prefer to live.' The drug problem remains pervasive in Colombia and we Lions appreciate the effective methods the Leos are using to oppose it."

Triminol continued, "We have approximately 400 Leo members in Colombia and their ages range from 14 to 21. About half of the members are male and half are female. The Leo clubs started in Colombia around 1970. The most recent club organized in Bogota is made up mostly of members who are not children of Lions. They are young people from universities who have been influenced by the Leos and they liked what they saw. They wanted to participate in the same projects. Because of what the Leos are doing and their good example, they wanted to be part of it. They raise money in all kinds of ways, with beauty contests, festivals, dances, they may gather old newspapers to be sold, they may have raffles. We even have Little Leo Clubs with children ages five to eight. These youngsters raise money by dancing or other little projects and they buy toys for children during Christmastime. They may make little pillows, or buy pencils and books for public schools. Later on when they reach the age, they can become Leos officially. Mothers or members' wives supervise the youngsters."

At an International Leo Club forum in 1983 Leos from all over the world attended and were asked what being a Leo meant to them. They came from many different countries and spoke many different languages and took turns talking to the group. Each of them had good reasons for saying why he or she was a member. But it was one young man who, through an interpreter, gave a reason that all of the gathering understood immediately as their own. "I became a Leo," he said, "because Leos are the friends of people who otherwise might have no friends." Unselfish and unstinting in their commitment to helping others, Leos all over the world work to help those less fortunate.

The pledge composed by a Leo club in India describes reasons for becoming a Leo in words that translate beautifully in every language.

> *I pledge of my hands*
> *Extended and open,*
> *To help those in need.*
> *I pledge of my heart,*
> *Reach for it and it will be touched.*
> *I pledge of my ears*
> *To hear another's outcry;*
> *My eyes to see*
> *The plight of others;*
> *My knowledge to bring a man*
> *Closer to his dreams.*
> *I pledge of myself*
> *For the betterment*
> *Of my community, my state and my country.*

During his term as international president, Harry J. Aslan spoke of the development of leadership qualities and experience among Leos. President Aslan said, "It may very well be that 15 or 20 years from now these Leos will be our legislators, mayors, business and industrial executives, school and hospital administrators, and other governmental and civic leaders. The training they received in their Leo clubs will help them make rational judgments and decisions. Being Leos has given them the opportunity to learn sensible values about those most important qualities of life—decency, honesty, and respect for others. Their membership in Leo clubs provided this opportunity to become good and useful citizens. They learned to enrich their own lives through community service and aid to the less fortunate."

In 1984, Constantiaberg Leo Club members in South Africa collected more than 11,000 sweaters and jerseys during a week-long period. Eighty schools, ten libraries, and ten supermarkets had collection boxes where the clothing was gathered. "Jersey Week" was publicized with posters and strong support from free radio, television, and newspaper advertising. The Leos began with a kickoff celebration that attracted a large gathering of Lions and media representatives who helped with the proceedings.

Strong school support contributed to the project's success. The Leos presented a trophy to the school that collected the most jerseys. Leos donated the sweaters and jerseys to child welfare organizations, senior citizen centers, and needy families in the area.

Members of the Kingston, Nova Scotia, Canada, Leo Club donated $700 to the New Kingston Skating Rink to finish a dressing room. In addition, the Leos brightened up the arena by painting the grandstands and another dressing room.

The Lethbridge Community College Leo Club in Alberta, Canada, raised $800 for the Canadian Suicide Prevention Foundation.

The Leo Club of Siliguri Greater, India, organized six free surgical camps that attracted thousands of participants. As a result of their efforts, physicians treated 897 people and performed 260 operations.

In May 1987, International President Sten A. Akestam wrote in *The Lion*, "Leo Clubs demonstrate to youth the necessity for citizens to volunteer their time and talent on behalf of their communities. Leo membership teaches them how to exercise leadership abilities and how to work with others to plan, coordinate and conduct service projects. It also instills in them something else—the knowledge that they belong to an *international* organization, that they are part of an *international* youth movement of over 107,500 members, one that is recognized and respected in 103 nations. Leos are bringing both quality to life in the communities in which they are active and quality into their own lives because the spirit of humanitarian service is a quality which will last a lifetime."

Leos understand that young people who lack awareness of the past and a vision of the future are likely to live in an impoverished present.

To improve the quality of lives everywhere, Leos generate long-term solutions for deep-seated problems around the world. Improving literacy is one of these objectives.

This became the target in June 1988, when the International Board of Directors authorized a new Leo project. While promoting the teaching of reading and writing, the new program aims at much more. To that basic objective, the project adds a new dimension: cultural literacy—the understanding of one's time and environment.

The goals of the "Literacy and Culture" project combine a dual vision: 1) To promote reading and writing skills; and, 2) To create increased cultural awareness, international understanding, and an informed public.

Tailored to global needs, the program will provide young people everywhere with expanded knowledge of the great traditions of philosophy and literature of their own cultures. Designed to create enlightened human beings in all parts of the world, it will create greater appreciation of the important points of individual cultural heritages.

The program was designed in two phases.

In the first phase, the United Nations provided information to help pinpoint literacy levels around the world, and supplied sample materials used for teaching, reading, and writing, particularly in developing countries.

In the second phase, a letter outlining the Literacy and Culture Project and its goals was sent to all Leo clubs. Clubs were asked for information on literacy programs already being conducted in each club's area by either private or governmental organizations. The letter also asked the clubs if they could use materials or funds to either develop new programs to meet local needs or to take part in existing programs to make them more effective.

Clubs are encouraged to solicit help from professionals where the needs outstrip the club's capacities. However, members are asked to remain assistants.

Leos are urged to organize exhibitions and workshops designed to promote literature as well as conferences and seminars devoted to cultural activities. Theater presentations, motion picture screenings, and musical programs are suggested as activities to promote cultural literacy.

To motivate the clubs, an annual competition has been developed. The first competition began in the 1988–89 fiscal year. Leo clubs selected as prize recipients must use the money to develop a new project in their area or to enhance existing literary or cultural projects. Project reports are reviewed and weighed by the Youth Programs Committee at the June board meeting using specific literacy and cultural criteria. The committee then recommends projects to the board for approval.

Activities that Leos may support in connection with the literacy and culture program are extensive:

- Book collection and distribution.
- Teaching or tutoring students in accordance with local regulations.
- Conducting fundraisers to buy books and materials for schools or students.
- Offering scholarships and grants as incentives to area students, with the help of local businesses and schools.
- Sponsoring concerts to raise money for literacy projects.
- Corresponding with or meeting with clubs in Club Twinning to exchange ideas, materials, and culture.
- Teaching basic job and work skills to the functionally illiterate and then helping them find employment.
- Working with literacy organizations and foundations in common efforts to promote literacy.

- Sponsoring Braille sections in local libraries and providing Braille literature for this purpose.
- Improving library environments by cleaning desks, books, and study areas, painting walls and replacing light bulbs.

In the preface to his book, *Cultural Literacy*, E. D. Hirsch, Jr., wrote, "To be culturally literate is to possess the basic information needed to thrive in the modern world. The breadth of that information is great, extending over the major domains of human activity from sports to science. It is by no means confined to 'culture' narrowly understood as an acquaintance with the arts. Nor is it confined to one social class. Quite the contrary. Cultural literacy constitutes the only sure avenue of opportunity for disadvantaged children, the only reliable way of combating the social determinism that now condemns them to remain in the same social and educational condition as their parents."

The new Leo program, ambitious and well thought out, aims at enabling young people everywhere in the world to profit from the treasures of their own cultures. Designed with an international perspective it provides precise suggestions and directions for success.

Leos are enthusiastic about the results. One 19-year-old Finnish woman said, "As we learn more about our heritage I see an increase in pride in our country's history. Our nation's background is a source of cultural wealth many of us hadn't paid much attention to until we began this project."

Leo clubs assure that Lionism's enduring message will have an ever-growing impact. Wrote Austin P. Jennings, past international president: "I am certain all of us realize fully the immeasurable value of our Leo Club program in molding young men and women to accept the responsibilities of good citizenship and to understand the prominent place volunteerism has in the community. Across the earth, Leos are providing assistance to people in need and initiating other community services, thus enhancing the image of our proud emblem. The success of this program is undeniable evidence that young people want to be involved in meaningful activities and are more than willing to accept the guidance and advice provided by their sponsoring Lions. Remember always, that the enthusiasm they develop for voluntary service—for the principles of Lionism—will be with them all their lives."

True literacy opens lives to profound knowledge and economic success and also to other people and other cultures. As Leos implement their sense of service through major projects like Literacy and Culture they enrich the association's tradition. In more than 100 nations around the world Leos make essential contributions to more effective lives.

Lavishing time, energy, and compassion in an elaborate chain of service, they systematically transcend limitations by recognizing the intrinsic worth of each human being.

CHAPTER ELEVEN

Social Services

I

DRUG AWARENESS

Caravans of horses and donkeys wind slowly through the Burma hill country to destinations in Laos and along the border with Thailand. The objective: a dozen or so refineries in Laos and along the Thailand-Burma border. The cargo is deadly. It brings immeasurable wealth to a few and addiction, degradation, and death to countless others. Here in Southeast Asia's Golden Triangle, a remote mountainous area where Burma, Thailand, and Laos meet, is manufactured the potent heroin that hits the streets in major cities in the United States and Europe. It's called "China white."

A batch of opium that costs $170 in northern Burma is worth, after inexpensive processing and dilution, $2 million as heroin in Western cities.

Cocaine begins as coca leaves in Bolivia and Peru. These are refined into coca paste in primitive laboratories. The paste is flown to secret labs in Colombia and processed first into what is called coca base, then into cocaine hydrochloride, the pure white powder that is smuggled into the countries in which it is used. Wholesalers dilute it with an inert substance before passing it on to street dealers who cut it again.

The profits are enormous. Five hundred kilos of coca leaves are worth

$500 and yield 2.5 kilos of coca paste worth $750. When it becomes cocaine powder—if it is 55 percent pure—it has a street price of $200,000 a kilo.

The global drug trade may run up to $500 billion a year, more than twice the value of all U.S. currency in circulation.

To gain a perspective on that amount, it is more than the total combined sales for 1987 of 15 major international companies. These include Ford Motor, International Business Machines, Mobil, Toyota Motor, General Electric, Texaco, American Telephone and Telegraph, Volkswagen, Nissan Motor, Bayer, Toshiba, Amoco, Honda Motor, Proctor and Gamble, and Boeing Aircraft.

The illicit drug trade is probably the fastest growing industry in the world and undoubtedly the most profitable. Lions Clubs International has mounted a multifaceted approach to deal with the problem.

On February 25, 1983, an International Symposium on Drug Awareness was held at the International Headquarters in Oak Brook, Illinois. Chaired by International President Everett J. Grindstaff, the meeting included international vice presidents, international directors, and a number of experts from around the world.

Many international organizations took part. Representatives of Lions club drug programs came from Australia, Germany, Italy, Norway, Thailand, and the United States.

The participants carefully considered various recommendations for fighting the drug epidemic. They voted to call their effort the Lions Drug Awareness Program, with the focus on prevention and education. They concluded that drug abuse should be defined as "the abuse of any licit or illicit drug, including alcohol or tobacco."

The group decided on a five-year commitment to emphasize and promote the program "or until respective official governmental sources state that the problem no longer exists."

The report on the 1983 symposium noted that "already at least 153 districts in 22 countries have reported formally adopting Drug Awareness as a district program and have appointed a District Drug Awareness Chairman to promote and coordinate it."

The Federal Republic of Germany is one of the nations in which Lions have made a difference in the drug problem with a program to stop addiction before it begins.

"One of the problems with a prevention program is that people generally don't believe that evil will come," said Dr. Herbert Schafer. "Parents invariably feel that drug addiction won't strike their child, and if it happens, cannot understand how it happened."

Director of Law Enforcement for Bremen and Bremerhaven in the Federal Republic of Germany, Dr. Schafer is one of the Lions in District 111-0 who developed the addiction prevention program that has taken hold in the country. He is a member of the Bremen (Hanse) Lions Club.

"Prevention means working with hope in the future," Dr. Schafer continued. "It takes time and patience, but if we persist, we can be sure that we'll save some of our young people from the misery of drug addiction. We can see some results already. For instance, where marijuana is concerned, there was a powerful movement ten years ago in Germany to legalize it. There was endless talk about its not being harmful. Today, that has turned around. People are aware of its dangers and at least some of that awareness results from the Lions prevention program."

Dr. Schafer's remarks are supported by data from the National Institute of Drug Abuse in the United States. This shows that, aside from alcohol, marijuana is the first drug most young people try. If they are buying marijuana on the street, as most of them must, then they will be exposed to the rest of the drugs, too.

The Bremen program got its start in May 1981, at a district meeting in which more than 700 Lions participated. The program was adopted unanimously by the group. The project cooperates with all appropriate agencies but does not receive any financial support from the government. About 50 percent of the Lions clubs in Germany take part in the program.

The addiction prevention program aims at stopping *all* drug abuse, including such prescription drugs as tranquilizers and sleeping pills. Ambitious and specific, it is designed to provide information and motivation to young people to avoid *any* chemical dependency.

Herbert Baumgarte, of the Delmenhorst Lions Club, is chairman of the prevention program. "We've prepared a workbook that is the backbone of the program," he explained. "This was developed by several Lions, including Bernd Isler, Dr. Horst Liebig, and me. The age of drug abusers is getting younger and younger and our aim is to prevent young people from experimenting with drugs. Drug abuse cuts across all social and economic classes."

"We've directed our program at schools and teachers," Lion Baumgarte continued, "and the workbook gives the teachers factual information on the problem and what to do about it. It also includes tips on the best ways to use the information. In many schools in Germany there is a teacher responsible for informing other teachers and the students about the drug problem. This is the person we concentrate on with our prevention program because he or she will be most influential and best qualified to use our material."

Lions in Germany have an official position against legalizing marijuana and feel that their program has been effective in building public support for that stand. They point out that young people who do not smoke at all are far less likely to experiment with marijuana. Also, boys and girls growing up in homes where parents do not smoke are much less likely to smoke themselves.

Although ten or 15 years ago it was popular to say that marijuana causes no damage, a growing body of evidence negates that view. Chromosome damage in the regular user has been reported to be three to seven times higher than in those who abstain from the drug. Changes in personality added to severe mood swings have been noted after only six months of steady marijuana use. There is also a reduced ability to perform complex physical tasks and a drastic decrease in the user's motivation.

The effectiveness of drug prevention programs is often hard to measure. However, there are many cases like a young man we'll call Karl. Karl lives in Bremen and said, "I heard one of my teachers talk to our class using the workbook the Lions provided. Then, as part of the program, I heard a former addict talk about what had happened to him as a result of drug abuse. He was in his 30s and had been down a rough, rough road created by his addiction. I knew that he knew exactly what he was talking about.

"I had been smoking marijuana and treated getting high like a joke. I was 16. Suddenly, it wasn't funny anymore. There just wasn't any way I could ignore what had been said. Several days later I went to see the teacher who had talked to us and told him about my marijuana use. He put me in touch with a small group of people my own age who had been experimenting with drugs. The leader of the group was a former addict who had recovered and I haven't used drugs since. That was nearly three years ago. I finished high school and am going to college. That talk several years ago was a major turning point in my life."

Dr. Horst Liebig is a chemist and one of the architects of the program. "The family is the key in producing human beings who can face life without chemical support," said Dr. Liebig. "I started talking about the chemical effects of drugs on the mind to parents, teachers, and Lions clubs in 1978. At that time, I was discussing the physical, not the social, aspects of drugs."

"Our current program started in 1981," he continued, "and we've used a variety of methods to promote it. For instance, the Nienburg Lions Club near Hanover has devised a play spotlighting the dangers of drug use. We're interested in teaching the young people who are at risk and giving them enough information and motivation to prevent their trying drugs. Each heroin addict will cost the country $330,000. Simple mathematics points to one of the reasons for battling the problem."

The German Lions believe that the country's laws are adequate to do everything possible from a legal standpoint. Their objective is to develop moral strength within young people so they will make right choices and not be attracted to drugs.

Dr. Liebig has said that the Lions clubs are developing their own approaches to expand drug prevention activities. He has found that young people taking part in these different initiatives remember what they see and hear.

A young woman from Bremen supports Dr. Liebig's words. "The Lions program made an indelible impression on me," said Gretchen. "I was 15 when I came in contact with it and had heard a lot about drugs, but didn't really have any solid knowledge or understanding about the question. Some of my friends had experimented with them and wanted me to try marijuana. After learning the facts I wasn't about to take a chance. There's nothing glamorous about drug addiction unless you're ignorant. Thanks to the Lions, I know better and I'm not ignorant about drugs and have no intention of using any drugs." Gretchen is now 18 and has just started a drug-free college career thanks to the Lions prevention program.

Studies show that lifelong attitudes toward drugs are formed during or before adolescence. Taking aim at this group, the German Lions are making vigorous strides to give young men and women positive support in resisting the drug plague.

Lions' approaches to the drug problem take varied forms. In Japan, ten Lions clubs in District 333-A sponsored a citizen's rally against drugs. It was followed by a parade during which Lions handed out leaflets.

Finnish Lions in Multiple District 107 work with the "Free of Drugs" organization to toughen laws on abuse of alcohol and other drugs. Tasmania, Australia, Lions of District 201-T1 erected a drug informa- tion center in Hobart while the Tall Ships were docked there. Between 30,000 and 40,000 persons visited the exhibit each day of the four-day period.

The Turkish Ministry of Health assigned the Lions District 118-T Drug Awareness Committee to coordinate all drug awareness programs in the country.

In 1977, Italian Lions, in cooperation with the Rotarians, started the Italian Association for the Prevention of Drug Abuse in Milan. It is supported by 30 Lions clubs and 30 Rotary clubs.

"The program has succeeded because of close cooperation between the two organizations," explained Past International Director Giovanni Rigone, a member of the Pavia (Host) Club. "Our initial effort has grown into a center that is widely used as a resource by the government and other agencies in Italy. Today, it features a library of more than 1,000 volumes dealing with the drug problem and 25,000 indexed articles on the subject."

As sometimes happens, the inspiration for the drug prevention pro- gram was sparked by the tragic death from drugs of the son of a Milan Lion. A team of Lions and non-Lions then met with parents and teachers who had resolved to face the addiction problem and work on ways to fight it.

The Milan Lions estimate that they have spoken to 500,000 parents and teachers about the problem since their wide-ranging program began in 1977. They have written and printed three books for different age groups that deal with drug abuse and attitudes that may create suscep- tibility to addiction.

"The spirit of the program is to prevent drug experimentation in young people," said Carlo Martinenghi, a member of the Varese (Europa) Lions Club. Carlo was governor of District 108-1B when the project started. "However, we don't go directly to the children but instead try to educate parents and teachers. From the beginning, that is where the emphasis has been. We prepared a slide program with tapes to implement this goal. This was developed after extensive research by our scientific adviser and is technically accurate.

"This program is presented in two evening sections of 90 minutes each," Carlo continued. "Among other things, it points up signs to look for that may indicate drug use. We believe that in Milan there are about 30,000 addicts and it's difficult to measure the impact of this kind of approach. However, we feel that the long term effects are positive. Along with expanding public awareness of the problem and the need for preventive measures, the Lions' example has increased government involvement in this situation."

A facility for documentation, education, and prevention, the drug prevention center operates on a budget of $60,000 a year. In 1984, the government gave $18,500 to the association to develop a booklet for pupils: "How to Decide About Drugs." As it points to the critical role of parental vigilance in dealing with the drug problem, the center's influence continues to grow.

"Our association is now working in other towns, including Rome, Palermo, Genova, Turin, Florence, Venice, and Salerno," Rigone said. "We can see a difference in attitudes as a result of what we've been doing. We keep emphasizing that the drug problem is a problem of the individual. We're trying to strengthen the home environment so that children will make the right choice, will learn to accept limits in life and respond to discipline. Our books and slide presentation are an extension of the educational process."

"There's no question that the influence is spreading," added Martinenghi. "It is touching many more lives as it has moved outside of our district. We feel this project is unique in Lionism. The worldwide drug problem is staggering and our aim is to try to do something to stop it before it begins for some of our young people."

Extensive research armed the members with accurate information and adequate understanding of the problem and the approach.

"This has been a demanding job to equip ourselves to meet the requirements of the program," explained Sergio Simonetti, a member of the Milan (Duomo) Lions Club. "One outgrowth of our success is that we have become a government resource for the drug problem. As one example, the government is using us to speak to soldiers at army bases. For the past two years we've been training officers in what we've learned in preventing drug addiction."

"As a result of our persistent effort through the association, we see more and more interest and response to our approach," said Vincenzo Sessa, of the Cinisello Balsamo Lions Club. "I certainly agree with the basic concept that the best way to fight drug addiction is to prevent it. It seems to me that in the past the government has not given sufficient weight to the important role of prevention. However, that is changing and I feel this new awareness on the part of our officials stems, at least in part, from what we've been doing since 1977 to increase it. Certainly, if the government vigorously fights the problem it can be a big factor in reducing it."

Farsighted in their concepts and pragmatic in their approach, the Italian Lions are energetically battling a plague that affects nearly every corner of the world. Their commitment to addiction-free living is daily translated into healthy lives for young people who are helped by their program. And as invariably happens, the Lions are helping themselves, too.

In 1984, Sergio Simonetti put it this way: "We have seen many benefits since we began this in 1977. In fact, I've seen benefits in my own home. I have a son 15 and a daughter 20, and this program has helped me be a better father."

When drug awareness and education approaches have not prevented addiction, the Lions are ready with highly effective treatment facilities. Employing advanced therapeutic techniques, they give the drug abuser a chance for a new life.

In Malmedy, a lovely Belgian town, the Haute Fagnes Lions Club supports an enlightened program to help addicts recover. Founded in 1982, it is called the Post Cure Center for Drug Addicts. It serves 30 residents at a time who come from all over Belgium and range in age from 16 to 60. About one-third of the residents at the center are from the immediate area around Malmedy.

"Essentially, what we try to do is build a new person," explained

Oswald Heck, a past president of the Haute Fagnes Lions Club. "In our experiences, a drug addict has generally lived a dishonest, irresponsible life. When he comes to the Center the purpose is to change these self-defeating attitudes and behavior patterns so that he or she will no longer run to drugs instead of facing problems."

Dr. Emil Binot, director of the center, worked at a similar facility in Canada in 1968 and 1970. It was there Dr. Binot got many of the ideas incorporated in the Malmedy facility.

"The patient stays here as long as necessary," said Dr. Binot. "He cannot use drugs or alcohol while he's here or he's thrown out. We find that of our patients, about 25 percent are alcoholics, 25 percent use marijuana or heroin, 25 percent abuse tranquilizers and other prescription drugs, and about 25 percent abuse a combination of these."

When a patient arrives at the Malmedy Center he or she is completely free of drugs. The patients come directly from a hospital and have had at least three weeks of detoxification. That, however, is just the beginning. At the center the recovering addict is given a chance to learn new skills and values to avoid a relapse into drug use. The emphasis is on complete freedom from drugs.

Regular therapy at the center includes family therapy groups designed to improve these critical relationships. Obviously, there are no quick or easy answers for the drug epidemic. Extensive research, however, spotlights the family as the crucial factor in a young person's drug use. The family provides the child with emotional support and role models for correct values and behavior.

"A good family provides clear communication, closeness, and good role models," said one Lion. "A good family shows no compulsive behavior, no gambling, drug use, or excessive alcohol intake. The parents set an example of honesty and responsible living and do not lie to themselves or others. A facility like the one in Malmedy functions as a family, with the discipline and guidance that go with the relationship— and that might not have been provided when the addict was growing up. Gradually he becomes capable of independent living without drugs."

"That's exactly what happened to me," said one of the graduates of the Post Cure Center. "I had been through treatment programs before but each time went back to drugs. At Malmedy they taught me that I was the one who caused my troubles—nobody else did. I spent six months at the center and have been drug-free since finishing their program five years ago. I had become a master at manipulating others to get my own way and blaming everyone but myself for my difficulties. They showed me how to change and grow up, at the age of 25."

He works as an automobile mechanic and supports his wife and two children. He received some of his vocational training while a resident of the center.

The Haute Fagnes Lions Club is 34 years old. Responding to Dr. Binot's request for help with the project, they obtained a building that had been used as an old people's home. After raising money, they remodeled and refurbished the building. Much of the work was done by the patients themselves.

While living in the center, each resident is responsible for work performed there. He makes his own bed, cleans, gardens, works in the kitchen, and does other tasks as part of his rehabilitation.

"We made a study of 164 patients one year after treatment," said Robert Denis, who is a member of the Haute Fagnes Club. "We found that after 12 months 55 percent were doing well and the remaining 45 percent were marginal. In the last five years we've seen a dramatic upsurge in drug addiction in Belgium and this facility is meeting the problem and dramatically changing lives."

Residents are taught to change those habits and attitudes linked to addictive behavior. They are encouraged to select realistic goals and helped to work toward them. Staff members support and monitor progress.

"We've been very fortunate with our anti-drug program here in Malmedy," said Ernest Drosch of the Haute Fagnes Club. "In seven years we've had some wonderful results. We have no money problems and our club members are excited about our success."

Added Manfred Dollendorf of the Haute Fagnes Club, "Dr. Binot had the idea for the center and our members have been able to make it work. We've brought a variety of skills and experience to bear on the project, and by working together have seen some good things happen in dealing with drug addiction."

As with all successful treatment programs, the Post Cure Center in Malmedy aims at total abstinence. Staff members stress that one drink, one marijuana cigarette, one snort, or one injection will lead back to total addiction.

Emphasizing responsible behavior as the road out of the addiction maze, the Post Cure Center is rebuilding drug users into men and women of conviction and commitment. Drug abusers who nearly killed themselves living on their own terms recover by adopting living patterns consistent with a drug-free life.

Working tirelessly both in their own communities and with Lions and professionals outside their own areas, Lions around the world are responding to the need spotlighted by International President Everett Grindstaff in *The Lion* in September 1982.

He wrote: "Lions, become involved in the fight against drugs—now! The future of your children, your grandchildren and the fine young people of your community depend on whether concerned adults will become aware of the deepening tragedy and take a stand to fight this cancer which is afflicting all communities."

II

LIONS-QUEST *SKILLS FOR ADOLESCENCE*

In June of 1984 the association introduced Lions-Quest *Skills for Adolescence*, the major initiative for implementing the drug awareness program. Lions-Quest was created through the joint efforts of Lions Clubs International and Quest International in Granville, Ohio, a leading developer of programs for young people.

The program was designed by 75 educators, researchers, psychologists, and curriculum developers working in cooperation with Lions Clubs International and Quest International. It helps young people combat peer pressure and make responsible decisions for a drug free life.

The program teaches students specific skills in understanding adolescent changes, making and keeping new friends, learning to manage feelings, strengthening family communication, resisting peer pressure, and developing a substance-free life style.

The curriculum helps children become independent adults—responsible, decisive, able to function better as family members and students.

All teachers and group leaders who offer the course are required to participate in a three-day training workshop conducted by professional trainers to prepare them to teach the course. Program materials are only available to men and women who have completed the training.

Parent participation is a cornerstone of the program. Research invariably shows that drug education programs are far more effective when parents are involved. While youths participate in the course, a series of four parent seminars are held. They reinforce the goals of the classroom lessons, paralleling information presented to the students. A textbook, *Surprising Years*, guides parents through the course and gives them tips on how they can help their own youngsters.

Lions-Quest participants are enthusiastic. Hank Richardson, a Lion and principal of Monte Vista Middle School in San Jacinto, California, and his superintendent, also a Lion, first read about it in *The Lion*.

"I'm sold on this program," says Richardson. "We're going to be offering it to all our kids in grades six to eight, and we're hiring a new teacher specifically to teach it. This is a whole new thrust for Lions. They're really beginning to link up with educators and kids."

In West Union, Iowa, Jon Antes, Lions club drug awareness chairman, reports, "Our membership is up, our participation is up and our camaraderie is up. I think most of this can be attributed to having a program such as *Skills for Adolescence*." In February 1987, the Lions Clubs International Foundation approved a $500,000 grant to adapt the *Skills for Adolescence* program for other languages and cultures and to promote and coordinate its international expansion.

Although based on research among American youngsters, the program's philosophy appears to address the needs of teens everywhere and its spread throughout the world has been swift and decisive.

Joyce Phelps, director of training for Quest International and veteran Lions-Quest trainer Bev Fisher have traveled to many countries, meeting with Lions, educators, and government officials to help set up the Lions-Quest program outside the United States. "The teachers in Sweden couldn't get enough of what we had to offer," Fisher said. "Even though there were differences, the teachers saw that *Skills for Adolescence* works and could be adapted and operational in a short time."

Lions-Quest travels well to other lands. Joyce Phelps and Bev Fisher agree that cultural differences around the world have been the most interesting and challenging aspects of the explosive growth of the program.

In Uppsala, Sweden, a picturesque university town just north of Stockholm, 18 schools used the *Skills* curriculum as part of a pilot program led by the Lions of Multiple District 101. Impressed by the work of the Lions, the WASA (insurance company) foundation awarded the Lions-Quest program a grant of $333,000 to fund teacher training workshops for two years.

Encouraged by the Swedish experience, the Lions of Iceland sent a team of eight educators to the United States to study the program. After their return, the Lions conducted a pilot program with the Ministry of Education. Multiple District 109 Lions and the Department of Education are providing financial support for the program which will be implemented in the middle grades throughout Iceland.

Multiple district councils in Denmark, Finland, and Norway piloted the program during the 1988-89 school term.

When conducting their workshops abroad, Quest trainers found it necessary to make subtle changes in approach. "One important difference between American and British teaching styles is that teachers in England are likely to be more formal," said one. "The important thing is that we've been able to adapt the basic principles and methods. Once we did that, the teachers were much more comfortable."

Though no two countries have initiated the *Skills* program in quite the same way, Lions-Quest officials have found more similarities than differences. "I think there's a special sensitivity among people who work with adolescents that transcends cultural and national boundaries," said another trainer.

Since its introduction at the 1984 International Convention, the Lions-Quest *Skills for Adolescence* curriculum is available in six languages—English, Icelandic, Spanish, French, Norwegian, and Swedish—and the program has been implemented in 19 countries. By the end of 1990 more than 18,300 schools worldwide had the program in place, affecting well over two million students and their parents. It had reached more than five million students and parents since it began.

"Other drug awareness thrusts include such varied activities as developing speakers' bureaus that provide experts in the field of substance abuse, establishing lending video libraries to educate interested groups on the devastating effects this tragedy has for families and communities, and, through retirement home visitations, presenting programs to the elderly on the potential dangers of prescription drugs."

In 1984, the *Skills for Adolescence* curriculum was introduced simultaneously in the United States and Canada. An office was set up in Canada headed by Past District Governor Bill Moody in Ontario. The administration of the plan which worked well in the United States had to be greatly modified into a distinctively Canadian program.

Drug Awareness Chairman Bill McGregor was one of many Canadians who lauded *Skills for Adolescence.* "Lions-Quest is one of the most significant programs our international association has ever been involved in," he said. "It gives information and skills to our youth to help them develop a successful, drug-free lifestyle."

The Lions of Multiple District 105 were the first outside North America to express an interest in Lions-Quest and they began to circulate the curriculum in the United Kingdom almost as soon as the program became available in North America. The Lions involved the Teachers' Advisory Council on Alcohol and Drug Education (TACADE) and began a series of Lions-Quest presentations to local education authorities. Where there was local interest, *Skills* was begun with a half-day "Launch" introduction to the program. After the "Launch" presentation, local Lions clubs began arranging funding for teacher training workshops and curriculum materials. In a period of only 18 months, Lions, working with TACADE, got the program into over 400 schools.

In the United Kingdom one in six schools is implementing Lions-Quest very effectively. An English 13-year-old underscores the success of the life skills aspect of the program:

"I had a problem when I first came to this school because I was so shy I would not mix with other children. When I was a second year pupil I had a lesson called Skills. It was all about mixing with other children. This helped me to overcome my problem and now, in my third year, I have a lot more confidence than I had before."

In Vesoul, France, Lion Denys Gobry reports a change in students' attitude as a result of the *Skills* program: "They are happy to come to school, they pay attention to each other, this is building their quality of attention and concentration." What is more, "Twenty-four parents came to a parent meeting. Some of them thanked us warmly for starting this remarkable experience." In France, three districts are piloting the distribution of the program under the auspices of the French Lions.

A teacher attending a workshop in Spa, Belgium, commented on "the quality of the trainer, the quality of the materials, the quality of the listening."

The La Cote Lions Club of District 102-W, Switzerland, sent two educators to the United States where, in Chicago and Columbus, Ohio, they met with representatives of Lions Clubs International and Quest International. Based on the report of the two teachers, Daniel Pellaux and Martine Bovay, the Lions of Cote created a Foundation for the Prevention of Drug Abuse. Established by Lion Max Graf, the foundation is implementing the Swiss Lions-Quest program.

Alan Moore, past district governor 201-VI, Melbourne, Australia, reported that "the response by teachers to the workshops has been fantastic. With the enthusiasm they have we will have no trouble obtaining more teachers in the future." New South Wales and Victoria, Australia, are piloting Lions-Quest after official support came from Lions District Leadership.

A team of district governors from Multiple District 202 in New Zealand met with officials of the country's Department of Education who gave the Lions a go-ahead for a successful pilot program. Because the Department could not fund the program, the Lions of New Zealand pledged $32,500 for teacher training, curriculum materials, evaluations, and administration costs. In a little more than a year, more than 1,400 students were enrolled in *Skills for Adolescence*.

The Spanish version of *Skills*, "Destrezas Para La Adolescencia," will go into 200 public and private schools as a community project of the Lions of Puerto Rico, the Puerto Rican Community Foundation and the Office of Education.

In late 1988, eight educators from South Africa came to the United States to study the Lions-Quest program and other facets of American education.

Sponsored by the Lions of Multiple District 410, they visited many different schools and educational facilities. Their visit provided another graphic demonstration that the association's global sweep speaks to human needs everywhere. Customs, cultures and languages may differ; but the needs of children are the same the world over. In South Africa the contrasts among people are substantial. However, educators from at least four segments of the country clearly recognized the value in the kind of teaching and training of teachers and parents provided by *Skills for Adolescence*.

Lions Clubs International has a long tradition of commitment to young people and education. *Skills for Adolescence* is another link in the chain of helping young men and women successfully meet the challenges of today and tomorrow. The process instills awareness that success in life is connected with responsibility to oneself and others.

Youths participating in Lions-Quest *Skills for Adolescence* develop healthy relationships, sound values, and positive attitudes. The program aims at producing men and women with mature approaches to living who function successfully each day as effective members of their communities.

III

DIABETES EDUCATION AND RESEARCH

Diabetes kills, maims, and blinds. More than 200 million people worldwide suffer from the disease and at least 50 percent do not know they have it. In addition to blindness, diabetes causes kidney disease, heart attacks, strokes, gangrene leading to leg amputation, and other serious complications.

There are two types of diabetes. Type I, insulin dependent diabetes, appears most frequently in children, adolescents, and young adults, but can develop at any age. Its onset is usually abrupt. Symptoms are severe and obvious. It is caused when the pancreas stops producing insulin, and without injections of insulin, Type I diabetics would die. They need to take insulin throughout their lives.

Type II, non-insulin dependent diabetes, is more common and accounts for 80 to 90 percent of the cases of diabetes in the world. This often appears when a person becomes overweight and there is a reduction in the ability of the body cells to react to insulin. Most of its victims are over 40. The disease can often be controlled by weight loss or, if necessary, oral medication.

Diabetes cuts life expectancy by 33 percent. More than half of all heart attacks occur in diabetics. The earlier a person develops diabetes, the higher the risk. A Type I diabetic is 25 times more likely than others to become blind, 17 times more prone to kidney disease, five times more likely to develop gangrene leading to limb amputation, and much more vulnerable to strokes. Diabetics are at risk for diabetic retinopathy as well as glaucoma and cataracts.

In 1982, International President Everett Grindstaff talked with an official from the American Diabetes Association about the devastating effects created by the disease. He took the initial steps in implementing a program to deal with the problem.

His background as a former president of the Texas Lions League made him well qualified for the mission. In 1973, the Texas Lions League for Crippled Children assumed full responsibility in the state for diabetic summer camps for children. They immediately expanded from one to two sessions; one at the original site of Camp Friendswood near Houston, the second at Kerrville, the site of the Texas Lions Camp for Crippled Children. In the early years about 30 children attended the diabetic camps. By 1982, over 325 diabetic youngsters were enjoying the two two-week sessions.

Because of the special health problems of the diabetic campers there are stringent safeguards. This includes a larger medical staff as well. There are complete medical, nursing, dietary, psychological, and educational programs for the youngsters. The goal is two-fold—treatment of the medical problems suffered by the children and extensive education and training to help them better cope with their disease.

Camping activities are extensive: hiking, games of all kinds, swimming, and anything else that campers enjoy at summer camps.

Each child attending the camp is sponsored totally by the Texas Lions League, which also finances the medical and educational program, thus making this one of the most unusual camps in the United States for children with diabetes.

"A number of these kids have learned to administer insulin shots to themselves for the first time," said Past International President Grindstaff. "They see other children doing it and think, 'If they can give themselves injections, so can I.' "

Sparked by Past International President Grindstaff and other concerned members, Lionism's involvement in battling the disease became official at a meeting held February 29 to March 1, 1984. Coming from all over the world, Lions representing international diabetes programs and Lion authorities in the field converged on International Headquarters in Oak Brook, Illinois. They were there to develop a plan of action to reduce new cases of blindness caused by diabetic retinopathy through diabetes education and research.

Participants included representatives from the American Diabetes Association in Alexandria, Virginia; the Juvenile Diabetes Foundation International in New York City; the Joslin Clinic in Boston, Massachusetts; the University of Wisconsin, Madison, Wisconsin, and the World Health Organization, Geneva, Switzerland.

Lions from Africa, Asia, Europe, North America, and Australia represented international diabetes programs. Called the "Lions Diabetes Awareness Program," its main objective is to reduce the new cases of blindness caused by diabetic retinopathy. A degenerative disease that affects the small blood vessels nourishing the eye, it is a leading cause of new blindness throughout the world.

As one of the first steps in the association's emphasis, Robert B. Chronister, Ph.D., an associate professor in the department of anatomy at the University of South Alabama School of Medicine, received a $48,000 LCIF grant for his first major project in diabetic retinopathy. He had, however, already shown significant findings in preliminary research. Dr. Chronister's concern is related amines, chemicals liberated by one nerve cell to talk to another nerve cell.

Dr. Chronister said, "Although diabetic retinopathy is thought to result from changes in the microvasculature in the eye, we have recently demonstrated that there is also a defect in the retinal nerve cells. This defect may well reflect the first diabetes induced alterations in the eye. Our research seeks to characterize the functional changes in retinal neurons resulting from diabetes."

Dr. Chronister added, "My feeling is that current treatments for retinopathy are solely related to treating the vascular disease, but at the same time, there may be a neuronal component to the disease which might point to new means of treatment."

"Without the grant, there's no way that we could begin building up the information to look realistically at this problem," he emphasized.

The more than $1.6 million raised through LCIF for diabetic retinopathy research has led to some other invaluable discoveries. For example, laser treatment of diabetic retinopathy uses the laser beam to seal bleeding and damaged blood vessels. This increases the underlying blood flow to the eye so the retina receives more nutrients and oxygen. This has been extremely successful in preventing blindness in patients with diabetic retinopathy.

Vitrectomy is an even newer treatment for advanced diabetic retinopathy. The damaged vitreous is removed and replaced by an artificial solution. The vitreous is a clear jelly-like fluid filling the eye. Vitrectomy is often successful and can restore vision when scar tissue has caused loss of sight. About six out of ten persons who have undergone vitrectomy surgery have improved vision. On the other hand, 20 percent experience no improvements and 20 percent actually experience greater loss of vision.

The emphasis begun in 1984 is helped by momentum developed in Lions' programs operating before the meeting at International Headquarters. In Brazil, Lions in District L-5 implemented an Awareness and Diagnosis Program in February 1983, during the term of District Governor Carmine Campagnone. The Lions provided simple blood sugar tests for more than 5,000 people in the first year. Dr. Carlos Alberto Magna, a member of the Campinas Jequitiba Lions Club, has been in charge of the program.

"Our program is two-fold," said Dr. Magna. "We want to educate people, to make them more aware of diabetes, what it is and what can be done about it. We made a videocassette, which we show at various meetings and public gatherings, and we published a brochure explaining what diabetes is and how it can be controlled.

"But we also knew realistically that when people get a piece of paper they scan the information and then throw it away. It's not that often they do anything about what they have just learned. So we decided that in order to have more impact on the public we should supplement the educational aspect of our program with what we call the practical aspect—free blood sugar examinations."

District L-5 works with both children and adults. For children, exam sessions are set up at various schools throughout the area on Friday morning. Women from the neighborhood also bring their preschool age children for testing.

The Brazilian Lions also work with adults on Saturday morning. Usually they set up their exam tables at a busy public park where there is a lot of traffic. Passersby are encouraged to have a blood test and to take any literature pertaining to diabetes. Each of the district's clubs is assigned a weekend to coordinate and man the exam tables. They get a great deal of volunteer help from wives, sons, and daughters.

"There are six and a half million diabetics in Brazil," Dr. Magna concluded, "and we want to inform and alert as many as we can. We hope to call attention to potential problems for people who otherwise would not have had early, and necessary, medical care."

Projects devised by Lions, Lionesses, and Leos are as imaginative as they are effective and include:

- *Club programs* stressing diabetes prevention.
- *Articles* on the prevention of diabetes in Lions district or multiple district publications.
- *Large print and audio visual materials* for the blind and visually impaired.
- *Diabetic camps* offering educational and recreational camping experiences for diabetic children.
- *Diabetic day camps* as an alternative to the diabetic residence camps.
- *Preliminary screenings* for hidden diabetics in the community.
- *Research* support through fund-raising programs.

The first Lions Clubs International Diabetes Institute in the world is the product of the Lions of Victoria, Australia. It serves the more than 140,000 families in Victoria. Australian Lions provided major funding for the center.

Dr. Paul Zimmet, a specialist in diabetes, said, "The Institute offers quality care and education, backed up by technology for both clients and health professionals who use its resources. Through its research facilities and ongoing collaboration, nationally and internationally, the Institute will be at the forefront of prevention and control programs for diabetes mellitus." Zimmet is foundation director and a member of the International Diabetes Federation.

He added that a retinal camera for eye screenings, to detect early changes in the eye, was made possible by donations from local Lions clubs.

Research supported by Lions clubs points to the critical role of fiber-rich foods in diabetes control. Fiber prevents blood sugar levels from becoming too high by slowing passage of food from the stomach and slowing digestion of starch and sugar in the intestines.

Emphasizing the importance of careful eating for diabetics, the Lions in District 201-Q3 in Australia, produced a dietary guide book called the *Australian Diabetic's Guide to Good Eating*. Lavishly illustrated and printed in full color, the 8½ x 11 inch book provides quick, easy-to-read information on what the diabetic should eat and what to avoid. Colorful and eye-catching, it can save the life of a diabetic needing fast, specific information. The Lions enlisted help from nutritionists and the National Library of Australia in the project.

In 1921, two Canadian scientists, Dr. Frederick Banting and his graduate assistant Charles Best, changed the future for diabetics when they discovered that insulin derived from animal pancreases and injected into diabetic humans controlled the disease. Insulin injections were so effective that diabetics who would have been dead within a year or two before its discovery were now able to live relatively long lives. Insulin is a hormone normally produced by our bodies in an organ called the pancreas. It enables body cells to convert certain foods we eat into energy.

Unfortunately, adding to the problem of diabetes is a worldwide shortage of insulin. There's a shortage of insulin in most of the nations in Africa, Asia, Central America, and South America, as well as in Poland, Romania, and Turkey.

Insulin is expensive. The pancreas of animals slaughtered for food, in most cases pigs and cows, are used to produce insulin. Professionals in diabetes organizations, clinics, and hospitals have approached Lions involved in the diabetes awareness program for help in obtaining supplies of insulin. Many experts have told Lions of their frustration at trying in vain to save the lives of people with diabetes when sufficient supplies of insulin are not available.

Dr. Christos Theophanides of District 117 in Cyprus is a champion of diabetics in developing nations. Through his involvement in the Diabetes Awareness Program and his work with the International Diabetes Federation in Brussels, Belgium, he has made Lions much more aware of the unique problems affecting diabetics in underdeveloped nations. In cooperation with the Lions of Australia, Dr. Theophanides has devised LIDA or the Lions International Diabetes Aid Project—an all out effort to get supplies of insulin to diabetics in areas of need.

During their multiple district convention in 1988, the Lions of South Africa asked Dr. Theophanides for guidance in planning effective diabetes projects. "By the time I left South Africa," Dr. Theophanides said, "I had done two radio programs, a TV talk show, and lectured twelve times to Lions, the South African Diabetes Association, and the medical profession." In addition to this, Dr. Theophanides has lectured twice at diabetes awareness seminars held during the Lions annual convention and appears in the film "Don't Be Blind to Diabetes."

When the sole insulin manufacturer in South America went out of business, the Lions of Argentina leaped into action to establish an insulin bank. For several years these Lions have been working with professionals to get supplies of insulin to those in need. Although a new insulin plant has recently opened it does not begin to meet the demand for insulin in South America.

India has also been hit hard by the insulin shortage. One Lion in India said, "We're trying to do our best to serve people who have diabetes. But what our people in India need is insulin. How can we say we are involved in helping them and then let them die because we cannot obtain insulin?" Lions, worldwide, are working together to solve this deadly problem.

Where there's a need there's a Lion, a Lioness, or a Leo.

The Lions of District D-3 in Guatemala sponsor diabetes programs in the community aimed at educating the public on diabetes, its causes, and methods of treatment.

District 114-O in Austria sponsored a ski camp for children with diabetes. The main objective of the program was to instruct children with diabetes to control the disorder during athletic activities.

Lionesses and Leos of District 334-A in Japan helped the Lions Clubs in sponsoring a major diabetes campaign including education materials, lectures, referral information, and free detection screenings.

Lionesses in District T-2 in Chile have been trained to become knowledgeable about diabetes and to correctly perform diabetes detection screening. More than 150 Lionesses have become proficient and perform regular protection screenings throughout the district. The goal is to train 300 Lionesses in this capacity.

Leos of District 321-A in India sponsored a diabetes detection camp for free public testing. A total of 355 people were tested and people with diabetes were given free medicine.

Lions are also supporting research into the use of pancreas transplants for diabetics. This involves planting a healthy pancreas in a person with diabetes. So far 223 of these have been performed in the world and 69 percent of these transplants were considered successful. However, some patients still need insulin injections after the transplant.

The insulin pump is another promising research project. The purpose of the insulin pump is to provide a continuous supply of insulin in order to eliminate the need for insulin injections in people with Type I diabetes. About the size of a standard transistor radio, it looks something like a calculator with a variety of programming buttons on it. It is connected to the body usually near the abdomen by a small needle. Insulin is delivered by the pump through plastic tubing and injected into the abdomen by a needle which should be replaced every three days.

Another important area of research is the transplanting of insulin-producing cells. Type I diabetes develops when the islet cells in the pancreas stop producing insulin. Theoretically, if healthy islet cells are transplanted, insulin will be produced. While there have been some short-term successes with these transplants, after about eight weeks the insulin production by the transplanted cells has stopped. Researchers are attempting to determine why these attempts were not successful. With further experimentation, they hope to perfect the technique.

Diabetes remains a virulent scourge. Known cases of the disease are increasing at the rate of six percent a year, even though 80 percent of all new cases could have been prevented.

Knowledge is the number one weapon in the fight against diabetes. The award-winning 20-minute film "Don't Be Blind to Diabetes" provides specific information to people at risk of diabetes to help them avoid blindness and other crippling complications. Unlike presentations designed for diagnosed diabetics, "Don't Be Blind to Diabetes" is geared to high risk groups and the millions of people who have the disease without knowing it. By reaching these individuals before serious problems develop, countless men, women, and children may be saved from blindness.

Speaking with vision and conviction, Past International President Judge Brian Stevenson said, "I firmly believe that we can live to see diabetes erased from the earth if we continue to press our work for this cause."

Powered by their unwavering commitment on every continent, Lions, Lionesses, and Leos are consistently active in diabetes research, education, and testing. The global impact spells hope and health for millions of human beings.

CHAPTER TWELVE

Lionism Today

LIONS promote world understanding with a personal approach. What could involve Lions in a more direct way than driving a caravan of donated emergency vehicles on an eight-day, 3,000-mile odyssey from Indianapolis, Indiana, 1,400 miles through Mexico and another 200 miles to Guatemala City, Guatemala? The idea was born in November 1984, when Past International Director Jim Cameron of Urbana, Indiana, went to Guatemala with a group of eye doctors as part of the Volunteer Optometric Services to Humanities team (VOSH).

"While I was there, four Lions from that area talked to me about getting a pickup truck they could use for an ambulance," said Cameron. On his return, he broached the idea of obtaining used emergency vehicles and donating them to Lions clubs in Guatemala. He found an enthusiastic reception among fellow members of the Urbana Lions Club.

"The very next year we returned with an ambulance and a fire truck, and since then the project has gotten bigger every year. This past year, we delivered 12 vehicles—ambulances, fire trucks, a school bus, and a van.

"We followed the Gulf coast, through Tampico, Veracruz and then down to the Isthmus of Mexico. We drove straight south to the Pacific and then down to Guatemala.

"There were 40 of us who drove down in 1988, and 20 others who flew. We started with 14 vehicles—six ambulances, three fire trucks, two school buses, a pickup truck, a van, and an old Datsun 210 auto."

The caravan of donated vehicles, which started as the project of Cameron's Urbana club, has become an Indiana international project, with clubs all over the state donating about $40,000 in 1988, including $24,000 in air fare. Among the volunteer drivers there were two Lions from Sweden, Past District Governor Conny Kingsfors and Bengt Stembeck, who paid their own air fare in order to drive in the caravan.

Lions buy used ambulances, fire trucks, and buses for prices which range from $800 to $2,000, although sometimes the old vehicles can be had for nearly nothing. The Madison Township Lions Club in Indiana bought a fire truck from the town for only $1.00.

"That was really a donation from the town of Wakarusa for all the past services the Wakarusa Lions and the Madison Township Lions clubs have done for the area," explained Past District Governor Raymond Enfield of District 25-G.

More typical of the vehicles which go to Guatemala was the 1964 General Motors fire truck with only 8,200 miles on it. It was donated by the Noble Township Lions Club, which paid the Noble Township fire department in Wabash, Indiana, $1,000 for it. Most of the vehicles have been well maintained with much mileage left in them, Enfield explained.

The caravans become, in effect, relief trains to Guatemala. Each vehicle is loaded with medical supplies, blankets, clothing, and eyeglasses donated by clubs around the country. One bus alone on the 1988 trip had 14,000 pairs of eyeglasses aboard, all in plastic bags along with precise prescription information.

Not only do Guatemalan cities get fire trucks, ambulances, eyeglasses, and needed supplies, but international Lionism is strengthened.

The caravan has become a means of forming new Lions clubs. If a city that doesn't have a Lions club asks for a vehicle, the Lions request that they form a Lions club. At least six new clubs were formed between 1986 and 1988 as a result.

As news of the Indiana project spread, clubs in other states got interested. When the caravan was featured on a San Antonio, Texas, TV station, a past district governor who saw the show phoned Cameron and offered caravaners rooms at a motel at half price. The next morning that club paid for breakfast, $196.50 worth.

Other Lions clubs, hearing of the Indiana project, have sent vehicles to a city on the Baja Peninsula in Mexico and a town in Chile in the Andes Mountains.

Driving a donated vehicle to Guatemala demands determination. "The buses only go about 45 miles an hour. If you try for 55, they shake and vibrate," said Enfield. "All the ambulances made the trip to Guatemala in quite good condition, but we did have trouble with the school buses and the fire trucks. They are made for around town driving and if driven hard they have a tendency to break down."

Enfield reports he thought Guatemala would be warm, "but as we went up in altitude it started to rain and get cold. By the time we got to Guatemala City, the guys riding outside on the fire truck were frozen." Enfield added that some stretches of road are very poor. "You have to be careful because you could bend a rim going into a pothole."

Even the U.S. portion of the trip can be difficult. Jim Ross, past district governor from Indianapolis, said that on the 1988 trip, one of the school buses broke down between Louisville, Kentucky, and Nashville, Tennessee. Another gave out just outside of Nashville in a heavy rainstorm. The $1 fire truck from the Wakarusa fire department, a 1951 Ford, lost its wipers in the same storm.

The two drivers of that vehicle, Ray Klein and his wife, Helen, "wound up tying a string to the wipers," Ross said.

"I would pull one way and she, the other," explained Klein. The couple was so busy with the wipers that they missed a turn and got separated from the main group.

Ross himself, with Cameron's son, installed new brakes on a bus that developed brake problems. Near Austin, Texas, one of the fire trucks dropped a drive-shaft, but a sympathetic Ford dealer in Austin was able to find the parts and repair the truck.

Sometimes repairs were accomplished almost by magic. The only car on the trip, an old Datsun 210, hit a pothole, broke a right rear spring bolt and "was running about four inches out of line," Ross said. "Jim Cameron said that if we couldn't fix the car we would have to leave it. The Datsun must have heard him because it hit a chuck hole, straightened up, and never ran sideways again." The caravan did eventually lose a fire truck and a school bus to breakdowns and had to jam all supplies, donated materials, and 40 people into the remaining vehicles.

Ross explained a typical day, which usually began at six o'clock in the morning. "We tried to eat breakfast. A lot of times that was impossible. We took a lot of junk food with us, canned this, canned that. We didn't stop for lunch because you lose two hours with that many people. We stopped every three hours for gasoline, and we usually quit about nine or ten o'clock at night. Eight days of that gets tiring. It's not exactly a vacation."

Word of the caravan's approach got around fast. At many of the towns along the way caravaners were greeted by welcoming crowds. Enfield said that one community had a big banner across the street that said, "Welcome, Jim Cameron." The caravan and the crowd stopped all traffic for a few minutes for an impromptu ceremony of appreciation right in the middle of a busy city street. "When we presented an ambulance or a fire engine, the ceremonies got much longer. Everybody who was anybody was given an opportunity to make a speech."

As the fleet of vehicles neared Guatemala City, the skies opened up in torrential rains and temperatures dropped rapidly. Ross said the Lions "kept noticing a big neon sign as they entered the city, but our interpreter told us there had been a volcanic eruption and what we thought was a neon sign was a river of lava running down a mountainside."

District Governor Alfonso Barahona and the Guatemalan Lions meet the caravan each year on the Mexican/Guatemalan border. Barahona, who serves as Cameron's contact in that country, also takes charge of delivering much of the clothing and medical supplies the Lions bring with them.

On the other side of the world, a Lions project started with an operation on a 12-year-old Indian girl. It soon expanded into a global medical mission linking Lions clubs in India and Canada.

A moving story of international medical teamwork, it began when the Weston, Ontario, Lions Club and the Chembur, India, Lions Club arranged an operation on the girl to correct crippling scoliosis, the damaging curvature of the spine. In 1969 she was flown to Toronto where Dr. John Hall, an orthopedic surgeon, implanted special steel rods in her back in a highly technical operation. The successful procedure transformed her life.

Altogether, the cost of the operation and of flying the girl to Canada totalled $8,000. With costs like those, the Lions could help only two Indian children a year on a continuing basis. After thoughtful consideration they devised an alternative. They asked Hall if he would train Indian doctors brought to Canada to do the operation. Better yet, could he himself go to India and conduct training sessions? Hall not only could but would.

Before Hall's departure, Lions did extensive groundwork. They appealed successfully for donations of supplies and equipment. J. B. Watt, past president of the Weston Lions Club, approached a Canadian company and obtained five copies of a film showing a scoliosis operation. The company which made the special steel rods used in the operation provided them at half the usual cost.

One company provided body braces required for the post-surgical therapy at cost. Another firm donated an orthopedic table. A local doctor gave the Lions $450 worth of instructional slides and films.

Early in 1970, Hall flew to India with anesthesiologist Dr. John Relton and physiotherapist Gordon Plorin. Once there, the surgical team did 15 scoliosis procedures. At each operation, Indian doctors either assisted or observed. The three Canadians also lectured at Indian universities where more Indian doctors learned about the operation. Copies of the scoliosis film were provided to universities in Bombay, New Delhi, Lucknow, Calcutta, and Madras.

The Lions had done nothing less than bring a new surgical technique to India. Now Indian doctors perform this surgical miracle on Indian patients in Indian hospitals. In the words of Past President Watt: "The success of this mission has gone beyond our most optimistic expectations in that 15 children have been cured, Indian doctors are now able to perform the technique, Indian brace makers are now able to manufacture the braces needed, and films have been left at five major universities to assist in teaching young doctors."

Another international medical mission sponsored by Lions in Columbus, Ohio, brought Dr. Benjamin B. Caplan, a member of the Downtown Lions Club of Columbus, to Santa Cruz, Bolivia. In making the 5,000 mile flight, Caplan was fulfilling a promise made to another Lion, Dr. Abraham Telchi of Santa Cruz, to bring polio vaccine to protect the children of the town.

Telchi, a member of the Santa Cruz Lions Club, was doing post-graduate work at Ohio State University in Columbus in the spring of 1969. He visited the Columbus club and made a plea for polio vaccine. The Lions sprang into action immediately to support Caplan who eventually spent almost $13,000 of his own money to bring 25,000 immunizations for polio to Bolivia. Lederle Laboratories furnished the vaccine and also guaranteed its safe arrival and proper storage after it reached Santa Cruz.

Caplan, Alma Brill, a registered nurse, and Daniel Waitzman, a pharmacist, all good friends for many years, left Columbus in November—springtime in Bolivia.

The last lap of the trip was a flight from La Paz. "Because the runways at the Santa Cruz airport cannot accommodate jets," Dr. Caplan said, "we went by propeller aircraft. It was somewhat disconcerting to look out the window and see some of the peaks of the Andes at a higher level than our plane. Several weeks earlier there had been an accident on this run in which 76 people had perished. Our only comfort was that this plane held just 30 passengers, so we felt much safer."

In Santa Cruz the three were greeted by Oscar Justininao, president of the Santa Cruz Lions Club, Dr. Riserio Rojas, director of the Santa Cruz Health Center, Dr. Telchi, and several other Lions and officials.

The next morning was spent passing out two drops of oral Sabin vaccine to each child who visited the health center. There was a festive air, with vendors selling ice cream and candy as they moved among the parents and children who had gathered at the center. An old Indian woman sat in the courtyard peddling apples and another vendor sold handmade banjos. "We noted that Santa Cruz was blessed with very beautiful and healthy children," commented Caplan. "It filled us with joy to realize that we were helping protect them from polio."

A similar visit was made to La Belgia, a town of about 5,000 people, 40 miles from Santa Cruz. "Over and over, in our contacts with the people of Bolivia, in newspaper accounts of our work and in interviews of us on a local radio station, friendship and good will were clearly evident," said Caplan.

During the team's three-week stay, 21,200 immunizations were given and an additional 8,000 booster doses were shipped later in response to Telchi's request. The team was honored at a dinner hosted by Telchi and attended by 20 leading citizens. "We were honored with gifts and told to regard their homes as our homes," Caplan reported.

On the trip home, the trio was met at La Paz airport by Dr. Walter Arzabe Fuentalsas, the Bolivian minister of public health, Dr. Mario Landivar Catera, the assistant minister, and Dr. Luis Gallardo Larcin, general director of public health. On hand also were the president of the La Paz Lions Club, Marcos Kavlin, and fellow members Victor Jaurequi and Walter Freudenthal. Cordiality, warmth, and good wishes quickly dissolved the language barrier.

When Caplan was named "Lion of the Year" by his club, he told his fellow members that "it impressed us deeply that we accomplished more than immunizing children. We believe that the project has improved relations between peoples of two different cultures. We are grateful to have been part of this program of international good will."

In his inaugural address, International President Joseph L. Wroblewski said: "I have never ceased to be impressed by the way Lions on the international level, speaking scores of languages and representing many cultures, can join in a single purpose to help people in need. Lionism truly does cut through differences in culture, race, religion, and politics."

Lions have a knack for making those cultural differences disappear. In Nicosia, Cyprus, the Nicosia Lions Club worked with the Tel Aviv, Israel, Club to give a four-year-old Nicosia girl suspected of having leukemia the medical attention she needed. Highly advanced treatment, unavailable in Nicosia, was given the child, Angela Petrou, when the Nicosia club financed her trip to Israel. Once there, the Tel Aviv club arranged for her hospitalization, visited her often in the hospital, and kept the cards and gifts coming.

In remote Robinpet Village, India, 1,300 villagers now have a reliable source of pure drinking water because Lions joined in that "single purpose to help people in need" International President Wroblewski described in his inaugural speech.

Robinpet Village had made many appeals to governmental and municipal authorities for fresh, safe drinking water. When the Lions Club of Ootacamund, India, offered to help, the villagers were skeptical. If government, with all of its resources could not help, what could a single Lions club do?

The Ootacamund club asked for assistance from the Lyn Lions Club in England, which quickly provided both funds and guidance. An analysis determined that it would be possible to pump pure water from a well some distance from the village to a nearby distribution point and finally to the village itself. The idea looked good on paper and the club built a pumping station. But how could the Ootacamund club—far from the village—see that the system was maintained so that it would continue to meet the needs of the villagers?

With typical Lions zest, the club struck a deal with a nearby private school, the Lawrencewood School. The headmaster agreed to arrange for a permanent crew of workers to keep the system pumping, with the costs to be paid monthly by the Ootacamund club. So once built, through the international cooperation of two clubs and one school, pure water continues to flow to Robinpet Village.

Lionism originally came to Japan from the Philippines. Therefore, it was natural for Lions of Japan's District 334-E to decide to do something about the health needs of the men, women, and children who live on some of the 7,200 islands which make up the Philippines. Because of inadequate medical facilities, many suffered from a variety of diseases. In 1977, District 334-E sent a medical team to four different locations for four days.

The medical mission got full support from the Filipino Health Ministry, local physicians, the governor of the state of Sulacan, and the Bulacan state hospital. Initially, many Filipinos expressed strong anti-Japanese feelings. But when local newspapers publicized the team and its purpose, hostility based on memories of World War II faded away. The free treatment offered by the team attracted some 8,000 people.

Preliminary studies indicated that the team, which included specialists in internal medicine, dentistry, and ophthalmology, should place emphasis on inoculations to prevent TB. In make-shift clinics set up in warehouses and town halls, the days began with long lines of Filipinos.

Physicians, dentists, pharmacists, pathologists, and general assistants dispatched from District 334-E, together with doctors and nurses from local hospitals and their assistants totalled 130 people. Barely stopping for meals, the group treated 3,107 patients.

Stories about the team's work ran in newspapers and on radio and television all over the Philippines, and the Japanese press gave the story good coverage. The team capped its work by receiving keys of honorary citizenship from the mayor of Manila and letters expressing gratitude from the governor of Bulacan state and the governor of District 301-D in the Philippines. Since the initial mission, District 334-E has continued its service activities in the Philippines and even expanded them to include preventive medicine.

When a cry for help came from Singapore, the Lions Club of Northshore Pakeke, New Zealand, answered. The club is composed of retired Lions who have been answering the call to service for most of their lives. The club banner reads "As elders we serve." In 1985, the International Year of the Child, this group heard an appeal from the Lions Club of Singapore (East).

The two-year-old son of a member of the Singapore club suffered from a serious congenital heart disease and was going to Auckland, New Zealand, for an operation to be performed by Sir Brian Barrett-Boyes, a distinguished heart surgeon. Both parents, only one of whom knew English, would accompany their son, Kar Wee Tan, for a one-month stay in this unfamiliar country. Unfamiliar, but friendly, thanks to the Northshore Pakeke Lions and their wives. The Tans' home away from home was provided by Lion Syd Hewetson and his wife, Mary.

The warmth of a welcome which was to extend throughout the Tans' stay in New Zealand began at the airport where the couple and Kar Wee were greeted by President Ron Mogridge. The heart operation, performed at the Mater Hospital, was a complete success, and the Tans began to relax a little in their new household. After Kar Wee left the hospital he was even able to go for a few short trips around Auckland to shop for souvenirs. The family then flew back to Singapore, but not before Lion Tan attended a meeting of the Northshore Pakeke Lions Club. Club banners were exchanged in a simple ceremony in which Tan thanked every member who had welcomed and helped his family.

The story of the Tans is a little story—about one club reaching out to another culture to help one small boy and his family—but also on a world scale, there is a willingness among Lions to lend a hand when famine or disaster strike. After a June 1971 earthquake devastated Peru, more than 200 Spanish-speaking Lions clubs mobilized to help. Thousands of people were killed and hundreds of thousands were left homeless by the quake which shifted mountains and opened up holes in the earth wide enough to swallow entire villages in Peru's northern Andes area. While relief poured in from all over the world, the 200 Lions clubs in the Americas, the Caribbean, and Spain donated an estimated $150,000 in goods and $50,000 in cash. In Peru, 59 Lions clubs provided $20,000 worth of materials. Lions clubs in the Dominican Republic, Puerto Rico, Venezuela, and Uruguay gave generously, even though they were fighting the ravages of heavy rainfall at the time of the Peruvian disaster. Considerable donations came from Lions clubs in Argentina, Ecuador, Guatemala, Panama, Paraguay, El Salvador, and Mexico. Spanish-speaking clubs added new luster to the Lions' motto: "We Serve."

In a District 308 project, Singapore Lions sent food and other needed provisions to Vietnamese refugees living in camps in Malaysia.

After a destructive cyclone in Sri Lanka, the Amstetten, Austria, Lions Club shipped a large quantity of vitamins to the Lions Club of Mirigama to meet the nutritional needs of victims.

The Cap Rouge Club of Quebec, Canada, provided $6,000 to help homeless men, women, and children in Southeast Asia.

The Aix Mazarin Club in Marseilles, France, provided $1,250 to buy food for residents of refugee camps in Africa.

The Chioggia-Sottomarina Lions Club of Italy sent $1,000 to the Vietnamese refugees fund.

In a "one franc for one child project," the Nice (Baie des Anges), France, Club raised $9,000 for refugees who fled Cambodia.

Lions in Norway and the United States cooperated in a wintertime activity generating international warmth and understanding. In February 1975, they sponsored the first "Race for Light." The event drew 54 skiers from the United States, Canada, Norway, and Africa to the slopes of Breckenridge, Colorado. All of the skiers were blind.

The first "Race for Light" was not really a contest nor a test of speed or endurance. It provided an opportunity for blind people to enjoy an athletic experience ordinarily open only to those who are sighted—ski touring. An instructor or guide skis on a trail which parallels the trail used by the blind skier. The instructor/guide warns of turns, bumps and hills ahead, becoming, in effect, the eyes of the skier.

The "Race for Light" was modeled after the internationally famous "Knights' Race" in Norway. Started in 1965, the event attracts hundreds of visually handicapped men and women from the United States and 19 other nations. The skiers respond to the challenge of open ski trails, add a new dimension to their lives, and gain a closer contact with nature as they join their fellows in a shared experience. They learn a great deal about skiing, too. Blind and partially blind skiers are introduced to new training techniques in both cross-country and downhill skiing.

The Breckenridge "Race for Light" was a joint effort of the Lions clubs of Norway and Colorado and the Sons of Norway Foundation. It was hosted by the Summit County Lions Club. Assisting in the preparation of the course and obtaining accommodations for the skiers were the business community and many private citizens who invited skiers to spend their week at the event as guests in their homes. United States and Norwegian National Guardsmen helped out with traffic and communications and staged special ceremonies. Cross-country ski equipment for skiers and instructors was furnished by Norwegian equipment manufacturers.

Doreen Borgersen of Norway is typical of many of the participants— a blind person who has resolved to live as normal and full a life as possible by fighting the restrictions placed on her by her handicap.

She explained, "If you are blind, you are naturally forced to live a restricted life no matter how willing you are to try new things. Every time you want to leave your house to go downtown to shop, for example, and even if you have a dog guide, you must still always be aware of the trouble you can run into.

"I became blind nine years ago. For the first five years, I did nothing. I simply stayed home and took care of my family as best I could. But I began to realize that I was making myself a prisoner. No one was doing it to me. I had to learn to live not only with my blindness but with the fact that I did not necessarily need to be a prisoner.

"That is why I decided to learn to ski four years ago. And really, it is why I came to Colorado with other blind skiers to participate in this event."

The capstone of the first "Race for Light" was a banquet on the final night at which each skier received a certificate and gifts. Among the featured speakers that evening was then First Vice President Harry Aslan. He presented a special Lions Club International award to Erling Stordahl, director of the Beitostolen Recreation and Rehabilitation Center for the Handicapped in Norway. A Norwegian Lion, blind since the age of 12, Stordahl is credited with bringing the sport of skiing to the visually handicapped of Norway. His Beitostolen Center is heavily supported by the Lions of Norway.

Two cultures can blend happily when Lions clubs in different countries decide to team up. The result of such cooperation is that many are helped—and international understanding expands. One story of such cooperation begins in Algeciras, a rail terminal and port located in the southernmost part of Spain. Lions in that city joined with the Lions Club in Ashland, Ohio, to help 45-year-old Miguel Gonzales Lopez. Blind since birth, he was employed as an administration officer at the Spanish Organization for the Blind. The Algeciras Lions Club and the Lions Club of Ashland cooperated to help Gonzales obtain a Pilot Dog. Lions Pilot Dogs, Inc., in Columbus, Ohio, welcomed Gonzales as a member of the Eighth Class of 1983.

Before coming to Columbus, Gonzales studied English every day so that he could better understand his training with his Pilot Dog, Zack, a black Labrador retriever. Zack was one of a litter bred specifically for dog guide work and had been raised in the home of Heidi Lutz in Zanesville, Ohio.

Despite language differences which sometimes made communications between Gonzales and his instructors difficult, the training went extremely well. Zack and Gonzales became close friends. An inseparable team, they trained together for four weeks. They traveled throughout the city, up and down elevators and escalators, on and off buses until they had mastered every possible situation. Graduation day arrived and Gonzales returned to Algeciras with Zack. When Dr. Jorge F. Wenzel of the Ashland club returned from Spain after a visit to the now totally independent team, he reported that Gonzales was "happy as a lark with his Pilot Dog."

The Lions Club of Ashland and Wenzel were implementing a resolution to support Pilot Dogs which Ohio Lions endorsed in 1960. Between

1960 and 1984, Lions of Ohio donated more than $1.4 million to the project of furnishing dog guides to sightless citizens—at no cost to the blind person being helped.

Commenting on the results of the efforts of the clubs, Dr. Wenzel said: "For us who are constantly working for blindness prevention and easing the life of the already blind, we sometimes forget the impact of our work, not only on the person, but on the community that surrounds him or her. In this case, two parallel communities are benefited and inspired; one, the friends and neighbors of the blind, and two, the Lions club community that discovered the world of service is not their immediate town, but the whole world. How good it is for the creation of a better image of the United States in every corner of the world."

In the little village of Hani in Ghana, Lions turned an archeologist's idea into a glowing example of international cooperation. It began in 1972 when Dr. Joanne Dombrowski, a lecturer in archeology at the University of Ghana visited Hani, a poor, rural village 300 miles inland from the Atlantic Ocean. Struck by the educational difficulties faced by the villagers, Dr. Dombrowski resolved to find a way to provide books to Ghana. She wrote her mother, Grace Dombrowski, a school counselor in Gary, Indiana. By late 1973, local school children mobilized by Mrs. Dombrowski had collected crates of used but usable books—ready to be shipped to Ghana.

She turned for help to Gary area Lions, who agreed not only to pay shipping costs for the books already collected, but to build a library for them in Hani. The effort became a project of District 25-A under the leadership of Past District Governor Dr. E. W. Griffith and his wife. In the next two years, Lions shipped three and a half tons of used books. District 25-A Lions continued to help collect books and financed the library's construction.

The people of Hani supplied the labor while the University of Ghana organized the transportation of supplies and supervised construction. In early 1975, the library was dedicated in ceremonies attended by Dr. and Mrs. Griffith, representing the Lions, and Mrs. Dombrowski, representing the citizens of Gary. Since then, there has been continuing support for the project. That includes a promise to raise not only Hani's educational level, but health standards as well, with the shipment of medical supplies for emergency use in the village school.

The Cyprus School for Deaf Children looked forward to its 21st birthday and completion of a new "dream school" to house 116 youngsters and 61 adults from the school's Cooperative Factories for the Deaf. Completion of the school would mean that every deaf child on the island now had a chance to get the proper training and instruction in new, fully equipped facilities. But war in 1975 intervened. The students were among the 220,000 people who lost homes and possessions and ended up in refugee camps. The 21st birthday was "celebrated" in the Refugee School for Deaf Children while troops occupied the new school.

As has happened so many times in the past, these children, and all of the refugees on Cyprus, were the beneficiaries of a massive, coordinated effort mounted by Lions all over the world.

In Guildford, England, William Blake, president of the Guildford Lions Club in 1974–75, checked the first consignment of clothing donated by British Lions for Cyprus refugees. That shipment arrived in Athens by plane and was transferred by truck to a Cyprus-bound freighter. The Lions Clubs International Foundation forwarded $6,000 to Cyprus to help rebuild the school. Money from U.S. Lions clubs also flowed in to help the deaf children.

Thousands of packages of food came from Lions in Denmark, Germany, Italy, England, Norway, Finland, Greece, and other countries. An initial appeal for tents to house the refugees who were both Greek and Turkish Cypriots, brought immediate response from Lions clubs.

Another story of Lions extending help across borders and continents began in the summer of 1979 in San Jacinto, Uruguay. The day was warm and 24-year-old Raul Techera and some of his friends decided to go swimming.

"The lake has high cliffs around it and we would dive into the water. It was fun. There was nothing special about it," said Techera. "When I jumped off the cliff, I saw I was going to land in shallow water which was only about three feet deep. Hitting the bottom knocked me unconscious."

Friends pulled him out of the water and on the way to the hospital he realized he could not move his arms or legs. Doctors told him he had permanently damaged his spine. His life would be spent in a wheelchair.

Two years later, Raul's father, Milton Techera, a member of the San Jacinto Lions Club, picked up a copy of *The Lion* and read about a Lions program in Arizona. It would change the life of his son. The story was about another Lion in Paradise Valley, Arizona, whose mobility was restored by intensive therapy received at the Lions Foundation of Arizona (LFA) in Phoenix. The president of the San Jacinto club, at Milton Techera's request, contacted then District Governor of 21-A, Leroy Gavette. Gavette, a member of the Glendale (Evening), Arizona, Lions Club, in turn contacted the Rehabilitation Clinic at the Foundation.

After a review of Raul's medical records, the clinic determined that hospitalization might be necessary. They referred the case to Dr. Norbert Dugan, head of the Spinal Cord Injury Service at the Institute of Rehabilitation Medicine at Good Samaritan Hospital, Phoenix.

Dugan thought that Raul might be helped—but how were the Techeras to pay for the air travel to the United States plus a long course of treatment? District Governor of J-3 in Uruguay, Lorenzo Odella, wrote Gavette about the problem. Within two months, the Glendale (Evening) Lions had raised enough money to cover expenses for the Techeras' ten-week visit. Meantime, the San Jacinto Lions raised the air fare and what seemed like an impossible dream became a reality.

Six weeks into a therapy program which was a cooperative effort of the hospital and the LFA staff, Raul regained the movement of his arms and legs. "I hope with what I have received and learned that I can someday learn to walk and return to work. I would also like to play soccer, basketball, and volleyball again," said Raul.

Lions make the world better in countless ways. Norwegian Lions and the Lions of Wisconsin teamed up to provide a piano for Leslie Lemke, a mentally handicapped Wisconsin youth of Norwegian origin. Blind and severely handicapped at birth, Lemke was abandoned by his family and raised by May Lemke, a nurse at the hospital. Though Lemke did not begin to speak until he was 26, at the age of 16 he suddenly sat down at a piano and played Tchaikovsky's Piano Concerto No. 1 after hearing it performed on television.

The Norwegian Lions have long had an interesting view of how handicapped people can be helped. They concentrate on what the handicapped person can actually do. The non-handicapped parts of the body—or mind—are trained so that the individual can experience the joy of accomplishment.

When the Norwegian Lions read in a newspaper about Lemke, they invited him and his foster mother to come to Oslo for the weeklong, Lion-sponsored "We Will Festival." Mentally handicapped people from all over the country are invited to take part in dance, song, and musical theater presentations. The event is designed to give talented, though handicapped, persons a distinguished performance venue for their talents. The festivals are held in the Oslo Concert Hall and are often attended by members of the royal family, parliament, government, and health officials.

Though Mrs. Lemke, at 84, was too ill and weak to make the trip, two of her daughters accompanied Lemke to Oslo. Scandinavian Airlines provided transportation in response to the Lions' request. The Norwegian Lions and the Lions of Wisconsin also teamed up to get Lemke a grand piano.

In Barranquilla, Colombia, ten-year-old Maria Gonzalez attends a special school that was started by the Barranquilla (Monarca) Lions Club in 1962. She goes to the special school because, although the world appears to her as it does to anyone else, to her it's a world totally without sound. Deaf since birth, Gonzales has never heard her parents' voices, the laughter of her little brother, the joy of music, or the rain falling on the roof of her family home.

But, with the loving support of the nuns who teach at the Lions-sponsored School for Deaf Children in Barranquilla, Maria Gonzalez will still be able to compete scholastically with anyone else. Fifteen teachers in the 22-room school teach 160 boys and girls 14 courses geared to the requirements of students ranging from five to 16 years of age.

"History is my favorite subject," said Gonzales, an excellent student with a cheerful disposition. "I like reading and spelling almost as much. The teachers at my school make learning new subjects interesting because they're willing to take the time to make sure we understand."

"We use modern techniques and equipment," explained Mother Maria de San Carlos, director of the facility. "For example, the audiophone is a machine that enables a hearing-impaired child to listen to a word or a phrase over and over and repeat it until he can say it correctly. These children need confidence when they come to the school and one of our primary objectives is to instill within each child the awareness that he can succeed; that he can learn to function in the outside world."

The School for Deaf Children cost $400,000 to build and equip; money was raised by the Barranquilla (Monarca) Lions Club through raffles, bingo games, dances, and other fundraising programs.

"In August, we have a day similar to the March of Dimes," said Past President Ramiro Besada. "This is called 'The Day of Love for a Deaf Child' and the spouses of club members collect money for the school. It is very successful and a good source of support for the institution."

"One of our main points in all of our projects is to make them practical," explained Enrique Arrieta, president of the club in 1980 and 1981. "At the school for the deaf youngsters we give them a solid grounding in academic subjects, but also teach them skills they can use for earning a living. They learn things like sewing, dressmaking, carpentry, and cabinetmaking, so they're equipped to support themselves when they finish the school."

Eighteen-year-old Juan Sanchez is an enthusiastic product of this training. Frightened and withdrawn when he entered the school 12 years ago, Sanchez was completely deaf, a result of sickness when he was four. Today he builds beautiful cabinets and furniture in a Barranquilla factory. Meticulous in his work and proud of his skill, Sanchez supports himself and enjoys the self-respect of a talented craftsman.

"It all started when I went to the School for Deaf Children when I was six," says Sanchez. "I was scared of everything and completely confused with my inability to hear anything around me. The sisters were very kind to me and slowly I learned how to read, write, count, and all the other subjects that are part of getting an education."

"I'm a good cabinetmaker," he adds, "and that's something else I'm grateful to the school for. It's changed my life, completely."

Sanchez is one of hundreds of hearing-impaired youngsters whose lives have been turned around by the school. The School for Deaf Children is only one of the major projects initiated and supported by the Monarca Lions Club.

Since its inaugural meeting at the Hotel del Prado on July 5, 1945, the Monarca Lions Club has devised and supported an extensive range of programs designed to improve the quality of life in Barranquilla. Homes for the homeless, clinics for the sick, education for those with limited opportunities; the Monarca projects bring an impressive blend of thought, energy, and good will to bear on community problems.

"In my opinion," said Besada, "these projects help us give our fellow human beings some of the good things we have received from God. We're all heavily involved in these activities and feel that most of our happiness comes from making God's children happy."

Lionism's international efforts succeed on such a vast scale because of each member's personal willingness to reach out to fellow club members around the globe to help those in need. As Past International President Judge Brian Stevenson observed, "Even as our service activities become more ambitious and far-reaching, we must never lose sight of the importance of personal involvement in achieving our goals."

Dedicated Lions in many places make millions of lives better—one life at a time.

CHAPTER THIRTEEN

The Lion: A Citizen of the World

LIONS who attended the 1944 International Convention in Chicago were looking backward at global devastation caused by five years of war, and forward to a future world that needed rebuilding, healing, and peace.

All Lions, but especially those at the convention, looked with hope to the United Nations, which had its founding sessions in San Francisco a few months later in April 1945. Private groups were invited to attend and help organize the world body. Lions came. Lions played an important role in writing the United Nations Charter. They stayed to make many contributions to many United Nations humanitarian and emergency relief programs.

Beginning in 1947, Lions Clubs International has maintained a consultative status to the Economic and Social Council of the United Nations (ECOSOC), the United Nations body concerned primarily with advancing the welfare of all people.

Since 1970, international presidents have made annual appointments of Lions to ECOSOC and to specialized, self-governing agencies within the United Nations. Lions of many nationalities and from clubs all over the world have worked with the U.N. on countless worthy projects, helped millions of people, and gained Lionism many new adherents.

"Without the participation of Lions in the United Nations, several thousand people who now belong to Lions clubs around the world might never have heard of the Lions, to put it mildly," is the belief of Past International Director Harold Curran. He was appointed to the Economic and Social Council of the United Nations, UNESCO, and served on the World Health Organization.

It was the traditional Lions' willingness to work in humanitarian causes anywhere in the world that brought them to San Francisco that summer of 1945. "We work with the humanitarian agencies of the United Nations on such matters as world health, food, education, and learning," explained Robert Uplinger, past international president who was appointed Lions liaison to the United Nations after Curran, in 1979.

"You learn what the United Nations is doing and recommend what we, as an international organization, might do in cooperation with them," he noted. "There are also weekly meetings. As representative, you are not on a committee, but you do go to briefings both by the United Nations and other groups. So really, what you are doing is gathering information most of the time."

So important is the role played by Lions in United Nations affairs that in 1978 Uplinger, on behalf of the association, was able to inaugurate Lions Day with the United Nations. It is a day of special, high-level briefings when Lions from all over the world are invited to attend. "The first year 35 people came. By 1989, 320 people took part," Uplinger said.

"We bring international officers in, presidents particularly. We start in the morning with a report from the current president on what he has seen during the year—an intermediate report, if you will. Then we usually invite the United Nations Secretary General, who summarizes world events. This takes about 45 minutes to an hour. Then we lay out a program which relates to the main service programs of Lions Clubs International."

What follows is a round of addresses from members of the United Nations Secretariat and from ambassadors to the United Nations from countries around the world. "At noon we have a luncheon in the United Nations' diplomatic dining room set with tables for ten. Invited are ambassadors from the Lions' countries, particularly those from countries where a Lion officer or director is actually present. Because most of the ambassadors and United Nations representatives are fluent in English, this is a good opportunity for questions on a one-on-one basis."

The day concludes with appearances by one or two more United Nations officials and a VIP tour of the United Nations Headquarters in New York City. On occasion, Uplinger explained, Lions clubs around the world have held simultaneous sessions in such places as Paris, Vienna, and Geneva. "There have been times when we radioed or transmitted by telephone the secretary general's messages to them. It's quite a network and everyone gets a taste of the United Nations on this day."

The purpose of Lions Day with the United Nations, in Uplinger's view, is not only to "acquaint people with the United Nations but to give them a broader view of what's going on in the world. They get a first-hand knowledge rather than a view which has been filtered through the press. You really end up after you attend one of these things with up-to-date knowledge."

Most recently, Lions Clubs International has also hosted a reception at the United Nations for ambassadors of Eastern European countries and China. "Until the last couple of years," Uplinger explained, "few full-fledged ambassadors from these countries attended. Now we are getting ambassadors from Russia, Poland, Czechoslovakia, Yugoslavia—even the People's Republic of China. One of the speakers this year was the ambassador from Hungary, which was particularly appropriate since the association organized clubs in that country shortly before."

"The biggest advantage," Uplinger explained, is that "they are becoming more knowledgeable about who Lions really are."

Uplinger feels that the first big step in Lionism's growing international role came at the time United States President Harry Truman asked Lions to help write the nongovernmental section of the United Nations Charter. "The idea of this section was that it would be a grassroots sounding board. Whether you were an American, an Englishman, a Frenchman, or a Russian, you could pass on thoughts and opinions to your representative at the United Nations," Uplinger said.

Lions joined in efforts to organize the United Nations late in 1944 when the State Department invited the association to send representatives to the Dumbarton Oaks Conference in Washington, D.C., and, a few months later, to the Bretton Woods Conference. These conferences resulted in the creation of the International Bank for Reconstruction and Development. In 1945, Lions Clubs International was one of 42 non-governmental agencies to send consultants to the American delegation at the San Francisco Conference—which actually wrote the United Nations charter.

As the charter took shape, it began to appear that the United Nations, like the League of Nations formed after World War I, would become merely a debating forum, hamstrung by its own bureaucracy, with little real authority. The American delegates became so embroiled in backroom debating and haggling that they had little time to confer with the nongovernmental consultants. Disillusioned, many of the Lions at the United Nations began to talk of packing up and going home.

Aware of this sentiment, the Lions representatives—then International President D. A. Skeen, Third Vice President Fred W. Smith, and Melvin Jones—decided on a course of action. They extracted a guarantee from the United States delegation to hold briefings on a twice-a-week basis with the consultants. They set up a dinner for the advisers which turned out to be much like a Lions club meeting. They were mixed up at the tables, sitting with strangers of widely different backgrounds. Before the affair began, it was announced that each guest would rise after dinner to introduce the man or woman at his left. The United States delegation acknowledged that the gathering, with its fellowship and good humor, did a great deal to preserve American optimism during those formative days.

At a meeting of the Lions representatives in his hotel room on the night following the official opening of the very first session of the General Assembly, Melvin Jones expressed the hope of Lions everywhere when he recounted the words of Isaiah 2:4: ". . . and they shall beat their swords into plowshares, and their spears into pruning hooks; nation shall not lift up sword against nation, neither shall they learn war anymore."

The nongovernmental sections of the United Nations Charter, as finally written, allowed the General Assembly to make agreements linking other self-governing organizations to the United Nations as specialized agencies. "We are the only service organization that since 1945 has remained an active participant in the United Nations," Uplinger said.

The first Object of Lions Clubs International closely parallels the second and third stated purposes of the United Nations. The first Object is "To create and foster a spirit of understanding among the peoples of the world." The second and third stated purposes of the United Nations are "To develop friendly relations among nations," and "To achieve international cooperation in solving international problems of an economic, social, cultural or humanitarian character."

The theme of peace has recurred many times in Lionism. In April 1982, during the tenure of International President Kaoru "Kay" Murakami of Japan, whose theme was "People at Peace," the association approved World Peace Day. On September 15, 1987, Lions Clubs International was recognized as a "peace messenger" by the United Nations at a special ceremony in New York for the role it played in the United Nations-designated International Year of Peace in 1986. The association's status as a leader in promoting good will was enhanced further when the board of directors approved a Policy Position on Peace in October 1987. International President Judge Brian Stevenson announced the policy on March 14, 1988, in conjunction with the tenth Annual Lions Day with the United Nations.

The policy was distributed in the ten official languages of Lionism: English, Finnish, French, German, Italian, Japanese, Korean, Portuguese, Spanish, and Swedish. Special printings in Russian and Chinese were made for distribution to Soviet and Chinese representatives at the United Nations on Lions Day.

General Wojciech Jaruzelski, then head of the Polish government, responded to the Policy Position on Peace: "I gave instructions that [the policy] be conveyed to the All-Polish community, including clergy . . . , women, youth, intellectuals."

From the office of the President of Israel came this response: "The sincerity and good sense of the document is far from the usual rhetoric . . . we are grateful for the material and its emphasis on the significance of even 'a single act of a single individual.' "

A copy of the policy was personally delivered by a Lion to a Soviet general and his wife by Kemp Forest, a member of the Lake Travis Lions Club near Austin, Texas. Forest made the 12,000-mile trip to see the Russian couple whom he had met 43 years earlier in the U.S.S.R. during World War II. The couple are now honorary members of the Lake Travis Club.

Lioness Jeanette Hedayati—now Lion Hedayati of the Graham (Tuesday), Texas, Lions Club—reported on the Graham Noon Lioness Club's grassroots movement paralleling the Policy Position on Peace at the Miami convention in 1989. "We sent letters of greetings to 1,800 Lioness clubs and district chairmen in 94 countries," she said. "We invited them to join in a united effort to write the leaders of our respective countries, expressing our desires for peace and urging the leaders to convene a world gathering for the purpose of establishing peace and consulting in a cordial, positive spirit toward solving the problems that afflict humanity." As a result, enthusiastic replies flowed in from more than 50 Lioness clubs in 21 countries.

Lions have spoken to the world again and again with the voice of peace. Peace projects undertaken by Lions are often so vast that they could be effectively organized worldwide only by Lions fiercely devoted to peace and driven by it as an ideal. One such project was the highlight in the administration of golden anniversary International President Edward M. Lindsey, who suggested it at his inaugural convention in New York in July 1966.

That project, the Peace Essay Contest, was hailed as brilliant when it was proposed. Many wondered, however, if it was practical. By 1966, Lionism had spread to 135 countries around the world. How could the anticipated massive flow of entries be handled and fairly judged?

The answer was contained in the Lions organization itself, beginning with the grassroots, individual Lions clubs. Any youngster between the ages of 14 and 21 could submit an essay to the Lions club closest to his or her home. There was no requirement that an entrant had to have a Lion in the family. The clubs appointed a committee of judges, publicized the contest locally, and sent the best entry up the line to the district judges. The winning district essay went to the multiple district level. Entries next were sent to the committees serving in each of the eight geographic divisions of the world. Eight essays emerged—one of them to be acclaimed as winner of the grand prize of $25,000 on July 8, 1967, the last day of the golden anniversary convention in Chicago. The winning essay would best articulate the selected theme, "Peace Is Attainable."

Under the direction of a special Peace Essay Contest committee headed by Past International President Aubrey D. Green, the Lions' machinery handled this vast project flawlessly. Within a month after the announcement of the contest, International Headquarters had mailed 200,000 entry forms to clubs. A month later, another 70,000 had been ordered and by the December 10, 1966, deadline, requests for forms reached nearly two million.

The contest captured international attention. Worldwide newspaper stories about the contest inspired millions of readers. *La Prensa* of Lima, Peru, announced a $1,000 prize to Peru's winner. Other newspapers followed suit with extra prizes at the local level. Lions clubs and districts offered their own scholarships and awards. As the deadline approached, essays poured in.

During an all-province tour of Canada, President Lindsey was presented with a $1,000 check from the Edmonton club to be given to the winner from Alberta. At Calgary, he told reporters that "If we get a million people thinking about how to attain peace, then the fringe benefits of the contest are more valuable than the essays for the $25,000 first prize."

Distinguished leaders from all parts of the world served as judges for the eight winning entries from the Lions geographic districts. The first judging panel included General of the Army Dwight David Eisenhower, honorary chairman; Homer J. Livingston, chairman of the board of the First National Bank of Chicago; Jose Figueres, former president of Costa Rica; Nobel Peace Prize winner Hideki Yukawa, physics professor at Kyoto University in Japan; Prince Bernhard of the Netherlands; and United States Secretary of State Dean Rusk. Rusk was also principal guest speaker at the golden anniversary convention.

One young woman and seven young men were in Chicago Stadium on July 8, all finalists, all nervous, all hoping that theirs had been selected as the winning essay.

They came from all parts of the world. There was William A. Curry of Carrollton, Alabama, winner in the United States and Affiliates Division. Andrew George Wyatt came from Wellington, New Zealand, winner in Australia, New Zealand, and Islands of the South China Sea and the South Pacific Ocean Division. Jose Benjamin Russo Zarza, of Asuncion, Paraguay, was the winner in the South and Central America and Caribbean Islands Division. Khalid Jamai of Rabat, Morocco, finished first in the Africa and Southwest Asia Division. Winner in the

European Division was Roger Schawinsky of Zurich, Switzerland. Montserrat Fong Campos of Mexico City, Mexico, was the winner in the Mexican Division and the only woman represented among the finalists. Masahiro Sahara, of Matsusaka City, Mie-Ken, Japan, came in first in the Orient and Southeast Asian Division.

Finally, President Lindsey ended the suspense by naming the first prize winner: A. Russell Wodell of Cranbrook, British Columbia, winner in the Canadian Division. Only 17 years old, Wodell had distinguished himself academically. He had graduated with honors from Mount Baker Senior Secondary School where he was president of the chess club and the drama club. He had served as secretary of the Mount Baker Centennial Committee and planned to enter the Faculty of Arts at the University of British Columbia.

Wodell called for restructuring of the United Nations to give it "the necessary power to enforce its aims, which will necessitate the establishment of the United Nations as a world government." Wodell also suggested "the creation of a special police force which shall be responsible for the maintenance of peace throughout the world." This force would include representatives from all nations with measures "to ensure that the police force itself cannot seize power and become a totalitarian body." Economic planning would be one of the functions of the federated world government proposed by Wodell, to correct "the great economic disparity in the world today." Without such a correction, "economic overbalance will lead to rebellion against the government, thus defeating its purpose."

The first Peace Essay Contest assembled the best words of youth to express ideas on how peace in the world could be attained.

Another worldwide Lions club project, the first Peace Poster Contest used art—a language which needs no translation—to dramatize those ideas. In fact, the official rules distributed to clubs in 1988 prohibited the use of words. Open to students, the Peace Poster Contest permitted paintings or drawings in any medium which carried out the theme, "Peace Will Help Us Grow." The Peace Poster Contest is patterned on the Peace Essay Contest. Winning entries moved from the clubs to judging at the district and multiple district levels, with 24 finalists selected by officers of Lions Clubs International and professionals in art and communications.

Entries came from 100,000 young people in 49 nations. Months of preparation were required before the winning poster was selected for eventual display at the Art Institute of Chicago, International Headquarters in Oak Brook, Illinois, and United Nations Headquarters in New York. From October 1–10, 1989, the poster appeared at the 44th International Eucharistic Congress in Seoul, Korea, at an exhibit hall in Olympic Park.

Created in delicate pastel hues, the winning poster depicts the white dove of peace above a flower, shown first as a tiny sprout and then in stages as it grows to maturity. It was called "a stunner" by one of the judges, Charles Stuckey, curator of 20th century painting and sculpture at Chicago's prestigious Art Institute. Another judge was Japanese artist Yutaka Takayanagi. Other judges on the six-member panel were: International President Austin P. Jennings; Michael Mahonec III, president of the New York City (Host) Club; Jan Ralph, of Australia, secretary, Art and Exhibitions for the United Nations; and Oleg Yershov, counselor, Embassy of the Soviet Union in Ottawa, Ontario, Canada.

Even to the casual viewer, this poster inspires a sense of tranquility, peace, and dignity. It shows a superb deftness of execution. Even more remarkable, it was conceived by a youthful artist who has lived all his life in Beirut, Lebanon, where death is dealt wholesale. Dodging shells fired randomly into apartment buildings or bullets sprayed from automatic rifles, no one is "safe" and anyone may be an enemy.

"I'm as old as the war and I hate it," exclaimed 14-year-old Mustafa Tahoukji, grand prize winner of the first Peace Poster Contest. "I have never known peace, but I dream of the day it will come to my country. I thank the Lions of the world who work every day toward the goal of world peace."

At an age when other teenagers are playing soccer or tennis, Mustafa has lived through practically every battle in the war and seen every army that has entered Beirut. His home is near the airport and the Palestinian refugee camps. As grand prize winner among 24 finalists, he received $500 and a plaque from President Jennings on Lions Day with the United Nations at United Nations Headquarters in New York on March 13, 1989. Mustafa, along with his mother and sister, were provided with transportation and hotel accommodations.

"Each artist took the time to imagine, even dream, what peace might be like, and each child who thought about the meaning of the theme and picked up a paint brush, pencil or pen, took the time to understand the importance of world peace," said President Jennings in announcing the winner. "That makes every participant an artistic peace ambassador in his or her own special way."

At the international convention in Miami in 1989, Past District Governor Georges Fernaine, a Lion for 27 years and a member of the Coast Lions Club in Beirut, spoke proudly of Mustafa. He also praised the clubs in Lebanon who worked to get more than 50 entries in the Peace Poster Contest from Lebanese youth. "Mustafa is studying painting in school and his professor thinks he will be a great painter. What delighted him in the United States was the opportunity to view great art in museums. The museums in our country have been closed for the past 15 years."

Fernaine and the 43 other Lebanese Lions who went to the Miami convention had to slip out of the country in small boats headed for Cyprus in order to board a regular airline flight.

"We will have to return the same way, risking shelling from Lebanese, Syrian, and Israeli forces when we enter the harbor."

Individual Lions don't just talk peace; they live it. Many of them have visited more countries than most diplomats. They have made firm and fast friends among men and women of all races, colors, and creeds. They know that bond of friendship which springs up almost instantly when one Lion meets another anywhere in the world.

The Lion as world citizen is typified by William Hiroshi Tanaka, Lions liaison to the United Nations in Vienna, Austria, and a past president of the Vienna (Cosmopolitan) club. He was a senior official at the United Nations Industrial Development Organization in Vienna for 16 years and is engaged in the export/import business. Tanaka has personally visited over 80 different countries on business or technical cooperation projects. Even his club is a unique microcosm of what the world could and should become. During a seminar on peace at the 1989 Miami convention, Tanaka described it "as the only Lions club where English is the main language in German-speaking Austria. More than 50 percent of our members hold passports from countries other than Austria, representing 20 different countries in all."

Tanaka said that because most of the club's members are engaged in international business or are from diplomatic or United Nations circles, "creating and fostering understanding among the people of the world is practically just an extension of their daily jobs."

The aptly named Vienna (Cosmopolitan) club quickly offered assistance to earthquake victims in Armenia as part of a Multiple District 114 activity. "Altogether, the equivalent of $100,000 was collected to build two houses in Leninakan in Armenia as part of the Austrian Village being built there." The club took similar fast action under its motto "Quick Help Counts Double" following severe earthquakes in Italy, Nepal, and Turkey.

"From all of my international contacts and friendships, I have come to recognize . . . that whatever color of skin, culture, language, belief, or political system, we are all human beings . . . sharing joys and sorrows, happiness and sadness alike," Tanaka said in Miami. "We all wear our Lions pin on our lapels with pride—proud to be members of the world's largest service club organization, larger in scale than the United Nations. Being a Lion automatically creates that warm feeling that exists between true friends. Such friendship strengthens mutual understanding and respect which is the basis of all peace," he told those attending an international relations seminar on peace.

Individual, inner peace lives among Lions, even in countries torn asunder by violence and terrorism. In Miami, Oscar Elejalde V, past district governor of District H-3 (Peru), called on all Lions to work to eliminate some of the underlying causes of discontent which make it possible for anti-democratic doctrines to take hold in a country. "In Peru, injustice takes different forms, such as extreme poverty . . . , the high rate of infant mortality, lack of adequate housing, hunger, malnutrition, endemic diseases, and the like," he explained.

"Insurgents are trying to impose a dictatorship by expanding anarchy and subverting law and order," he added. "More than 11,000 people have died in the last ten years as a result of the fratricidal struggles," Elejalde, a home builder and managing director of an international trading company, said in Miami. "Dollar losses have reached $15 billion, equal to Peru's national debt."

Despite that bleak picture, Elejalde sees Lions as "actual crusaders" who can "combat the original causes of discontent and misery in our own community in order to eliminate hopelessness." In Peru, Lions have acted on a national level to do just that, by approving a proposal called "Fasting" to help combat the country's hunger and malnutrition. Under this proposal, individual Lions are asked to fast twice a month. The money saved on meals goes to a district account, the funds from which are used to buy and distribute food among low income groups.

Through concrete actions like these, Elejalde asserts, "we are giving back to society a portion of what it has given us. Only with actions and attitudes such as these shall we be able to give some peace to those who suffer and, thus, protect the future of us all."

Past President Uplinger remarked that as the Lions representative to the United Nations he has seen an increased willingness of ambassadors from Eastern European countries to make reports on Lions Day at the United Nations. That willingness may indicate that a whole world is opening to Lionism.

In fact, the first Lions club in an Eastern bloc country was organized in late 1988 in Budapest, Hungary, with 27 charter members, eight of them women. The club charter was approved by Lions Clubs International on February 10, 1989. The historic organizational meeting was held at the Forum Hotel, Budapest's largest, on December 14, 1988. The session was covered extensively by Hungarian television, radio, and the press. At that meeting, then International President Jennings called the establishment of the Budapest club a significant breakthrough, a sentiment which was reiterated by the charter president of the new club, Dr. Laszlo Czegledi. "We are joining an organization that works for the common good in society." He said that despite many sad experiences in central Europe, "we still must believe in ethics, in truth, and in people's hope for a better life."

The key in chartering the first club in central Europe was its sponsor, the Helsinki (Hakaniemi) Lions Club of Finland. Other clubs from Germany, Austria, Italy, and Brazil have also made efforts to organize in Hungary. The prime mover was Past District Governor Leo Lindblom. He made several trips to Hungary for talks with government officials and prospective club members before completing the organizational work and gaining Hungarian government approval. Lindblom was instrumental in translating the association's constitution and by-laws into Hungarian and in presenting them to the minister of culture.

At the organizational meeting, Lindblom said, "Since we are members of the common family of Lionism, we work as members of this family for the common good."

Poland's first Lions club appeared in Poznan on April 22, 1989. Twenty-three members attended the first meeting.

Richard Piasek, of Poznan, a charter member, club secretary, and a sociologist, attended the Miami international convention. "We were helped in getting started by Swedish Lions," he said. "They had been sending orthopedic hospital equipment into Poland for some years. We have one meeting a month. We haven't started any projects yet, but we think we will work in three fields. One will be helping the crippled and handicapped, continuing the work of the Swedish clubs which helped us organize. The second area will be ecological problems, and the third will be educational, specifically youth exchanges. We hope we can find some help with that here at the convention."

Andrew Nowakowski, an orthopedic surgeon, charter member, and vice president of the Poznan club, even saw the possibility of forming Lions clubs in the Soviet Union. "It is possible, especially in the present situation." The most likely places for clubs to be formed within the U.S.S.R. would be Lithuania, Estonia, or Latvia, Nowakowski felt. Shortly after his comments at the Miami international convention, a Lions Club was formed in Estonia, and now there are clubs in Moscow and Lithuania as well. Within Poland, he believed that the next clubs would be organized in Warsaw and Gdansk, and this prediction came true as well. In his college days, Nowakowski took a course in ethics from the present Pope John Paul II.

Peace seems to be a more attainable goal when people's basic needs for food, housing, clean water, and health care are met. Lions have always understood this and worked unceasingly within their own countries and across countless borders to meet those needs.

Often, the efforts of just a few Lions working together within a single club can make a tremendous impact. The Lions Club of Sandila, India, is building a school that will eventually serve 400 children who cannot afford an education. "In that project, the government has given 3.7 acres of land with a value of $65,000 upon which the school is being built," H. N. Singh, charter president (1984–85) and former zone chairman explained.

"We began construction in 1986 and have completed six classrooms at a cost of $50,000. All together, there will be 12 rooms for children from kindergarten up to the 12th grade. We have applied for an LCIF grant and beginning in October 1989 we will begin giving financial aid to the school as well as books and other financial help."

Singh helped found the club in Sandila, a city of 20,000 people, because "we wanted to do something for the poor. Currently we are supporting 500 to 600 eye operations a year in addition to our work on the school."

For Singh, joining the Lions has made a profound change in his own life. "Becoming a Lion has made me a better human being by giving me an opportunity to work with others on projects which help the poor. Before I joined the Lions, I did things as an individual, like donating blood. Now I can work with other Lions on projects which make a real difference in the lives of people who are less fortunate than I am."

Because Lionism's concerns are humanitarian and international, Lionism can often slip across borders of nations even where governments are deeply suspicious of Lionism. Such was the case with Egypt, where President Gamal Nasser banned Lions in 1962 and this stayed in effect until 1975. "When we established the first Lions club in Egypt in 1954, a half dozen of us went to see Nasser and gave him a pin," explained Yanny Nawar, one of the founders of the Cairo, Egypt, Lions Club. "Later on he banned the Lions, but it was not really him. It was the confusion of the times."

The Lions came to Egypt as the result of the chance meeting of Nawar, a professor at Cairo University, with a few Lions from the United States who were visiting Egypt in 1954. Impressed by the United States Lions, Nawar and 15 others founded the club shortly afterwards.

"I also had the pleasure of introducing Lionism in Sudan, where we formed a Lions club in 1956, in Ethiopia in 1960, and in Libya in 1962," Nawar said.

For Nawar, as for most Lions, moving across a border into a country where there are Lions is to be always among friends. "In one instance, I was touring Europe by car and was having difficulty booking a room on the Italian Riviera. At one hotel I noticed the Lions emblem and asked who the Lion there was. I was told he was the owner of the hotel. When I asked him about the possibility of a room he answered: 'Look here, dear Lion, I will give you mine and I'll stay at home.'

"In West Berlin, I met a fellow Lion and he invited me to the Berlin Philharmonic Orchestra. It was a very delightful night. Whenever I wear my past president's badge at a Lions meeting anywhere, I get introduced all around and I am a friend among friends."

At one time, Lionism was viewed with suspicion as a "secret" organization and Lions meetings were banned by many Middle Eastern countries whose governments were not certain of Lionism's humanitarian and charitable purposes, Shaheer Nawar, Yanny's son, explained. "Eventually the Egyptian government began to understand the real meaning of Lions clubs and they started to send government representatives directly under the president to better understand what the Lions were. They found that we were people concerned about our communities and about international affairs. Now we are beginning to be seen very favorably in Egypt and many other countries."

"Now government officials are anxious to give speeches at the meetings and sometimes they even open themselves up to questions," echoes Yanny.

In troubled South Africa, Lions work side by side on humanitarian projects. Rick Loveland, a member of the racially mixed Midrand Lions Club, sees Lionism as a force "which can help break down the barriers. Working together, coming together with other groups of people—this does remove obstacles to understanding both internally in South Africa and on the international scene."

Loveland is manager of a manufacturing company. His wife, Trish, and daughter, Liza, are active supporters of Lionism.

"I'm going to be president of the Midrand club in 1989–90 and my wife is going to be working on starting a Leo club in our area. We've identified that as a very big need. My daughter is 16 and spends a great deal of time with Lion projects. She cleans up and paints houses for handicapped children, sells white canes, and works at fund-raising. She never misses a project."

Loveland, who has been a member of the 27-strong Midrand club since 1987, says that many South African clubs include members of all races. The Midrand club is part of District 410. Loveland estimates there are 71 clubs with "probably 3,500 to 4,000 members."

"Working as a Lion has made me a better person," said Loveland. "It has made me a better leader. It has given me a deeper appreciation of what is happening around the world and increased my understanding of the needs of other people.

"I think the future of Lionism looks very good. It improves communication between individuals, races, and nations. In South Africa, Lionism is a positive force in helping to solve our social problems. Unquestionably, the association's principles create harmony wherever people use them."

While all Lions are citizens of the world in the sense that they share a world view, many of them are also roving ambassadors for Lionism.

One of these ambassadors is Charles Robison, a member of the Des Plaines, Illinois, Lions Club and a Melvin Jones Fellow. With his wife, Katherine, Robison has visited 70 countries and all 50 United States—and managed to make a warm Lions connection in most of them.

"Visiting Lions clubs in foreign countries has become our hobby," Robison, a Lion for 41 years, explained. "On a five-and-a-half-week trip in 1985 to seven islands in the Caribbean, my wife, Katherine, and I met Lions and Lionesses in Aruba, Barbados, Curacao, Grenada, Jamaica, Nassau, and St. Kitts. At Bridgetown, Barbados, we joined a group of some 30 Lions and their ladies for an evening 'pirate ship' cruise. In Kingston, Jamaica, we attended a Lions club fundraising wine and cheese party at the residence of the consulate general of Switzerland."

In Aruba, Robison even joined in some typically Lionesque activity by spending a morning helping six members of the Aruba club paint bus shelters and put up signs which read "Aruba Decente" and "Keep Aruba Clean."

On a trip to South America, Robison recounts "the president of the Lions Club of Cuzco, Peru, his wife, and another Lion came to our hotel one evening. They took us on a night tour of the city, and to the top of a mountain overlooking the city where stands a huge lighted statue of Christ with outstretched arms." When the Robisons visited Buenos Aires, Argentina, they traveled by bus to a ranch where they enjoyed an outdoor barbecued beef dinner. "To enliven an otherwise dull trip, the bus guide asked people from each country represented to make comments. Few responded but I went forward, took the mike, and explained that back home before each Lions club meeting members sing "America" before dining. I sang the song as did a few other North Americans on the bus." In La Paz, Bolivia, "the president of the Club de Leones and two club officers met us for lunch. That evening they and their wives came to the hotel with the Lions district governor."

Robison feels that person-to-person contact "increases understanding of other races and cultures. Some of our best experiences in life have come as a result of meeting Lions overseas and realizing that Lionism is an interest which binds us all as brothers."

It would be difficult to find a more energetic Lions goodwill ambassador than veterinarian Dr. Ian W. Taylor, a Lion who has never missed a meeting since his first one in May 1958. A past president of the Wheeling, Illinois, Lions Club, Taylor is currently a member of the Arlington Heights, Illinois, club.

Like Robison, Taylor is a dedicated world traveler who has visited 57 different countries. In 1988, he even brought Lionism to the high seas aboard the Queen Elizabeth II. During a crossing from Southampton, England, to New York, Taylor presented a special plaque to ship's captain Alex J. Hutcheson.

That plaque travels today wherever the Queen Elizabeth II sails, displayed in a showcase near the main staircase. It reminds Lions and other passengers that Lionism crosses all national borders. It travels over them as easily as waves traverse the sea.

"The Lions Clubs International Directory is my Bible," said Taylor. In Morocco, that resulted in Taylor's attending six club meetings in ten days. He had sent his planned itinerary ahead to the clubs.

"I hadn't heard from any of the clubs, so I thought that was it. But when I got to Morocco and checked into the hotel, there was a message waiting for me which had been translated into English. The message said that my itinerary had been received and I would be contacted. Four out of the six clubs put on special meetings just for me. One of them was attended by 40 people. In one small, typical Arab town where I was to spend only a couple of hours, the club gave me a beautiful engraved brass tray, explaining that they were so happy that I, a visiting Lion, had contacted them. They seemed particularly happy that I was just an ordinary Lion from the United States. At every meeting, they always persuaded me to talk—though I don't take much persuading. Someone was always there to translate what I said at each of the six meetings."

The spectacular climax to Taylor's Morocco tour was a cocktail party in the capital, Rabat, given by the district governor and his wife. "After that, we were all loaded into cars for a trip to a feast at a nearby restaurant. It was a fitting climax to a wonderful international experience," Taylor added.

With the growth in sheer numbers, there has been vigorous expansion of humanitarian activities by Lions clubs worldwide, within national borders and across them. Lions have led the way in promoting peace and in generous efforts to eradicate hunger, disease, and poverty.

CHAPTER FOURTEEN

The Future

SUSTAINED accomplishment is the force that has propelled Lionism's explosive expansion around the world. Ever-sensitive to human needs, the association is active in the international arena with principles that dissolve all boundaries and meet basic human requirements.

On every continent Lions strive for peace where there is war, build homes for the homeless, bring food to the hungry, restore vision to the sightless, and hearing to the deaf. They provide opportunities to those without hope. Lions will continue to do these things. But the future will also bring many changes, including:

- Rapid formation of new clubs in Eastern European nations as they throw off communism and develop market economies.
- An emphasis on recruitment to reduce the average age of Lions and to bring in more women members.
- Development of a more global outlook among the Lions of the world.

When predicting the future, experts say we will eat better, exercise more, live longer. Work days will be shorter. Technology will free us of boring chores, both in the workplace and at home. The world will continue to shrink. Europe will become an economic force larger than the United States after the European Community becomes a trade free zone in 1992.

We will become more aware of the Earth's fragility and treat it with more respect. New scientific and technical marvels will continue to burst onto the scene with dizzying speed.

"We used to have one major advance every 25 years," a business executive said. "Now we have one every 24 hours." We will live in smart houses that control and regulate themselves and we will be able to watch TV on wall-size screens or on screens the size of a wristwatch face.

Health experts say they will be able to regrow some body parts and surgically transplant many more organs than now. Immunologists are working on ways to prevent insulin-dependent diabetes, multiple sclerosis, and rheumatoid arthritis. Some predict cures will be found as early as the year 2000.

The world's population—especially in the Third World—will continue to grow, and, on average, become younger. People will marry later, have children later, and become financially established later.

Scientific and technical developments may mean that Lions clubs will be undertaking different kinds of projects. But in many ways, Lionism and Lions will remain profoundly the same.

While man's next neighbors may be extra-terrestrial, Lions' goals for the future will remain down to earth. Lions clubs will continue to work on specific projects that change lives which otherwise might be without hope. Lions will do these things because, universally, they find that "in helping others, we find happiness for ourselves, and if we help more today than we did yesterday, then each tomorrow will hold greater promise for everyone," as then International President William Woolard phrased it in his inaugural address in Miami in June 1989.

Some, both inside and outside Lions, predict the decline of service organizations in this changed new world. Disagreeing emphatically is Past International President Woolard who in his inaugural address said, "I think we will be confronted with many more challenging opportunities in the next ten years than we have experienced in all of the preceding 72 years of our existence."

Enlightened leadership has played a major role in the association's international success.

"I find," said 1990–91 First Vice President Donald Banker, "that our leadership is increasingly professional. It is much more efficient in management programs than when I became a Lion in 1963. At International Headquarters in Oak Brook I find good business management and ideas and a willingness to put them into effect. In order to survive and compete in the world we have no choice but to become increasingly effective in management and leadership. There has been for the past five or six years a growing awareness of the need for long range planning and ways to implement the plans."

In October 1986 in Washington, D.C. the International Board of Directors commissioned a study by the Insititute for Alternative Futures. The study outlined future trends including changes in values, technology, global population growth, and growing age and wealth disparities around the world.

As a result of the study, Lions will be working harder in sight conservation. They will be active in diabetes awareness, drug education, youth exchange programs, and educational programs to fight illiteracy, but sight conservation will remain the number one priority.

"The Long Range Planning Committee has given Lions a sense of direction," said Past International President Austin Jennings. "The future of our association as far as long range planning is concerned is to provide a sense of unity of purpose. We are developing the largest program of its kind ever undertaken in sight conservation. It is a program of world dimension."

WOMEN IN LIONISM

Elly DuPre doesn't fit the profile of the average Lion today. Tomorrow she probably will. In the years to come, recruiting drives will lower the average age of members, bring in more women as members, and increase the number of clubs.

Elly DuPre is one of the more than 35,000 women who became Lions in the first three years after the constitution was amended in 1987 to invite women into full membership. Elly is young (40) and a member of the Hallandale-Hollywood Executive Lions Club, Florida, which boasts a 60 percent female membership. As executive director of the Broward Center for the Blind, she shares the typical Lions "can do" spirit with her male counterparts. Her club is committed to raising $1,000 to buy a voice adaptation program for the Broward Center, "and I've already ordered the stuff. I trust my club."

"Many service clubs which don't have service programs will die," DuPre predicts. "There's a trend away from service in general and more toward the materialistic. Until that pendulum swings back there will be some dry years trying to get young males involved, getting them off the racquetball court and into the noon meetings."

DuPre is typical of a new breed of Lions members who "are going to have a tremendous effect on our association over the next five or ten years," Lion Don Banker feels. "In my home state of California the new women Lions are young, aggressive business people who are very aware of what's going on and also aware of their own abilities. They are not afraid to assert themselves."

Women will bring a new enthusiasm to Lionism and its enterprise, Banker predicts, "because women realize that a Lions club is a method for them to involve themselves in the community, to become better known. It's interesting to note that the charter president of the new club in Poznan, Poland, is a woman. In Europe many of the Lionesses are becoming Lions and that's true in other parts of the world. In Malaysia, the Philippines, and right here at home Lionesses are making the switch. Despite the switchovers, Lioness clubs continue to grow and attract new members."

Rohit Mehta, 1990–91 Second International Vice President, is also enthusiastic about the future of Lionism in other parts of the world. "In India, we have Lions clubs which are composed 100 percent of women members. Some of these members are former Lionesses, but many women choose to remain as Lionesses."

There is an intrinsic appeal for women in Lionism, Past International President Austin Jennings feels. Sometimes this appeal is culturally based. "There is an emerging need to be a part of something beyond the home. Young women in Japan are joining because Lionism offers them a chance to become involved in service and in the life of the community outside the home." Past International President Jennings says that clubs, increasingly, are extending membership invitations to leaders in government, business, and industry who are women. "We don't have to make a major issue out of it. It's just going to happen in the natural course of events."

Past International President William Woolard adds, "The 1987 decision to admit women was one of the smartest things we've ever done."

Kenneth Olson of the New Britain (Evening), Connecticut, Lions Club sees healthy future growth for Lionism as more and more women become members. "Women have a wider perspective and they will help Lionism share in that perspective. Women have a different understanding of what is needed in the community and they will direct clubs into new activities. These activities might be in helping children or in child care, perhaps funding child care centers for women who wish to work during the day in order to get off welfare. As women around the world work for equal rights, including the right to equal opportunities and to guide their own destinies, Lions should encourage them to join Lions clubs in order that they may reach their potential of helping other people as members of Lions clubs."

Lions of widely differing geographical and cultural backgrounds share Olson's view. One is Thomas Gordon of the Lions Club of Xolotlan in Managua, Nicaragua. His wife, Deanna Alana de Gordon, has been a member of her husband's club for a year. "I think the idea of lady Lions is wonderful," said Tom Gordon. "Women are good workers, they're more understanding. They are often more serious about the things which need to be done. They will make a great contribution to Lionism."

Ruth Spies of the Davenport (Host), Iowa, Lions Club with 55 members joined the club with an ulterior motive, to provide glasses for students in a literacy program she started before becoming a Lion. "I started the literacy program in Davenport five years ago. Currently I have 17 students, both English and non-English- speaking that I am teaching to read."

The constitutional change that permitted women to join Lions clubs does not seem to portend the decline of Lioness clubs. These will continue to grow and prosper. As then International President Woolard said in his inaugural address in Miami in 1989, Lioness clubs "provide special opportunities for service for many thousands of hard-working people who prefer membership in a Lioness club. Some hold dual membership in a Lions club and in a Lioness club. I plan to do all I can to support the Lioness program, with increased membership and anything else that will make it a stronger organization. I want it to be clearly known that Lionesses are a very important part of the family of Lionism."

HEARING-IMPAIRED PROGRAMS

Research going on around the world today will make the Lions' work for the hearing-impaired more fruitful than ever. Researchers at the University of Michigan's Kresge Hearing Research Institute, for instance, are developing drugs to improve inner-ear blood flow and metabolism, offsetting the effects of noise or medication.

Hearing aid technology is moving forward in giant steps. New digital aids use microchip technology to amplify only the most important speech frequencies while reducing background noise. Large, body-mounted units of this type are available now. Tiny behind-the-ear versions are expected within five years with miniaturization of batteries and improvements in microchip and computer technology. Users will be able to tune the new aids to different noise environments.

As noted in Chapter Six, there are those who can't be helped by hearing aids because of damage to the hearing nerve. Even in these cases there may be nerve fibers remaining that can still send signals to the brain. The cochlear implant electrically stimulates nerve fibers that remain in the ears of the deaf or severely hearing-impaired in such a way as to give hearing sensations.

The part implanted in the ear is a 22-channel electrode array with a like number of electrical contacts. Each electrode delivers a different hearing or pitch sensation. The contacts carry signals from a receiver/ stimulator that is surgically placed in the bone behind the ear. The microphone and speech processor select and code the sounds most useful for understanding speech. The unit is carried by the user on a belt or in a pocket.

"Future developments will be in the external parts of the cochlear implant," explained Diane Meyer, Ph.D., director of the Audiology Center at the University of Illinois Eye and Ear Infirmary at Champaign, Illinois. "As better speech processors become available they can be simply attached to the implanted parts without further surgery. So this, our first patient, can benefit from advances made years from now," Meyer said. She is audiology consultant to the Lions of Illinois Foundation.

"Lions were the major source of funding for our center," Meyer continued. "Their contributions within the state and their vision will make it possible for many people to benefit not just once from technology, but again and again."

Lions clubs around the world work on a host of different projects for the hearing-impaired. They send repaired and renewed hearing aids to areas and communities that need them. They set up mobile hearing screening units to help find hearing loss, provide sophisticated testing equipment for hospitals, and furnish specialized instruments like telephone amplifiers for individuals who are hearing-impaired. They back closed-caption TV programming. Clubs adopt individuals around the world who need surgery or special equipment to restore or improve their hearing.

DRUG AWARENESS

Twenty-seven-year-old Stephanie turned to alcohol at 15, when heavy drinking seemed the only way to dull her loneliness and stifle boredom. Before her 22nd birthday, she was hooked on cocaine, too. "I tried to quit many times, but couldn't," she said. Last year, at 24, she checked into the Lions Center in Malmedy in Belgium. She suffered through the rigors of withdrawal, then followed a schedule crammed with classes on addiction and therapy.

"It took me out of my life. The fog I'd lived in slowly began to lift," said Stephanie. She hasn't had a drink or a drug since she got out 18 months ago. She works steadily as a secretary and looks ahead to a drug-free life.

Significantly, at the 1924 International Convention in Omaha, Nebraska, Lions first voiced concern as a body at the problem of drug abuse, encouraging communities to crackdown on drug addiction.

In many nations, Lions sponsor thoughtful education and prevention programs to help keep drugs out of the community in the first place. It's not easy to teach but prevention is good medicine. Drug experts now say that effective programs must begin in kindergarten. They deliver facts about drugs without resorting to scare tactics. These programs increase students' confidence by emphasizing individual worth, show students how to resist peer pressure, and improve the school atmosphere so that even low achievers form an attachment to the institution. Experts encourage healthy, wholesome "highs" like rafting or ski trips to achieve some of the thrill that drugs provide. Special efforts must be directed at high risk students such as children of drug abusers or those from disadvantaged backgrounds. Confidential counseling sessions outside the normal curriculum also help.

In the early 1970s, so-called "informed scientific opinion" declared that cocaine was not a dangerous drug. These scientists believed that cocaine was not addictive and did not lead to use of other drugs. History has proven the stupidity of these views.

In the 1960s, marijuana was often called a "recreational drug" that was harmless in all respects. At the time, many scientists and physicians supported that theory with supposed documentation. Painful experience has shown otherwise.

The latest on marijuana is a study from the National Cancer Institute of the United States showing that if a mother smokes marijuana during pregnancy she increases her child's risk of developing a rare form of leukemia by as much as 11 times. This is nonlymphoblastic leukemia which accounts for 15 percent of childhood leukemias. That is only one of marijuana's many damaging side effects.

The Lions' approach, focusing on drug education as a way to reduce demand, is a strategy that has many experts on its side. Michael Darcy, president of Gateway Foundation in Chicago, Illinois, counsels that "as long as there is a demand for drugs there are going to be suppliers who will meet that demand. In the future, we will have to concentrate on the demand side rather than the supply side of the equation."

"What I like about the approach of Lions Clubs International is that they are interested in worldwide prevention programs designed to discourage experiments with mind-altering drugs."

Statistics bear out the effectiveness of drug education. Illegal drug use declined by about 25 percent in the United States between 1985 and 1988, according to a $2.5 million survey conducted by the Research Triangle Institute of North Carolina. The survey was commissioned by the National Institute on Drug Abuse. William Bennett, President Bush's drug czar, and Louis Sullivan, U.S. Secretary of Health and Human Services, called the overall drop in drug use "dramatic." Both credited recent campaigns waged in schools, the news media, and workplaces for much of the decline.

The survey estimated that the number of Americans using at least one illegal drug dropped from 37 million in 1985 to 28 million in 1988. Bennett labeled the decrease in occasional drug use "a triumph of changed attitudes."

On every continent Lions implement vigorous drug prevention programs that change attitudes and stop drug abuse before it begins.

LIONS-QUEST—SKILLS FOR GROWING

Lions have long recognized the wisdom of the educational approach with its aim of "changing attitudes." Since 1986 Lions have increased their support and participation in the Lions-Quest program as an effective weapon against drug abuse. Almost five million young people in 18,000 schools have benefited in the Lions-Quest *Skills for Adolescence* program. More than 20,000 men and women have been trained as instructors worldwide.

The newest addition to the *Skills* curriculum is aimed at children from kindergarten through fifth grades. After being piloted in 41 schools in North America, *Skills for Growing* was implemented in 1,400 schools in the 1989–90 school year, with expansion to 3,000 schools planned for 1990–91. The program builds upon the success of Lions-Quest *Skills for Adolescence* which is aimed at the 10 to 14 age group.

Skills for Growing was developed through a cooperative effort of Lions Clubs International, the National Association of Elementary School Principals (NAESP), National PTA, and Quest International. Cooperating organizations include the American Association of School Administrators, Just Say No Foundation, and the National Council for Juvenile and Family Court Judges. Also behind the program are the National Federation of Parents for Drug-Free Youth and the Pacific Institute for Research and Evaluation.

A comprehensive program for the elementary grades, *Skills for Growing* brings together parents, educators, and community leaders to teach basic life skills, including:

- Making wise decisions
- Communicating effectively
- Setting goals
- Accepting responsibility

- Building self-confidence
- Developing self-discipline
- Solving problems
- Resisting negative influences

Past International President Austin P. Jennings said that Lions Clubs International chose to co-sponsor the new program "because of the strong community support built into the *Skills for Growing* curriculum. This is an opportunity for Lions Clubs to bring together the resources within the community to create a positive environment in the schools."

The Quest approach is endorsed by Rox Campbell, president of the Lions Host Club of Edmonton, Alberta, Canada. He dreams of "a drug free society where substance abuse is no longer a problem and where children can make the right choices in how they want to live."

Campbell was quick to act when an opportunity to make his dream a reality came along. The chance came when Margaret-Ann Young, principal of the Aldergrove Elementary School in Edmonton turned to the Host Club for help after her school was picked to pilot the Lions-Quest *Skills for Growing* program.

"The club immediately picked up the challenge and fully funded the $5,500 cost of materials and training for teachers and support staff at a three-day workshop held in Edmonton," Campbell said.

"My dream is to have every child realize his or her potential and with that become productive and happy members of society," explains Principal Margaret-Ann Young. With the kind of support she's getting from the Host Lions Club, she is that much closer to seeing her dream fulfilled.

DIABETES AWARENESS

Lions will continue to play a key role in the fight against diabetes. They have screened millions for the disease and have alerted millions more to its danger by educational and media projects. Lions Clubs International has produced and distributed a wide variety of printed materials on this disease. In 1988, it produced a film/video *Don't Be Blind to Diabetes.* Available in many languages, the film has gone into international distribution.

Through 1989, the Lions Clubs International Foundation provided $1.8 million in grants. This money was used for widely divergent projects including public information and funding research in medical centers all over the world. Much of that research has looked into the causes and treatment of diabetic retinopathy, responsible for much of the blindness in the world today. Typical is the grant of $200,000 to the Kobe School of Medicine in Japan. It will be used to help a group of scientists led by Shigeaki Baba, M.D., of the Kobe University of Medicine to study the relationship of diabetes to the immune system.

Most diabetes researchers are now convinced that Type I, or insulin-dependent diabetes, is an autoimmune disease. They theorize that the body's immune system mistakes the beta cells that produce insulin as "enemies" to be attacked and destroyed.

That theory goes back to the 1960s when scientists noted that people with other autoimmune diseases were usually prone to diabetes. In the 1970s, blood studies among sets of identical twins by Stuart Soeldner, M.D., of the Joslin Research Laboratories in Boston, Massachusetts, strengthened that suspicion. Soeldner studied the blood of twins where one had diabetes and the other did not. He found insulin-attacking cells in the blood of non-diabetic twins long before they actually contracted diabetes.

Dr. Baba will use the LCIF grant, along with a $100,000 grant from the Japanese government, to look for a specific gene that will identify people at high risk of developing diabetes. Ultimately he, and researchers like him, hope to discover ways to shut down the gene responsible for destroying insulin-producing cells. A shut-down could slow the onset or reduce the severity of the disease. It might even prevent the disease from developing in individuals from a family with a history of diabetes.

Other scientists are at work on an artificial pancreas for diabetics. The most promising approach so far is to harvest insulin-producing cells from human or animal donors and enclose them in a plastic membrane before implantation. The membrane would act as a pancreas, allowing the insulin to be secreted while protecting the foreign cells from the person's immune system.

Another promising breakthrough is the Eli Lilly development of

Humulin, human insulin synthesized by means of recombinant DNA technology.

The DNA molecule is the basic building block of life. It carries the genetic information that determines the future of each cell. DNA molecules can be changed in a complex series of scientific steps to foster production of desired traits. In this case, bacterial host cells have been programmed, through the insertion of desired genes, to produce the Humulin proinsulin molecule. That is precisely what the normal pancreas does. Vast quantities of these host cells can be produced by fermentation. The proinsulin molecules are processed and purified to yield insulin that is structurally identical to human insulin.

All types of insulin are proteins that are made from chemical building blocks, amino acids. Human, beef, and pork insulin all have 51 amino acids linked together. Insulins obtained from animal sources have one or more amino acids that differ from those of human insulin. The structure of Humulin is identical to that of insulin produced by a healthy human pancreas. One of the benefits of this synthesis is that patients may be less likely to react allergically to Humulin than to animal source insulin.

LEOS AND LITERACY

There are 889 million individuals in the world who are unable to read and write. Usually they are poor and undernourished, as well. They are barred from participating in the bright promises of the future because they are unable to fill out a job application or understand a newspaper. An international project entitled "Literacy and Culture," proposed for Leos and approved in June 1988 by the International Board of Directors, brings the talent and energy of the 104,000 Leo club members to bear on the worldwide problem of illiteracy.

How this worldwide army of Leos can work with other organizations, including UNESCO, in the fight against illiteracy was sketched out by Past International Director Rodolfo Alfredo Marinelli at a seminar for Leos held at the International Convention in Miami in June 1989.

The Leos Literacy and Culture Project involves two major thrusts. The first of these is teaching non-readers how to read, write, and manipulate numbers. Where qualified, Leos are doing this themselves. In other cases they are helping to provide the teachers, materials, and organization required.

The second aspect of the project is to develop interest in and awareness of the participants' native culture, as well as other cultures, by sponsoring events such as concerts, art displays, and poetry readings. For those lacking opportunity for such activities, this dual approach "can break this wall, which in the world of today, is a wall of ignorance," Marinelli said.

"Nothing less than a well-educated mankind will end the isolation of large numbers of people and allow them full participation in building a better future. Leos are particularly well suited to wage an effective fight against the scourge of illiteracy because as young people, they themselves are building their own futures," Marinelli added.

Leos like the concept. A survey of Leos in many parts of the world showed literacy was the subject which interested them the most, ranking ahead of leprosy eradication and work among those who suffer from AIDS. Marinelli explained that the Literacy and Culture approach:

- gives Leos a "main thrust," long-range program;
- builds a greater sense of public awareness of Leos by identifying them with a specific area of activity;
- is able to show significant results for relatively low costs;
- complements similar programs like the UNESCO literacy program and many local programs;
- can be adapted to almost any country or region.

The program offers great flexibility. Leos are doing the work themselves. Some clubs are contracting with teachers and assuming responsibility for paying their fees; building schools; donating essential materials such as books, pencils, and paper; providing scholarships to students in need; caring for small children in order that parents may attend classes; and generally addressing their communities' needs in regard to the process of literacy. In the few locations where illiteracy rates are very low, Leos are encouraged to help support the literacy efforts in other areas of the world.

The cultural aspects of the Literacy and Culture Project involve an extensive range of activities including supporting local theatrical groups as well as creating their own performances; conducting essay, visual art, poetry, and musical contests in local schools; and organizing concerts for the public. Leo clubs are also sponsoring exhibitions by local and national artists and performers, funding libraries, and establishing inter-cultural relationships through twinning clubs and youth exchange programs.

"No one has a better opportunity than our youth, by means of this program, to improve the future of humanity," Marinelli concluded.

THE ENVIRONMENT

Lions are builders. They also carefully preserve what is important. During his 1972–73 term International President George Friedrichs encouraged Lions clubs to carry out environmental service projects.

In keeping with these interests, the guest speaker at the final session of the 1973 International Convention was Shirley Temple Black, former child movie star. She stressed the need for global consciousness in addressing problems of environmental quality. Black highlighted the need to acknowledge "our spiritual kinship as human beings, as the great law transcending nations, ideology, and every other private interest." At that time she was serving as Special Assistant to the Chairman of the President's Council on Environmental Quality.

Today, many Lions are concerned with preserving the world's rain forests.

Tropical forests exist on only about six percent of the Earth's land surface. However, they support more than 50 percent of all living species, protect water supplies, help regulate global climate, and prevent soil erosion. They contain many of the plants that have important medical uses for such ailments as arthritis, heart disease, and cancer. Man is relentlessly destroying these areas at the rate of 50 acres a minute; even faster in some places.

Trees change carbon dioxide into oxygen and help preserve the planet's breathable air. The world's forests are critical factors in the world's climate and the nursery for at least half of the world's plants and animals species. The widely-publicized "greenhouse effect" is one of the deadly results of forest destruction.

The Amazon rain forest is home to at least 60 million species of life. An incredibly complex natural laboratory, it is a place to study anything from evolution to global warming to medical uses of plants. With more than 2.5 million square miles of green carpet, fertile valleys, rain forests, and savannah, the Amazon rain forest is two-thirds the size of the 48 contiguous U.S. states. Seventy percent of the Amazon lies within Brazil; the rest occupies parts of Ecuador, Peru, Bolivia, Colombia, Venezuela, Guyana, and Surinam.

A longtime student of the destruction of the fragile rain forest is Past International Director Zander Campos da Silva of Goiania, a city of 1,200,000 people in the central part of the country near Brasilia, the capital. A Lion since 1965, Campos da Silva was elected to the International Board of Directors in 1984.

"Saving the Amazon rain forest is an issue that has excited Lions throughout the world," he said. "Lionism began in Brazil on April 16, 1956. We now have 1,763 clubs and 45,600 members at work on more than 2,000 projects in our 29 districts. Preserving the world's forests is one of the most important goals for us and for everyone in the world because of the danger of global warming."

At the close of the summit meeting in France on Sunday, July 16, 1989, the leaders of the seven major industrialized nations recognized global warming as a "serious threat" to the planet. They agreed to pursue "determined and concerted" policies to protect the world's environment.

French President Francois Mitterrand, the summit host, read the 22-page final communique while flanked by his summit partners from the United States, Britain, West Germany, Italy, Canada, and Japan.

The leaders declared: "Decisive action is urgently needed to understand and protect the Earth's ecological balance. We will work together to achieve the common goals of preserving a healthy and balanced global environment."

The promise of international cooperation in protecting our ravaged environment is long overdue. The problem cuts across all national boundaries. Stopping the savage destruction of the world's forests is critical for the health of human beings everywhere.

SIGHT CONSERVATION

Lions have been identified with service to the blind since before 1925, when Helen Keller appeared at the International Convention to ask Lions to become Knights of the Blind.

Lions will no more move away from sight conservation than the Green Bay Packers will stop playing football, suggests Norman Dahl, a Lion for 37 years and a former District 1-A Governor. "The great Green Bay Packers coach, Vince Lombardi, had a seasonal rite," explains Dahl. "He would gather all his professional players around him, hold up a football and say simply, 'This is a football.' Lions do the same thing every few years—they start with the basics, and for a Lion, sight conservation is a basic of basics."

The same theme was echoed by Past International President Woolard: "Sight conservation and prevention of blindness have been major parts of our service activities in America and indeed in most of the clubs throughout the world."

New technology and medical advances will multiply Lions efforts. Over the next few years and into the next century they will be able to do more to prevent blindness and restore sight to more people than at any time in the past.

Ophthalmologists may be able to correct vision problems by reshaping the corneal surface, according to Morton Goldberg, M.D., of the Wilmer Institute, Johns Hopkins University, Baltimore, Maryland.

A whole new generation of lasers will be used to correct ordinary eye problems like nearsightedness and farsightedness, Goldberg predicts. The technique involves eye sculpturing. A narrow circle of light is directed by computer over the eye's surface. Microscopic layers of the cornea are vaporized to flatten or steepen the eye's curvature. The procedure, now undergoing its first clinical trials, uses an unusual kind of laser called an excimer, originally developed to etch silicon chips.

Instead of burning cells away as ordinary lasers do, the excimer relies on the high quantum energy of its ultraviolet light to destroy the molecular bonds in the cell. "This new laser technology will be used to change high refractive areas or very marked levels of nearsightedness or astigmatism. After surgery, patients will have normal sight or reduced dependence on glasses or contact lenses," Goldberg explains.

Improved conventional surgical methods and laser surgery will combine to further refine glaucoma therapy. "Better eye drops are being developed all the time," he adds.

Multiple District 22 Lions in Delaware, Maryland, and Washington, D.C., are supporting the eye research center at the Wilmer Institute which Dr. Goldberg directs. "They have pledged $1.5 million toward the center and recently obligated $100,000 to sponsor research into visual rehabilitation of diabetic retinopathy patients who would not benefit from current medical or laser therapy."

Wilmer Institute scientists are collaborating with the National Aeronautical and Space Agency to apply space age technology to build a pair of special glasses to help those with markedly reduced vision to navigate better and read a little bit better. Computers and scanning devices have improved. Already developed are machines that scan typed sheets and convert what they read into synthesized, audible language. Other machines permit a blind person to type on a keyboard. The machine then reads aloud what they have typed.

On the horizon: tiny TV cameras mounted on eyeglasses will transmit electronic images directly to the brain's visual cortex. Scientists are working on "liquid sunglasses"—eye drops that absorb most of the sun's ultraviolet rays, thought to be a major contributor to cataracts.

Scientists are developing new eye adhesives which will make eye surgery safer and easier and reduce post-operative problems, according to Dr. Jeffrey Robin. Dr. Robin is associate professor of ophthalmology at the University of Illinois College of Medicine at Chicago.

"Advances in our understanding of how we see will continue," Dr. Robin said. "Over the next ten to 20 years we may be able to prevent macular degeneration and cataracts. Lions have been most supportive of eye care and eye research around the world. They fund eye banks and raise money for studies of harvesting eye parts. Lions run eyeglass programs and eye clinics all over the world."

The Lions International Sight Symposium held in Singapore in the spring of 1989 zeroed in on areas where Lions' efforts would have the greatest effect. There, members of the Lions Clubs International Long Range Planning Committee, Service Activities Committee, and executives from the Lions Clubs International headquarters in Oak Brook heard presentations by world health experts.

Members of the symposium concluded that sight conservation programs would translate into large and measurable results. For instance, providing Vitamin A to children in Third World countries would prevent blindness or death in millions. Vitamin A deficiency causes xerophthalmia or "dry-eye," one of the most common causes of blindness around the world, especially in children. It appears first as a spot on the white surface of the eye. Eventually it causes a complete meltdown of the cornea and blindness. In millions more people, blindness is caused by cataracts and could be corrected by relatively simple surgery. Trachoma causes "something like 25 percent of world blindness, and is the most common blinding disease around the world," Dr. Bjorn Thylefors told Lions at the symposium.

Thylefors, who is director of the Prevention of Blindness section of the World Health Organization based in Geneva, estimated 360 million trachoma cases occur each year. "We feel that six to nine million of those cases are blind due to the disease" which is caused by an infectious virus-like organism called chlamydia. The infection leads first to an inflammation on the inside of the eyelid, then to under-lid scarring. The scarring tends to destroy the normally transparent part of the cornea causing it to become opaque.

Trachoma and other sight-robbing diseases are presently targeted for eradication by the far-reaching SightFirst program of the association, launched at the 1990 International Convention in St. Louis, Missouri. It is a direct outgrowth of the investigative work of the International Board of Directors and the Sight Symposium in Singapore. Indeed, it is the most elaborate and detailed service program in which Lions Clubs International has ever been involved.

SightFirst: Lions Conquering Blindness

What greater challenge could Lions face than to reverse the course of blindness by the end of this century?

That is the ambitious aim of SightFirst, Lions Conquering Blindness, Lionism's most far-reaching global program. Undoubtedly the biggest Lion project ever conceived, its goal is to eliminate the world's backlog of blind who need treatment and build the systems needed for nations to keep up with new cases.

SightFirst asks Lions to play a leading role in effectively reversing the course of blindness by the end of the 20th Century. It is a battle against blindness that the world had been losing—losing so badly that there were 40 million blind people in the world in 1990. Experts predict that number could double by the year 2015.

Most frustrating of all is that most blindness is preventable—or reversible once it occurs. Eye care specialists estimate that 80 percent of those who are blind today would not be if proper health measures had been taken. Significantly, 90 percent of those with vision loss live in developing countries—countries with resources too meager to train people, buy equipment, and set in place the programs which would prevent and cure blindness.

Because most blindness is either preventable or treatable, the world-wide Lions attack on blindness has a good chance of eradicating the disease.

SightFirst projects include vision screening, building medical facilities, training medical or other professionals, sending teams of cataract surgeons into remote areas, establishing eye banks, and distributing used eyeglasses, activities which have already been brought to the status of high art by Lions.

Blindness was selected for the major international service initiative after extensive study and analysis by the International Board of Directors. SightFirst was officially launched in St. Louis at the 73rd International Convention in July 1990. Planning for the massive initiative began with a study initiated by the board's Long Range Planning Committee. World sight conservation leaders provided information to the Sight Symposium held prior to the April 1989 board meeting in Singapore. Many of these same experts met with key staff people at International Headquarters in early 1990 to develop a workable plan.

"For nearly 75 years, Lions have given clear evidence of their will to succeed in whatever course they embarked upon," said 1990–91 International President William L. Biggs. "Our SightFirst program will, I am confident, prove to be a decisive step toward our ultimate goal: To Conquer Blindness."

Lions, Lionesses, and Leos around the world support SightFirst by organizing activities, providing funding, or providing transportation, food service, clerical help, or other support required on site. Clubs also run publicity campaigns to support SightFirst activities or organize educational programs using literature and speakers bureaus.

By donating to Lions Clubs International Foundation (LCIF) or providing more Melvin Jones Fellowships, clubs help underwrite this massive assault on blindness. The cost, to be funded by LCIF, is expected to exceed $100 million in the first six years alone.

SightFirst requires Lions Clubs International to work closely with the World Health Organization (WHO), the International Agency for the Prevention of Blindness (IAPB), and other governmental and nongovernmental agencies.

Projects are conducted on the national or multiple district level or at the district level if the district encompasses an entire country. District and multiple district sight chairmen and district governors determine the potential of specific projects, set goals, and determine costs. Each SightFirst project ties into, or actually becomes a part of, a national program. Key players in SightFirst projects are professionals in the field of sight conservation who serve as technical advisors. Hired by Lions Clubs International and assigned to specific geographic areas, they work closely with the involved country's ministry of health and local health and sight conservation organizations.

One provision which will make the effects of SightFirst felt far into the 21st Century is that projects must eventually become self-sustaining. Local governments or local health organizations must continue the project after Lions have ceased active support.

Fully 50 percent of the world's blind are blind from cataracts in which the natural lens becomes clouded. Many of the SightFirst projects will be devoted to providing teams of ophthalmologists and other medical specialists to perform cataract surgery. Other kinds of vision loss targeted by SightFirst are:

- Diabetic retinopathy, a complication of diabetes which may cause blindness.
- Trachoma, a scarring and granulation within the eye caused by a contagious infection.
- Onchocerciasis (river blindness), a parasitic infection which causes blindness.
- Xerophthalmia, a Vitamin A deficiency usually found in children.

Currently, the battle against blindness is being lost. To win it, huge obstacles must be overcome: lack of medical services in remote areas, poor transportation and communications, and insufficient understanding, even among professionals, of the need for blindness prevention and treatment.

The odds were long when Helen Keller called upon Lions in 1925 to become "Knights of the blind in the crusade against darkness." They are still long, but improving.

SightFirst will be the global thrust that will dramatically reduce the odds of the spread of blindness. The scope of the program was clearly defined in an official statement passed by the International Board of Directors, in October 1990.

SIGHTFIRST
A MAJOR INTERNATIONAL SERVICE COMMITMENT
OF
LIONS CLUBS INTERNATIONAL

THE CHALLENGE:

Forty million people living in the world today are blind. Eighty percent are needlessly blind because their blindness could have been prevented or can be cured.

THE GOAL:

SightFirst: Lions Conquering Blindness will eliminate reversible and preventable blindness worldwide, while fostering present and future Lions service with the visually impaired.

THE PROCESS:

SightFirst is an umbrella which brings together all of the sight related activities that Lions have been involved in since Helen Keller challenged the Lions to become the knights of the blind in 1925; all of the sight related activities that Lions are currently involved in now; and all of the sight related activities that Lions will become involved with in the future.

The success of SightFirst is dependent upon three levels of commitment and involvement.

The first level and very foundation of SightFirst requires the development and continuation of all of those sight related activities that Lions support around the world today. All Lions clubs are encouraged to continue to develop ways to assist those who are blind through those successful programs developed and used in the past and to expand those efforts into the future.

The second level of commitment is to our Lions Clubs International Foundation. The success of SightFirst will require extensive programs beyond current involvement. LCIF will be the funding source for those new major projects approved and initiated to reverse or prevent blindness. Every Lions Club needs to conduct at least one project every year to support the funding of SightFirst through LCIF.

The third, and only new component of SightFirst, includes all that Lions around the world will do to eliminate preventable blindness in the future. Lions Clubs International will work closely with other organizations dedicated to blindness prevention.

This cooperative effort will provide every district with opportunities to determine blindness prevention needs in their area, to develop programs that will meet those needs and to receive assistance and direction that will ensure the success of the proposed program.

In summary, SightFirst is all that has been done, all that is currently being done and all that will be done to reverse or prevent blindness worldwide, while continuing to work with the visually impaired.

Daniel Burnham, the architect who drafted Chicago's magnificent Lake Front Plan in 1909, wrote: "Make no little plans. They have no magic to stir men's blood and probably themselves will not be realized. Make big plans: aim high in hope and work. . . ."

Lions have always heeded that advice. They go forth in a crusade against blindness with SightFirst, to realize a great plan which truly has the magic to stir mens' blood.

Born during the fury of the First World War, Lionism came of age in the peace that followed World War II. In the final decade of the 20th Century, the association extends the vision affirmed by its founders in 1917. It recognizes the intrinsic worth of each human being.

With undiminished vigor the association moves into the 1990s numbering 1,380,000 Lions, 148,000 Lionesses, and over 100,000 Leos. *The Lion* magazine is published in 19 languages. Nearly 40,000 clubs in 171 different nations and geographical areas lift spirits and hopes with practical designs for effective action. The 800 members at the end of 1917 have been multiplied countless times.

A circumstance arose shortly before entering the final decade of the century that tested the capability of Lions Clubs International to depart from its long-standing way of choosing its leadership. Never before had anything of this nature occurred in the history of the association. It was, most assuredly, a situation of critical importance, one that was born in tragedy.

Mathew Seishi Ogawa, of Tokyo, Japan, was serving as first international vice president when he died in September 1989. Donald E. Banker, then second vice president, automatically advanced to the position of first vice president and chose to serve a full term in that office, thus necessitating a special meeting for the selection of a Lion to serve as international president during 1990–91. Following litigation and eventual settlement with a member club that believed the association's response to filling the vacancy was not appropriate, the special meeting was held at International Headquarters in June 1990 to select a president to serve during the ensuing year.

This was conducted in accordance with the provisions of the International Constitution and By-Laws. A total of 159 votes were cast by current and past international officers and directors, resulting in the selection of Past International Director William L. "Bill" Biggs, of Omaha, Nebraska, U.S.A., to serve as 1990–91 International President.

The outcome demonstrated clearly that the association was able to adapt to the demands of the moment, to change a particular method of operation when necessary.

Indeed, change is the process by which the future challenges our lives. While conscious of their international mission, members remain firmly rooted in their own communities. They face the future with determination and courage. Working in varied service areas on every continent, Lions experience the quiet joy and expanded usefulness that come from unselfish service.

Lionism's enduring principles ensure continuing growth and progress. Melvin Jones put it this way: "I hope there will always be a Land of Beyond for Lions International; a goal that will keep growing larger and larger as we approach it, yet will keep just out of reach, challenging us to run faster, work harder, think bigger, give more."

APPENDICES

APPENDICES

Past International Presidents

(1) 1917–18 Dr. W. P. Woods, Evansville, Indiana, U.S.A.

(2) 1918–19 L. H. Lewis, Dallas, Texas, U.S.A.

(3) 1919–20 Jesse Robinson, Oakland, California, U.S.A.

(4) 1920–21 Dr. C. C. Reid, Denver, Colorado, U.S.A.

(5) 1921–22 Ewen W. Cameron, Minneapolis, Minnesota, U.S.A.

(6) 1922–23 Ed S. Vaught, Oklahoma City, Oklahoma, U.S.A.

(7) 1923–24 John S. Noel, Grand Rapids, Michigan, U.S.A.

(8) 1924–25 Harry A. Newman, Q. C., Toronto, Ontario, Canada

(9) 1925–26 Benjamin F. Jones, Newark, New Jersey, U.S.A.

(10) 1926–27 William A. Westfall, Mason City, Iowa, U.S.A.

(11) 1927–28 Irving L. Camp, Johnstown, Pennsylvania, U.S.A.

(12) 1928–29 Ben A. Ruffin, Richmond, Virginia, U.S.A.

(13) 1929–30 Ray L. Riley, San Francisco, California, U.S.A.

(14) 1930–31 Earle W. Hodges, New York, New York, U.S.A.

(15) 1931–32 Julien C. Hyer, Fort Worth, Texas, U.S.A.

(16) 1932–33 Charles H. Hatton, Wichita, Kansas, U.S.A.

(17) 1933–34 Roderick Beddow, Birmingham, Alabama, U.S.A.

(18) 1934–35 Vincent C. Hascall, Omaha, Nebraska, U.S.A.

(19) 1935–36 Richard J. Osenbaugh, Denver, Colorado, U.S.A.

(20) 1936–37 Edwin R. Kingsley, Parkersburg, West Virginia, U.S.A.

(21) 1937–38 Frank V. Birch, Milwaukee, Wisconsin, U.S.A.

(22) 1938–39 Walter F. Dexter, Sacramento, California, U.S.A.

(23) 1939–40 Alexander T. Wells, New York, New York, U.S.A.

(24) 1940–41 Karl M. Sorrick, Springport, Michigan, U.S.A.

(25) 1941–42 George R. Jordan, Dallas, Texas, U.S.A.

(26) 1942–43 Edward H. Paine, Michigan City, Indiana, U.S.A.

(27) 1943–44 Dr. E. G. Gill, Roanoke, Virginia, U.S.A.

(28) 1944–45 D. A. Skeen, Salt Lake City, Utah, U.S.A.

(29) 1945–46 Dr. Ramiro Collazo, Marianao, Habana, Cuba

(30) 1946–47 Clifford D. Pierce, Memphis, Tennessee, U.S.A.

(31) 1947–48 Fred W. Smith, Ventura, California, U.S.A.

(32) 1948–49 Dr. Eugene S. Briggs, Edmond, Oklahoma, U.S.A.

(33) 1949–50 Walter C. Fisher, St. Catharines, Ontario, Canada

(34) 1950–51 Herb C. Petry, Jr., Carrizo Springs, Texas, U.S.A.

(35) 1951–52 Harold P. Nutter, Oaklyn, New Jersey, U.S.A.

(36) 1952–53 Edgar M. Elbert, Maywood, Illinois, U.S.A.

(37) 1953–54 S. A. Dodge, Bloomfield Hills, Michigan, U.S.A.

(38) 1954–55 Monroe L. Nute, Kennett Square, Pennsylvania, U.S.A.

(39) 1955–56 Humberto Valenzuela G., Santiago, Chile

(40) 1956–57 John L. Stickley, Charlotte, North Carolina, U.S.A.

(41) 1957–58 Edward G. Barry, Little Rock, Arkansas, U.S.A.

(42) 1958–59 Dudley L. Simms, Charleston, West Virginia, U.S.A.

(43) 1959–60 Clarence L. Sturm, Manawa, Wisconsin, U.S.A.

(44) 1960–61 Finis E. Davis, Louisville, Kentucky, U.S.A.

(45) 1961–62 Per Stahl, Eskilstuna, Sweden

(46) 1962–63 Curtis D. Lovill, Gardiner, Maine, U.S.A.

(47) 1963–64 Aubrey D. Green, York, Alabama, U.S.A.

(48) 1964–65 Claude M. De Vorss, Wichita, Kansas, U.S.A.

(49) 1965–66 Dr. Walter H. Campbell, Miami Beach, Florida, U.S.A.

(50) 1966–67 Edward M. Lindsey, Lawrenceburg, Tennessee, U.S.A.

(51) 1967–68 Jorge Bird, Rio Piedras, Puerto Rico

(52) 1968–69 David A. Evans, Galveston, Texas, U.S.A.

(53) 1969–70 W. R. Bryan, Doylestown, Ohio, U.S.A.

(54) 1970–71 Dr. Robert D. McCullough, Tulsa, Oklahoma, U.S.A.

(55) 1971–72 Robert J. Uplinger, Syracuse, New York, U.S.A.

(56) 1972–73 George Friedrichs, Annecy, France

(57) 1973–74 Tris Coffin, Rosemere, Quebec, Canada

(58) 1974–75 Johnny Balbo, LaGrange, Illinois, U.S.A.

(59) 1975–76 Harry J. Aslan, Kingsburg, California, U.S.A.

(60) 1976–77 Prof. João Fernando Sobral, Sao Paulo, S.P., Brazil

(61) 1977–78 Joseph M. McLoughlin, Stamford, Connecticut, U.S.A.

(62) 1978–79 Ralph A. Lynam, St. John, Michigan, U.S.A.

(63) 1979–80 Lloyd Morgan, Taupo, New Zealand

(64) 1980–81 William C. Chandler, Montgomery, Alabama, U.S.A.

(65) 1981–82 Kaoru Murakami, Kyoto, Japan

(66) 1982–83 Everett J. Grindstaff, Ballinger, Texas, U.S.A.

(67) 1983–84 Dr. James M. Fowler, Hot Springs, Arkansas U.S.A.

(68) 1984–85 Bert Mason, Donaghadee, Northern Ireland

(69) 1985–86 Joseph L. Wroblewski, Forty Fort, Pennsylvania, U.S.A.

(70) 1986–87 Sten A. Akestam, Stockholm, Sweden

(71) 1987–88 Judge Brian Stevenson, Calgary, Alberta, Canada

(72) 1988–89 Austin P. Jennings, Woodbury, Tennessee, U.S.A.

(73) 1989–90 William L. Woolard, Charlotte, North Carolina, U.S.A.

(74) 1990–91 William L. Biggs, Omaha, Nebraska, U.S.A.

The Extension
of Lionism

Country, State or Geographical Location	Oldest Club	Year Organized
1. UNITED STATES OF AMERICA		1917
Alabama	Montgomery (1)*	1922
Alaska	Anchorage (2)*	1944
Arizona	Phoenix (Downtown)	1923
Arkansas	Little Rock	1917
Arkansas	Texarkana	1917
California	Oakland	1917
Colorado	Colorado Springs (Downtown)	1917
Colorado	Denver	1917
Colorado	Pueblo (Charter)	1917
Connecticut	Bridgeport	1921
Delaware	Wilmington	1922
District of Columbia	Washington (Host)	1921
Florida	Orlando (Downtown)	1922
Georgia	Atlanta	1920
Hawaii	Honolulu	1926
Idaho	Malad City	1923
Illinois	Chicago (Central)	1917
Indiana	Lafayette	1920
Iowa	Des Moines (Host) (3)*	1920
Kansas	Wichita (Downtown)	1919
Kentucky	Paducah	1920

Country, State or Geographical Location	Oldest Club	Year Organized
Louisiana	Shreveport (Downtown)	1917
Maine	Portland	1923
Maryland	Baltimore (Host)	1921
Massachusetts	Springfield (Host) (4)*	1922
Michigan (Lower)	Grand Rapids	1919
Michigan (Upper)	Marquette	1919
Minnesota	Minneapolis	1918
Mississippi	Jackson (Central) (5)*	1921
Missouri	St. Louis (Downtown) (6)*	1917
Montana	Billings	1921
Nebraska	Omaha	1920
Nevada	Reno (Host)	1920
New Hampshire	Manchester	1923
New Jersey	Camden	1920
New Mexico	Albuquerque (Host)	1923
New York	Rochester (Downtown) (7)*	1921
North Carolina	Winston-Salem (Host)	1922
North Dakota	Fargo	1921
Ohio	Cleveland	1920
Oklahoma	Ardmore	1917
Oklahoma	Chickasha	1917
Oklahoma	El Reno	1917
Oklahoma	Muskogee	1917
Oklahoma	Oklahoma City (Downtown)	1917
Oklahoma	Okmulgee	1917
Oklahoma	Tulsa (Downtown)	1917
Oregon	Portland (Downtown)	1921
Pennsylvania	Pittsburgh	1920
Rhode Island	Providence (Central)	1922
South Carolina	Columbia	1922
South Dakota	Sioux Falls	1921
Tennessee	Memphis	1917
Texas	Abilene	1917
Texas	Austin	1917
Texas	Beaumont	1917
Texas	Dallas	1917

Country, State or Geographical Location	*Oldest Club*	*Year Organized*
Texas	Fort Worth	1917
Texas	Houston (Central)	1917
Texas	Paris	1917
Texas	Port Arthur	1917
Texas	San Antonio	1917
Texas	Temple	1917
Texas	Waco	1917
Texas	Wichita Falls	1917
Utah	Salt Lake City	1921
Vermont	Burlington	1924
Virginia	Lynchburg (Host)	1921
Washington	Everett (Central) (8)*	1920
West Virginia	Charleston	1921
Wisconsin	Milwaukee (Central)	1921
Wyoming	Cheyenne	1920
2. CANADA		1920
Alberta	Calgary	1929
British Columbia	Vancouver (Central) (9)*	1921
Manitoba	Winnipeg	1921
New Brunswick	Edmundston (10)*	1938
Newfoundland	Corner Brook (11)*	1948
Nova Scotia	Halifax	1945
Ontario	Windsor	1920
Prince Edward Island	Charlottetown (12)*	1952
Quebec	Montreal (Central)	1922
Saskatchewan	Moose Jaw (13)*	1928
3. CHINA, REPUBLIC OF	Taipei (Host) (14)*	1953
4. MEXICO	Mexico, D.F. (15)*	1931
5. PANAMA	Colon	1935
6. COSTA RICA	San Jose, San Jose (16)*	1944
7. COLOMBIA	Cali (Centro Monarch) (17)*	1945
8. PUERTO RICO (U.S.A.)	San Juan	1936
9. GUATEMALA	Guatemala (Central)	1941
10. EL SALVADOR	San Salvador	1942
11. HONDURAS	Tegucigalpa, D.C.	1942
12. NICARAGUA	Managua, D.N.	1942
13. VENEZUELA	Barquisimeto (Central)	1943

Country, State or Geographical Location	Oldest Club	Year Organized
14. PERU	Lima	1944
15. NETHERLANDS ANTILLES (The Netherlands)	Curacao	1946
16. BERMUDA	Hamilton	1946
17. ECUADOR	Quito (Central)	1946
18. AUSTRALIA	Lismore, N.S.W.	1947
19. SWEDEN	Stockholm	1948
20. SWITZERLAND	Geneva	1948
21. CHILE	Santiago (Central)	1948
22. FRANCE	Paris (Doyen)	1948
23. BOLIVIA	La Paz	1948
24. PHILIPPINES	Manila (Host)	1949
25. NORWAY	Oslo	1949
26. GUAM (U.S.A.)	Guam–Marianas	1949
27. ENGLAND	London (Host)	1949
28. DENMARK	Copenhagen	1950
29. FINLAND	Helsinki–Helsingfors	1950
30. ITALY	Milan (Host)	1951
31. URUGUAY	Montevideo (Anfitrion)	1951
32. YUKON TERRITORY (Canada)	Whitehorse	1951
33. ICELAND	Reykjavik	1951
34. NETHERLANDS, THE	Amsterdam (Host)	1951
35. GERMANY	Dusseldorf	1951
36. JAPAN	Tokyo	1952
37. BELGIUM	Bruxelles (Centre)	1952
38. BRAZIL	Rio de Janeiro (Centro)	1952
39. PARAGUAY	Asuncion	1952
40. LEBANON	Beirut	1952
41. MOROCCO	Casablanca	1953
42. SCOTLAND	Helensburgh (19)*	1952
43. AUSTRIA	Graz	1952
44. LUXEMBOURG	Luxembourg	1953
45. ALGERIA	Algiers	1953
46. LIECHTENSTEIN	Liechtenstein	1953
47. BAHAMAS	Nassau	1953
48. ST. PIERRE & MIQUELON ISLANDS (France)	St. Pierre-Miquelon	1953

Country, State or Geographical Location	Oldest Club	Year Organized
49. JORDAN	Amman	1953
50. PORTUGAL	Lisbon (Host)	1953
51. GREECE	Athens	1954
52. ARGENTINA	Buenos Aires	1954
53. CYPRUS	Famagusta	1954
54. CONGO, PEOPLE'S REP. OF	Brazzaville	1954
55. IVORY COAST, REPUBLIC OF THE	Abidjan–Lagune	1954
56. CAMEROON, UNITED REP. OF	Yaounde (Doyen)	1955
57. SENEGAL, REPUBLIC OF	Dakar (Boabab)	1955
58. NEW ZEALAND	Auckland (Host)	1955
59. IRELAND, REPUBLIC OF	Dublin	1955
60. CENTRAL AFRICAN REPUBLIC	Bangui	1955
61. HONG KONG (United Kingdom)	Hong Kong (Host)	1955
62. INDIA	Bombay (Host)	1956
63. PAKISTAN	Karachi	1956
64. CHAD, REPUBLIC OF	Fort Lamy–N'Djamena	1956
65. MALAGASY REPUBLIC	Tulear	1956
66. TUNISIA	Tunis (Doyen) (20)*	1968
67. GABON REPUBLIC	Libreville	1957
68. SURINAM (The Netherlands)	Paramaribo (Central)	1957
69. ZAIRE	Kinshasa	1957
70. SOUTH AFRICA, REPUBLIC OF	Cape Town	1957
71. BURUNDI, REPUBLIC OF	Bujumbura	1957
72. MALI, REPUBLIC OF	Bamako	1957
73. TOGO	Lome	1957
74. MALTA	Valletta	1958
75. NORTHERN IRELAND (United Kingdom)	Belfast	1958
76. NAMIBIA	Windhoek	1958
77. REUNION (France)	Saint-Denis	1958
78. SRI LANKA, REPUBLIC OF	Colombo (Host)	1958
79. BURKINA FASO	Bobo-Dioulasso	1958
80. KENYA	Nairobi (Host)	1958
81. SINGAPORE	Singapore (Host)	1958
82. KOREA, REPUBLIC OF	Seoul	1959

Country, State or Geographical Location	Oldest Club	Year Organized
83. THAILAND	Bangkok	1959
84. MALAYSIA	Kuala Lumpur (Host)	1959
85. RWANDA, REPUBLIC OF	Butare (18)*	1959
86. UGANDA	Kampala (Host)	1959
87. ZIMBABWE	Harare City	1959
88. SAN MARINO, REPUBLIC OF	San Marino	1959
89. ISRAEL	Tel Aviv	1960
90. TAHITI (France)	Papeete	1960
91. NIGER, REPUBLIC OF	Niamey	1960
92. GUYANA	Georgetown	1960
93. MALAWI	Blantyre	1960
94. NEW CALEDONIA (France)	Noumea	1961
95. MONACO, PRINCIPALITY OF	Monaco	1961
96. ZAMBIA	Kitwe	1961
97. BARBADOS	Bridgetown	1961
98. PAPUA NEW GUINEA	Port Moresby	1962
99. TRINIDAD and TOBAGO, REP. OF	Port-of-Spain	1962
100. TANZANIA	Daressalaam	1963
101. WALES (United Kingdom)	Wrexham-Maelor	1963
102. TURKEY	Istanbul	1963
103. CHANNEL ISLANDS (United Kingdom)	Jersey	1963
104. NEPAL	Biratnager (22)*	1971
105. FIJI ISLANDS	Suva	1963
106. NORFOLK ISLAND (Australia)	Norfolk Island	1964
107. DOMINICAN REPUBLIC	Santo Domingo (Central)	1964
108. SPAIN	Madrid	1964
109. ST. VINCENT	St. Vincent	1964
110. JAMAICA	Kingston	1965
111. NIGERIA	Lagos	1964
112. GRENADA	St. George's	1965
113. WESTERN SAMOA	Apia	1965
114. DJIBOUTI, REPUBLIC OF	Djibouti	1966
115. MADEIRA ISLANDS (Portugal)	Funchal	1966
116. ETHIOPIA	Addis Ababa	1966
117. VIRGIN ISLANDS (U.S.A.)	St. Croix	1966

Country, State or Geographical Location	Oldest Club	Year Organized
118. MAURITANIA	Nouakchott (23)*	1975
119. ST. LUCIA	Castries	1967
120. MARTINIQUE (France)	Fort de France	1967
121. BOTSWANA	Lobatse	1968
122. MAURITIUS	Port Louis	1967
123. DOMINICA	Dominica (loc. Roseau, Dominica, W.I.)	1968
124. ANTIGUA and BARBUDA	Antigua (loc. St. John's, Antigua, W.I.)	1968
125. GUADELOUPE (France)	Guadeloupe (Doyen)	1969
126. INDONESIA	Djakarta	1969
127. BRUNEI	Brunei (loc. Bandar Seri Begawan)	1970
128. FRENCH GUIANA (France)	La Guyane (loc. Cayenne)	1970
129. ST. CHRISTOPHER—NEVIS	Nevis (loc. Charlestown, Nevis West Indies)	1971
130. MACAU (Portuguese Overseas Province)	Macau	1971
131. BANGLADESH, REPUBLIC OF	Dhaka	1958
132. GRAND CAYMAN B.W.I.	Grand Cayman	1972
133. LIBERIA, REPUBLIC OF	Greater Monrovia (loc. Monrovia, Rep. of Liberia)	1972
134. HAITI	Port-Au-Prince (Central) (24)*	1982
135. BELIZE	Belize City	1973
136. BRITISH VIRGIN ISLANDS (Tortola & Virgin Gorda)	Tortola, B.V.I.	1972
137. SOLOMON ISLANDS	Guadalcanal (loc. Honiara, Guadalcanal Solomon Islands)	1975
138. ARAB REPUBLIC OF EGYPT	Cairo (21)*	1976
139. FAROE ISLANDS (Denmark)	Torshavn	1966
140. GIBRALTAR (British Colony)	Gibraltar	1977
141. TRANSKEI	Umtata	1973

Country, State or Geographical Location	Oldest Club	Year Organized
142. VANUATU	Port Villa	1978
143. BAHRAIN	Bahrain (loc. Manama, Bahrain)	1978
144. SWAZILAND	Mbabane	1979
145. LESOTHO	Maseru (25)*	1980
146. SIERRA LEONE	Freetown	1980
147. BOPHUTHATSWANA, REP. OF	Mafeking	1969
148. COMORO ISLANDS	Moroni	1981
149. BENIN, PEOPLE'S REP. OF	Cotonou	1981
150. GHANA, REP. OF	Accra (Host)	1982
151. EQUATORIAL GUINEA, REP. OF	Bata-Ceiba	1982
152. TONGA, KINGDOM OF	Nukua'Lofa	1982
153. SEYCHELLES	Mahe	1982
154. AMERICAN SAMOA	Pago Pago	1982
155. PRINCIPAT D'ANDORRA	Andorra de Veila	1985
156. COOK ISLANDS	Rarotonga	1985
157. MONTSERRAT	Plymouth	1985
158. ARUBA	Aruba	1947
159. CAPE VERDE (Portugal)	Ilha do Sal	1986
160. GUINEA, REPUBLIC OF	Conakry	1986
161. ALAND ISLANDS	Mariehamn	1955
162. GREENLAND	Ilulissat/Jacobshavn	1988
163. HUNGARY	Budapest	1989
164. POLAND	Poznan	1989
165. ESTONIA E.S.S.R.	Tallinn (Eesti-I)	1989
166. CZECHOSLOVAKIA	Prague (Eagle)	1990
167. ROMANIA	Bucharest & Craiova	1990
168. MICRONESIA, Federated States of	Pohnpei	1990
169. YUGOSLAVIA	Ljubljana	1990
170. RUSSIA	Moscow & Moscow (Centrum)	1990
171. LITHUANIA	Vilnius	1990

(1) Birmingham (First Club)—cancelled 1921
(2) Juneau (First Club)—cancelled 1929
(3) Sioux City (First Club)—cancelled 1920
(4) Boston (First Club)—cancelled 1942

(5) Clarksdale (First Club)—cancelled 1924
(6) Kansas City (First Club)—cancelled 1917
(7) New York City (Herald Square) (First Club)—cancelled 1917
(8) Seattle (First Club)—1920
(9) Spences Bridge & Dist. (First Club)—cancelled 1961
(10) McAdam (First Club)—cancelled 1935
(11) Bell Island (First Club)—cancelled 1953
(12) Montagne (First Club)—cancelled 1955
(13) Swift Current (First Club)—cancelled 1936
(14) Tientsin (First Club)—cancelled 1958
(15) Nuevo Laredo (First Club)—cancelled 1936
(16) San Jose (First Club)—cancelled 1944
(17) Barranquilla (First Club)—cancelled 1945
(18) Shangueu (First Club)—cancelled 1963
(19) Glasgow (First Club)—cancelled 1964
(20) Tunis (First Club)—cancelled 1968
(21) Cairo (First Club)—cancelled 1968
(22) Kathmandu (First Club)—cancelled 1971
(23) Port Etienne (First Club)—cancelled 1983
(24) Port-Au-Prince (First Club)—cancelled 1980
(25) Mafeteng (First Club)—cancelled 1984

Annual International Conventions

No.	Year	Place	Date
1	1917	Dallas, Texas	October 8–10
2	1918	St. Louis, Missouri	August 19–21
3	1919	Chicago, Illinois	July 9–11
4	1920	Denver, Colorado	July 13–16
5	1921	Oakland, California	July 19–22
6	1922	Hot Springs, Arkansas	June 19–24
7	1923	Atlantic City, New Jersey	June 26–29
8	1924	Omaha, Nebraska	June 23–26
9	1925	Cedar Point, Ohio	June 29–July 2
10	1926	San Francisco, California	July 21–24
11	1927	Miami, Florida	June 15–18
12	1928	Des Moines, Iowa	July 10–13
13	1929	Louisville, Kentucky	June 18–21
14	1930	Denver, Colorado	July 15–18
15	1931	Toronto, Canada	July 14–17
16	1932	Los Angeles, California	July 19–22
17	1933	St. Louis, Missouri	July 11–14
18	1934	Grand Rapids, Michigan	July 17–20
19	1935	Mexico City, Mexico	July 23–25
20	1936	Providence, Rhode Island	July 21–24
21	1937	Chicago, Illinois	July 20–23
22	1938	Oakland, California	July 19–22

No.	Year	Place	Date
23	1939	Pittsburgh, Pennsylvania	July 18–21
24	1940	Havana, Cuba	July 23–25
25	1941	New Orleans, Louisiana	July 22–25
26	1942	Toronto, Canada	July 21–24
27	1943	Cleveland, Ohio	July 20–22
28	1944	Chicago, Illinois	August 1–3
	1945	NONE HELD	
29	1946	Philadelphia, Pennsylvania	July 16–19
30	1947	San Francisco, California	July 28–31
31	1948	New York, New York	July 26–29
32	1949	New York, New York	July 18–21
33	1950	Chicago, Illinois	July 16–20
34	1951	Atlantic City, New Jersey	June 24–28
35	1952	Mexico City, Mexico	June 25–28
36	1953	Chicago, Illinois	July 8–11
37	1954	New York, New York	July 7–10
38	1955	Atlantic City, New Jersey	June 22–25
39	1956	Miami, Florida	June 27–30
40	1957	San Francisco, California	June 26–29
41	1958	Chicago, Illinois	July 9–12
42	1959	New York, New York	June 30–July 3
43	1960	Chicago, Illinois	July 6–9
44	1961	Atlantic City, New Jersey	June 21–24
45	1962	Nice, France	June 20–23
46	1963	Miami, Florida	June 19–22
47	1964	Toronto, Canada	July 8–11
48	1965	Los Angeles, California	July 7–10
49	1966	New York, New York	July 6–9
50	1967	Chicago, Illinois	July 5–8
51	1968	Dallas, Texas	June 26–29
52	1969	Tokyo, Japan	July 2–5
53	1970	Atlantic City, New Jersey	July 1–4
54	1971	Las Vegas, Nevada	June 22–25
55	1972	Mexico City, Mexico	June 28–July 1
56	1973	Miami, Florida	June 27–30
57	1974	San Francisco, California	July 3–6
58	1975	Dallas, Texas	June 25–28
59	1976	Honolulu, Hawaii	June 23–26

No.	Year	Place	Date
60	1977	New Orleans, Louisiana	June 29–July 2
61	1978	Tokyo, Japan	June 21–24
62	1979	Montreal, Canada	June 20–23
63	1980	Chicago, Illinois	July 2–5
64	1981	Phoenix, Arizona	June 17–20
65	1982	Atlanta, Georgia	June 30–July 3
66	1983	Honolulu, Hawaii	June 22–25
67	1984	San Francisco, California	July 4–7
68	1985	Dallas, Texas	June 19–22
69	1986	New Orleans, Louisiana	July 9–12
70	1987	Taipei, Taiwan, Rep. of China	July 1–4
71	1988	Denver, Colorado	June 29–July 2
72	1989	Miami/Miami Beach, Florida	June 21–24
73	1990	St. Louis, Missouri	July 11–14
74	1991	Brisbane, Australia	June 18–21

Index